D1031728

Macho Man

The Disco Era
and Gay America's
"Coming Out"

Randy Jones and Mark Bego

Westport, Connecticut
London

ITHACA COLLEGE LIBRARY
WITHDRAWN

HQ
76.3
.U5
J66
2005

4885569

$39.95

Library of Congress Cataloging-in-Publication Data

Jones, Randy, 1952–
    Macho man: the disco era and gay America's "coming out" /
Randy Jones and Mark Bego.
        p. cm.
    Includes bibliographical references and index.
    ISBN 978-0-275-99962-9 (alk. paper)
    1. Homosexuality—United States. 2. Gay rights—United States. 3. Village People.
4. Gay liberation movement—United States. 5. Celebrities—United States. I. Bego, Mark.
II. Title.
    HQ76.3.U5J66   2009
    306.76'6097309045—dc22   2008032412

British Library Cataloguing in Publication Data is available.

Copyright © 2009 by Randy Jones and Mark Bego

All rights reserved. No portion of this book may be
reproduced, by any process or technique, without the
express written consent of the publisher.

Library of Congress Catalog Card Number: 2008032412
ISBN: 978-0-275-99962-9

First published in 2009

Praeger Publishers, 88 Post Road West, Westport, CT 06881
An imprint of Greenwood Publishing Group, Inc.
www.praeger.com

Printed in the United States of America

The paper used in this book complies with the
Permanent Paper Standard issued by the National
Information Standards Organization (Z39.48–1984).

10   9   8   7   6   5   4   3   2   1

Contents

Acknowledgments

The authors would like to thank the following people for their help, assistance, support, and inspiration while writing this book:

Sunny Bak
Henri Belolo
Angela Bowie
Debbie Carvalko
Keith Collins
Tom Cruise
Agnes DeMille
Vince Desi
Alyse Dorese
Dodie Draher
James Edstrom
Chris Gilman
Keith Girard
Will Grega
John Hammond
Daniel Harmon
Bertie Hoover
Elaine Jones
Grace Jones
Harrison Jordan
Sergio Kardenos
Frosty Lawson
Michael Musto
Man Parrish
David Salidor
Colleen Simeral

Jacqui Smith-Lee

Marsh Stern

Derek Storm

Bruce Vilanch

Steve Walter and The Cutting Room, New York City

Mary Wilson

And the staff of The Palm West, 250 West 50th Street, New York City

Introduction

Welcome to our first book together. For four decades now, the two of us have been best friends, one-time roommates, business partners, and close confidantes to one another. We were born just 10 days apart and have shared in a countless number of experiences. We were both seniors in high school when the year 1969 ushered in Woodstock and the famed Stonewall riots. Randy is from North Carolina, and Mark is from Michigan. We were both college educated in our respective states, and both of us had a strong interest in show business and the entertainment world. We both studied theater, and each of us felt the magnetic pull that the excitement of living in Manhattan had to us.

Separately, we both gravitated to New York City in the early 1970s to pursue our careers. Randy's field of expertise was in dance and acting. His focus in Manhattan drove him to dance with the famed Agnes DeMille dance company and to audition as an actor in theatrical productions. Mark wasn't sure if he wanted to be an actor, a writer, or a broadcast journalist, so he pursued all three career aspirations. Both of us knew that we wanted to have something to do with show business, and we were each open to all sorts of opportunities and pursuits in the city. Ironically, before we met each other we both ended up as male models in the largely gay-oriented magazine, *After Dark*.

One of Randy's first and most high-profile jobs in the entertainment business was as one of the male dancers in disco star Grace Jones' act. (Although Grace and Randy have the same last name, they are unrelated.) With Grace, Randy traveled around America, where they performed in several of the top discotheques in the country. This was the perfect way for Randy to become acquainted with disco audiences and working on a road show. It was the perfect precursor to the global touring he would later do with the Village People show.

Mark, on the other hand, landed his first job in the publishing business, which came after he answered a want ad in *The New York Times*. The position that Bego successfully landed was as a "Guy

Friday" working for Praeger Publishers, which at the time was located in Greenwich Village. However, that job was short-lived, and Mark became the assistant to Alyse Dorese, the Contracts Administrator at Grosset & Dunlap Publishers on Park Avenue South.

Bego appeared in a theatrical production of *The Man Who Came to Dinner*, and wrote a yet-to-be-published gay/straight/bisexual pornographic novel he entitled *They Came in the Caribbean*. After working for Grosset & Dunlap for six months, one day Alyse called him into her office and said, "Look, I really like you, Mark, but obviously you don't want to type contracts for a living. And, you are not that good at it. I know, having read your porno novel, that you would rather be a writer than a secretary, so I am firing you. You have worked here six months, so you can file for unemployment insurance, and you can pursue your writing career."

That was exactly what he did. In his two years since leaving the publishing company, Bego took several odd jobs during this era. Ultimately, it was Alyse who championed the publication of Mark's first two published books: *The Captain & Tennille* and *Barry Manilow*. Also during this era he started doing freelance magazine articles, and for a while he took a job as a publicist for a music industry company called the Howard Bloom Organization.

Through his contacts at Howard's office, he met two very influential people: Bob Small and Marsha Stern. Bob invited Mark to be the official publicist for the upcoming Billboard Disco Forum in the summer of 1976, held at the Americana Hotel in New York City. One of the disco acts on the bill for that event was Grace Jones and her dancers, including Randy Jones. Although Mark and Randy didn't meet there, Bego was in the audience to catch Jones' pre-Village People act.

Two years later Bego was writing celebrity articles for a magazine called *Disco World*. His friend, Marsha Stern, was now working for a music and record production company called Can't Stop Music. The company was responsible for the success of a female trio they called The Ritchie Family. It was so successful in fact that they wanted to create an all male singing and performing group. Ultimately, they called the group Village People.

Marsha phoned Mark one day in the spring of 1978 and said to him, "We are representing this new group called Village People. Would you like to be the first person to interview them?" Always up for a new experience, he agreed, and Marsha set up an appointment for Bego to meet the group. To make a long story short: that was the day that Randy met Mark.

In the years that followed, Randy went on to become a million-selling recording artist with Village People, and Mark went on to become a million-selling book author. We remained friends throughout the years, and together we have done dozens of projects together. Mark coproduced Randy's act, Mark publicized Randy's theatrical performances, the two of us hosted parties and events together, Randy wrote the introduction for Mark's books, and the list goes on and on.

That is how we became the best of friends. Also throughout the years, we have discussed one day writing a book together. We have to admit that this book you are now reading is one that we would have never conceived of on our own. Originally, the two of us had been trying to sell a conventional autobiography on Randy, written with Mark. When we met with Praeger Publishers editor Debbie Carvalko, in the fall of 2005, she was intrigued about the idea of doing a book with us. However, it was she who conceived of and challenged us to write a manuscript of much more scope and dimension. Since she was currently editing books on psychology, historic and cultural events, and the developments of human society, she came up with an intriguing idea.

"Instead of writing a book about Randy's life and Village People," Debbie said to us, "why don't the two of you use Village People as a pivotal point of a book on a larger subject."

We looked at each other with quizzical expressions on our faces, not sure where this was leading. Then we turned back to Debbie, who continued, "What if you wrote a book about gay history, and how Village People became the center of modern 'straight society' that was able to accept gay images and gay music openly? Then you could write about how this global acceptance of Village People changed society and helped it evolve artistically and socially?"

At this point, we again looked at each other with slightly dumb-founded expressions on our faces. Then we looked back at Debbie, and said in unison, "We love it."

That evening, over dinner at a restaurant on Manhattan's riverside South Street Seaport pier, the idea for this book was born. Over the next several months, Debbie helped us to shape a proposal that everyone was happy with. Praeger agreed to our plan, and we started shaping the ideas that became this book.

Although she really wanted to continue as our editor, Debbie had other projects she was tending to, and—with our permission—she handed this book on to the Praeger editor who handles pop music books for the company. His name is Daniel Harmon, and he picked up the baton as our editor.

This book has changed and morphed slightly during its writing process, but the basics are all the same. The finished product, which you are about to read, has much more scope and depth than we had originally intended on it possessing. To be precise, this book has about 2,000 more years of scope than our first idea.

Through the writing process, we—Randy and Mark—have learned and discovered a lot of fascinating lessons about the changing sexual mores and customs of human society since the very beginning of civilization. On these pages, we have reported our findings in a very conversational way, which we feel has become both entertaining and informative.

Although the centerpiece to this book is the disco era 1975–80, when we first met, it is now part of a greater story. To understand the way in which the group Village People played a part in changing society and social perceptions, we first had to define the evolution of society in general. In other words, you cannot talk about change unless you know and fully appreciate what you are changing.

Once we signed our publication contracts, the two of us had several intellectual dialogues about the topics we wanted to discuss, similar to this one.

RANDY: "Okay, so how do we start?"

MARK: "Well, I think that we have to talk about 'gay liberation' and the Stonewall riots."

RANDY: "Well, that's fine, but what about historical figures who were gay?"

MARK: "Like Ancient Greece and Alexander the Great?"

RANDY: "Exactly. Back then it was common for Greek soldiers to have sex with their male servants and stable boys."

MARK: "Well, then there is all that Greek pottery depicting men having sex."

RANDY: "We can't forget Sappho and the Isle of Lesbos, where women had female lovers as well."

MARK: "And we certainly have to include Oscar Wilde and how he was prosecuted for having gay sex in the 1800s."

RANDY: "What about Andy Warhol?"

MARK: "And Tallulah Bankhead?"

RANDY: "I was just reading an article about the guy who cracked the Nazi secret codes; this guy by the name of Alan Turing."

MARK;   "Really? I've never heard of him."

RANDY: "He committed suicide rather than be prosecuted by the British
          government in the 1950s for being gay."
MARK: "Excellent, let's write about him for sure. Gay marriage. We
          have to talk about the controversy of gay marriage."
RANDY: "And Rosie O'Donnell."
MARK: "Ellen Degeneres."
RANDY: "Studio 54."
MARK: "Elton John."
RANDY: "Liberace."
MARK: "Rock Hudson."
RANDY: "Glam Rock."
MARK: "David Bowie."
RANDY: "Angela Bowie."
MARK: "We have to list all the unconventional Bohemians."
RANDY: "Everyone you've slept with?"
MARK: "Shut up."
RANDY: (laughing) "We had better start a list."
MARK: "Hand me a pen and a legal pad."

And, so it started. Of course, we couldn't list everyone in history
who risked their lives and their reputations to contradict the prevailing rules of society for their times, so we instead chose those figures
in history who interested us, and who either defined or changed the
times by their actions.

In the first chapter, we tackled the changing social attitudes toward homosexuality throughout history. For instance, in many societies it was highly acceptable to express love for members of one's
own sex, most notably in Ancient Greece where leaders like
Alexander the Great had a significant male lover for the majority of
his life, and the poetess Sappho routinely took female lovers. However, as modern religions took over in many prevailing societies, it
became forbidden to practice a gay lifestyle. But, just as the roles of
men and woman in society have changed and evolved, the roles of
gay and lesbian individuals have likewise changed.

Society as a whole made a moralistic shift when Christianity came
into fashion, and the Jewish religion basically broke off into two fac-
tions. The moral debate over gay tolerance continues. Today, while
gay images are all over the media, the "Religious Right" in America
proclaims that homosexuality is a sin against God and the Bible. At
the same time, throughout history there have been those who argued
the theory that Jesus Christ was in fact a homosexual and had a relationship with one or more of his disciples. This was the controversial

opinion of the famed Elizabethan-era British writer Christopher Marlowe.

Then, with the advent of mass media in the twentieth century, sexual identities again changed and morphed. In 1969, after years of repression and persecution, gay men finally revolted in New York City, and the famed Stonewall riots occurred in Greenwich Village. That was the birth of modern "gay rights" and the start of acceptance by mainstream society.

By the 1970s, sexual mores shifted to the point where sexual "swinging" from heterosexual activity to homosexual activity to bisexuality occurred. It was the "Me Decade," when a climate of "anything goes" occurred. The term "Me Decade" was first used in an August 1976 issue of New York magazine, in an article by Tom Wolfe. It perfectly labeled an entire generation that was totally self-absorbed.

Chapter Four is one of the most interesting chapters in this book, because in it we examine the significance of several places, events, and touchstone references that grew into the songs that Village People actually glorified in their greatest hits. It could easily be sub-titled, "Who put the 'Village' in 'Village People'?"

Then we come to the centerpiece of this entire book, the disco era, including the formation of Village People, both as a musical group and as a cultural phenomenon. Without their tongue-in-cheek references, Village People might have never found such acceptance on the radio and on the dance floors of discotheques around the world.

After the end of the 1970s, the times changed again. With the advent of AIDS, it looked like all of the progress of the '70s would be lost forever. It seemed that there would be a huge backlash from society. Eventually, the world realized that a mere virus could not differentiate between a gay and a straight person. What was originally looked upon as a "gay disease" was found to be much more of a pandemic threat than originally suspected.

Finally, we examine how society has again changed in the twenty-first century. Those of us who grew up in the "Baby Boomer" generation, and watched television shows like The Adventures of Ozzie & Harriet and The Donna Reed Show, could never have dreamed that a network television program like the gay/straight sitcom Will & Grace would become such a mainstream hit.

In August of 2008, when 10,708 international athletes marched into the Bird's Nest Olympic Stadium in Beijing, China, ten of them publicly identified themselves as being gay or lesbian. That's how far things have evolved lately. In the past, that never would have happened in sports.

Nowadays, as the controversy of "gay marriage" continues to rage, and in many states and countries has become a reality, it seems like some segments of society have come full circle to the ideas and ideals of Ancient Greece. At the same time, other parts of the United States, and the world in general, refuse to allow such things. But, then we are getting ahead of ourselves here.

On these pages we are going to discuss the homosexual and/or bisexual behavior and lifestyles of many well-known historic and modern people. In no way have we endeavored to "out" anyone or bring them "out of the closet" against their will. We are allowing for the admission of anyone's sexuality to be historically proven, either by self-declaration or via their writings, actions, or deeds.

While we could have devoted several chapters to the theories for why an individual becomes homosexual or heterosexual, we have chosen to leave that to the psychologists and biologists of the world. In this book we are not going to try and explain, justify, argue, deny, or promote any theories. Instead, we are going to talk about what does exist, what has actually happened, and some of the lives it has touched and influenced.

The two of us, as individuals, have had highly successful careers in "popular culture." Our lives have been based in our love for the creative world of music and movies, books, and television. This particular volume is also largely devoted to those topics. Chapter Seven presents our personal list of twenty-five of the most important gay-themed films that have been made. And, Chapter Eight presents a look at important gay rock songs. Naturally, we tackled some of the most obvious songs, but we have also included several surprises as well.

When you picked up this book, you no doubt suspected that this would merely be a book about Village People and the partying that we both did together at Studio 54 or at one of dozens of other dance clubs in the disco era. In reality, this is merely an important part of a much greater story.

We both learned a lot about society and its historic views on sexuality while writing this book. In fact, we learned so much while researching this book that one of the most daunting tasks we had was trying to fit everything and everyone into one volume. For fear that it would read like the New York City phone book, we had to pick and choose what to include. We made decisions about what we thought were the most important and most interesting people, topics, songs, and movies and put them into the book. In reality, we realized that each of these chapters could easily grow to become separate books unto themselves!

We hope that you find this book to be not only entertaining, but vastly informative as well. Come with us as we examine, salute, and delve into the whole concept of "sexual identity" and the role that each of us play in it.

Together we have gained a lot of knowledge in the constantly changing morals and mores of society. And, we are both honored and happy to be able to share our findings with you.

Chapter 1

Ancient Gay History to the 1900s: Icons and Diversions

Although we consider ourselves to be living in the "Modern Age" in the twenty-first century, and there are a great number of sexual freedoms practiced in most of the largest cities in the world, it isn't that way everywhere on the planet. Although there have been vast and sweeping changes made toward sexual tolerance in the last one hundred years, many provincial and narrow-minded prejudices still exist. Without debating modern religion, the Bible, reincarnation, Darwin, fate, or "live and let live" liberalism, it is safe to say that there is still a lot of prejudice in the world today.

Perhaps there will always be debates as to how society should or should not dictate the ways in which its citizens can express themselves sexually. What is tolerated or embraced in New York City is very different than what is tolerated in "small-town" America. What takes place in Stockholm, Sweden, or in Thailand is certainly different than what is considered acceptable in the modern Middle East.

In many societies that predate the proliferation of Christianity, a tolerance and acceptance of bisexuality and homosexuality was woven into the fabric of those cultures. In others it was not. One of the greatest societies in history, that of Ancient Greece for instance, had very different sexual mores than the world post-Christ.

Since that time, modern societies and religions routinely sought to impose its ideas on upon its citizens. Historically, individuals with homosexual feelings or desires were routinely ostracized or tortured for being different. As a result, gay men and women have had to seek professions and positions in society that would magnify their creativity and individuality so that their talents and crafts would outshine their sexual orientation. As evidenced by many of the

1

subjects of this book, many gay and lesbian individuals were often the celebrated artists, actors, and writers of their own eras. The gay individuals in many cultures were the faith healers, or the priests, the teachers, the inventors, the doctors, or the craftsmen and crafts-women.

In this way, gay people have often been the mediators, or the peacemakers. They have traditionally found positions for themselves that elevated their importance in society while allowing their personal lives to go unnoticed. They have also been the kings, the leaders, and the most revered people of their day.

However, they have often been ostracized or shunned by the masses. For this reason, often gay and lesbian individuals have lived dual lives, in which they had the secure shield of a heterosexual spouse and offspring, while keeping their same-sex lovers on the side.

Often the gay or bisexual people in society are actors and actresses. These are people who have learned to live in a world of "make believe." Perhaps that is because these people have had to "make believe" that they are straight, or "make believe" that they want to get married, when in fact their marriages to the opposite sex are merely one more "pretend" act in their lives.

Others found that by becoming sailors, soldiers, or athletes they could live out their lives in all-male or all-female settings without question. A perfect case-in-point is the author Herman Melville, who is discussed later in this book. A life in the military served many gay men or women well, in that there could be a same-sex bonding that conventional society did not provide.

Evidence of homosexuality being accepted dates back to the earliest of societies, starting with Ancient Egypt, going back to the era of 2450 BC, to Niankhknum and Khnumhotep, who were the royal manicurists to Pharaoh, King Niuserre of the Fifth Dynasty. Discovery of their existence in 1964 came in the ancient necropolis of Saqqara, by an Egyptian archaeologist named Ahmed Moussa. He discovered several tombs that faced the causeway leading to the ancient pyramid of Unas. It was there that he discovered a uniquely carved "relief" of two men in a loving embrace, kissing.

In other ancient cultures, there were traditions of soldiers having older lovers with whom they were intimate as part of their military training. In Sparta, homosexuality was engrained in their lifestyle. The older lovers would train younger soldiers in the arts of war. The young boys were referred to as the "beloved" in the relationship, and the older man was called the "lover." In battle, the lover and the beloved would fight side-by-side. Since there was a deep emotional attachment, the "lover" would not want to shame his "beloved" in Spartan battle, so he fought harder and with more passion.

Homosexuality was even more pronounced and accepted in Ancient Greece. Was it mere coincidence that the first Olympics found only men competing with each other? The games and competitions were held with the athletes in the nude, and the only spectators were men.

In the teachings of Plato and the other great scholars of Ancient Greece, it was believed that women were to be treated as nurturers and child bearers. However, passionate and devoted love was something shared between two men. It was not uncommon for the kings and warriors in Greece to have lovers and mates of both sexes throughout their lives.

The most famous and high-profile early homosexual male was undoubtedly the Macedonian-born king, Alexander the Great. And, from the same era of Ancient Greece came the roots of love of women for other women, on the Isle of Lesbos, as evidenced in the teachings and writings of Sappho.

Many people have no idea that some of their favorite heroes and heroines from ancient history were actually gay men and women. Historically, homosexuality was an accepted part of society. Over time, when religion became heavily involved in politics, it was banished. Then, in the last one hundred years, it has become acknowledged as a "lifestyle choice" in many societies and countries. However, regardless of what society did or did not accept, homosexuality has always existed whether or not it was publicly allowed.

RANDY: "It's fascinating to me to see how many historic figures we ran across, compiling our 'short list.'"
MARK: "We could have written volumes on this subject."
RANDY: "What we both agreed upon, however, was that the first person we needed to discuss was Alexander the Great."
MARK: "And this decision was not just because Colin Farrell recently starred as him in a hot film version of his life called *Alexander*."
RANDY: "But, it didn't hurt."

The first really big icon of historical "super hero" status who was gay was Alexander the Great. Born in Macedonia on July 20, 365 BC, Alexander's father was Macedonian King Phillip II. In his lifetime Alexander was an extremely successful warrior who conquered the majority of the known world at the time, including the Persian

Empire, which encompassed Anatolia, Syria, Phoenicia, Judea, Gaza, Egypt, Bactria, and Mesopotamia.

One of the things that Alexander's father insisted upon was the military education of all of sons. They were taught in boot-camp schools where intense male bonding was a common and encouraged occurrence.

In Macedon and other areas of the Greek empire, active homosexuality from an early age was believed to foster a unique "love thy brother" kind of masculinity, like teaching boys to hunt or to go off to battle together. There was no "don't ask/don't tell" nonsense; homosexuality in the military was right up front, in the open, and encouraged.

While Alexander was still a young boy amidst his schooling, he met and fell in love with one of his fellow students, a young Macedonian noble who was slightly older than he, a young prince named Hephaestion. From an early age, Alexander and Hephaestion were companions, lovers, and inseparable lifelong friends.

When Alexander was twenty years old, his father died and he ascended to the throne. From that time forward, he kept his male lover, Hephaestion, by his side.

When he was successful in leading his troops to conquer Turkey and Persia, he continued to march his troops east and into India, which at the time was considered to be the "edge of the world." Again, Hephaestion was right there by his side. In love with and devoted to Hephaestion, Alexander kept his male lover as part of his highest-ranking officers in the army.

It is said that Alexander was exceedingly handsome. Existing portraits of him made during his life as well as Roman copies that were painted are thought to accurately depict him as quite good-looking. He was of medium build, and by legend was said to have had a very pleasant scent to his skin and breath, which considering the hygienic conditions of the time was pretty amazing. He was also said to be in great physical condition. He loved strenuous exercise, and it was said that he could jump off and back on a chariot moving at full speed.

Likewise, his male lover, Hephaestion, was also said to be quite a hunk. Hephaestion was said to be even taller and more handsome than Alexander. When the conquered Persian Queen was first in the presence of Hephaestion and Alexander, she bowed to Hephaestion as she was presented to them. When it was explained to the Queen that she had bowed to the wrong man, Alexander said to the mortified Queen, "Never mind, Mother, Hephaestion is also Alexander." (1)

Every region that Alexander sought to conquer, he and Hephaestion did so victoriously. He not only conquered these regions, he made those countries' citizens part of the Greek empire. In this way, Alexander was able to integrate foreigners into his army, which lead many scholars to credit him with what they termed a "policy of fusion."

In a strictly political move, he married one of the daughters of Darius, the recently conquered Persian emperor. This did not signify the end of his relationship with his beloved male lover, Hephaestion. Quite the contrary. He also arranged for a political marriage for Hephaestion as well, to his wife's sister, so that Hephaestion's sons and daughters could be Alexander's nieces and nephews.

When he returned to Babylon with Hephaestion in 324 BC, he planned his next campaign, the invasion of Arabia. While plans were underway, in an uncharacteristic move Alexander ventured off to the nearby city of Hamadan to see the sights. Back in Babylon, amidst a weeklong celebration of games, feasting, and musical contests, his beloved Hephaestion became gravely ill with a fever caused by typhus. He was advised by his doctors to be careful with his food and drink. This was advice he rejected, as he wanted to be part of the celebrations. He continued to drink wine and eat chicken.

Eight days into this fever, Hephaestion's condition worsened, and Alexander was sent for. Unfortunately, Alexander did not make it back in time to bid his male lover farewell. Upon his return, he was beside himself with inconsolable grief. He had Hephaestion's doctors hanged for letting him die. He refused to eat or drink for three days, he hacked off his hair, and he had the manes and tails of his horses cut off to express his extreme mourning. Alexander also laid on the body of his beloved Hephaestion day and night, unable to let go of him. Finally, he planned for the most grand and elaborate funeral procession that his money and power could buy.

Although he had a wife and other lovers, with the death of Hephaestion he had lost the love of his life and his soul mate. His second male lover was a Persian eunich by the name of Bagoas. However, he did not replace Hephaestion in his heart. Nothing seemed the same, and it seemed that Alexander the Great had lost the zest and fire that had previously driven him to greatness.

What was even worse was that soothsayers predicted that Alexander would soon be joining Hephaestion in the afterworld. A year later Alexander developed the signs of fever and was confined to his apparent deathbed, descending his armies into chaos. It is suspected that the fever he contracted was malaria. Other theories are that he possibly had West Nile virus, typhoid, viral encephalitis, possible poisoning, or that he simply suffered from the consequences of a life of heavy drinking.

The day before his death his soldiers and generals broke through the phalanx of bodyguards to file past the bed of their beloved Alexander. At this point he was too ill to even speak and reportedly acknowledged their "goodbyes" with a nod or a knowing look in his eyes. He died on June 10, 323 BC.

Alexander the Great's legacy as a leader, a conqueror, and a fearless and beloved ruler is unquestioned in the annals of history. However, he will also be forever remembered as the world's first and most beloved gay hero.

RANDY: "What I find incredibly inspiring about Alexander the Great was the fact that he and his boyfriend Hephaestion were incredibly devoted to each other."

MARK: "Ancient Greek society found it equally acceptable to have male lovers and female lovers."

RANDY: "In this particular story, it is clear to me that his one true love was Hephaestion, and his marriage was more of a political move."

MARK: "It truly was. Alexander clearly felt an inseparable bond for his boyfriend and lifelong friend. And yes, conquering the enemy and then marrying the Persian princess seems like more of a strategic move than a gesture of love. Throughout history, it is the artists and educators who are always the most liberal. A lot of the people we are discussing in this chapter were influential by virtue of their creations and their imagination."

RANDY: "It seems that gay liberation and women's rights in society have often been closely aligned."

MARK: "Influential women in history often had to work twice as hard to have their voices heard."

RANDY: "Gay women have a history that goes back to Ancient Greece as well. That brings us to our first gay female historical figure Sappho."

The exact birth and death dates for Sappho are sketchy. Historians put her birth in Greece at somewhere between 630 BC and 612 BC, estimating her death to be around 570 BC.

Sappho was a very unique woman for many reasons. During her lifetime there were very few woman whose poems and writings were highly revered, let alone to have stood the test of time. And, she is the first woman who not only preached and lived a free life of woman-to-woman love, she championed it.

Unquestionably, like the James Brown song, "It's a Man's World" celebrates and illuminates, men have dominated society throughout the ages. However, throughout time, strong and influential queens, goddesses, empresses, and czarinas have broken through to lead their societies on to triumph and greatness. Sappho was that type of woman. Shackles could not hold her down.

She was born on the Greek island of Lesbos, and her teachings and poetry written on that island gave birth to the term "lesbian." Male-dominated society rejected much of Sappho's work and her poetry. Much of her biographical poetry was destroyed by men who did not want her to have power, and her reputation was besmirched by men who called her a "whore" and a "prostitute." For this reason, a lot of details about her highly compassionate and educated life have been lost.

However, on her female-dominated island of ancient Lesbos, Sappho was highly revered amongst women, and amongst some men. Fortunately, a large amount of her writing and poetry has survived the ages. She once wrote, "I tell you in time to come, someone will remember us." Indeed she was correct.

Sappho's initial time on Lesbos was her most influential one. She believed that women were nurturers by nature, and that they could live more peacefully away from male-dominated society. There was a prevailing belief amongst Greek men that sex with women sapped a man of his virility. There was a true celebration of men's love of other men. For that reason, most statues of men depicted them naked and virile looking, while statues of females were clothed. In other words, homosexuality was erotic and preferred, while sex with women was seen as being merely for procreation.

Paralleling this train of thought, Sappho felt that women lost much of themselves in the loss of their virginity. She felt that abstaining from sex with men kept them virtuous and strong. She did speak from a perspective of authority, since she was married and had a daughter. In reality, Sappho was a functioning bisexual, so she wrote her poetry with a knowledge that she had dealt with love and sex from both sides, similar to the Joni Mitchell song, "Both Sides Now."

Sappho truly believed that woman-to-woman love was the real true love, as it was a love shared by equals. When two women made love, it was mutually satisfying, in that neither party was submitting to the will of the other. It was the purest love that a woman could know.

It is believed that Sappho had her own school for girls, in the same way that Plato later taught boys. It is known that she sought to impart her knowledge and her opinions upon other women and girls.

In her lifetime there was a military coup on the Isle of Lesbos, and it was taken over by Pittacus, who overthrew the wealthy aristocratic families who were in power. For several of the next years she and her fellow poet Alcaeus were exiled to the city of Syracuse on the island of Sicily. By now Sappho was quite well known as a famed poetess in the Mediterranean. When the citizens of Syracuse found that Sappho was coming to live there, they constructed a statue in her honor to welcome her. It was as if the twentieth-century rock star Madonna had just announced her latest tour.

Finally, in 581 BC, when Pittacus had been deposed on Lesbos, Sappho returned to the beloved island of her homeland. Sappho was obviously an extremely well-educated woman and very much ahead of her time.

Unfortunately, after her death much of her nine volumes of writings was lost or destroyed by her detractors. Fortunately, enough fragments of her poetry have remained intact. Nowadays, it is hard to separate the concepts of lesbianism from the Isle of Lesbos and revered thoughts of Sappho: the first lady of female gay sex.

RANDY: "What I find inspiring about Sappho is that she was incredibly determined to be heard."
MARK: "And this was clearly an era before public figures went out and hired publicists to make them look good in the press."
RANDY: "Yes, look at how times changed. The powers-that-be tried to discredit Sappho by calling her a 'woman of loose morals.' At other times, that might be looked upon as a virtue."
MARK: "A couple of thousand years later, when they called Madonna that, she suddenly sold several million more copies of her *Like a Virgin* album."
RANDY: "You can say that again! Well, fortunately, Sappho and many of her writings survived. Now, let's jump ahead another thousand years, to da Vinci."

One of the most admired men of the Renaissance and in all of civilization was Leonardo di ser Piero da Vinci, as he was truly the person for whom the term "Renaissance man" most aptly fits. Born on April 15, 1452 AD, he was a painter, a scientist, a mathematician, an engineer, an inventor, an anatomist, a sculptor, an architect, a musician, and a writer.

Although he had many talents, ironically it was for two of his paintings that he is the most beloved and remembered: *The Last Supper* and the *Mona Lisa*. He was also notorious for being a homosexual in an era in which being gay was extremely out of the realm of society's range of approvable behavior.

In fact, his lifestyle and his sexual orientation was a matter of great controversy at the time—the fifteenth and sixteenth centuries. During this era, in Florence, Italy, citizens could anonymously accuse others of wrongdoing. To effect this form of finger-pointing, there were boxes set up around the city in which one could write down his or her knowledge or suspicion of wrongdoing, drop them into the box, and then retreat back into the shadows without revealing their own identity. In this way, someone could tip off a "witch hunt," without fear of personal reprisal.

At an early age, twenty-four-year-old Leonardo da Vinci was the subject of one such accusation. A note was left in one of the boxes claiming that da Vinci had sex with a teenager of the approximate age of seventeen, who was known to be a boy "of ill repute" by the name of Jocopo Saltarelli, and who, it was also noted, "consents to pleasure those persons who wish for that kind of deplorable thing."

Leonardo was arrested, tried, and released for a lack of evidence. This was fortunate for modern culture, or the world might have been prematurely robbed of one of history's true geniuses.

In his time, and due to the sketches and notes he left behind, da Vinci came up with a multitude of inventions that later became the helicopter, the submarine, the machine gun, and the automobile.

He is also credited with detailing, via his sketches and drawings, the first anatomically correct examinations of human bone structure, maps for elaborate irrigation systems, calculations for lunar eclipses, and unraveling how the human eye works.

As a young man who displayed a high aptitude as an artist, he was tutored by a highly revered artist by the name of Verrocchio. This was also an era in which his own homosexuality blossomed. While in Milan he employed a "studio boy" as his assistant. In the beginning of this working relationship, the boy, Giacomo Caprotti, was a mere street urchin who regularly stole household items. Da Vinci made a list of everything that turned up missing while Caprotti was around. According to his writings, Caprotti was a "thief, liar, obstinate, glutton." He was so mischievous that he nicknamed the boy "Salai," which is Italian for "little devil." However, in time the rambunctious youth began to mellow, as though he was a tamed wild animal. His role changed to the point where he grew to become not only Leonardo's pupil, but his lover as well. Salai ended up staying with da Vinci for his entire life.

In addition, Leonardo also befriended a young man whose name was Francisco Melzi. He was to become da Vinci's student as well has his lover and lifelong companion.

When he moved back to Florence, Leonardo continued to use young boys as his models. He would employ them for his sketches and drawings, and often he would take them to his bed as well.

Leonardo moved to Rome, where he lived from 1513 to 1515. While there he was commissioned for several paintings for the Vatican. He later took a trip to Bologna, where he became friendly with King Francis I. It was His Royal Highness Francis who invited him to come to France to continue his work. He accepted the King's offer, and during the winter of 1516–17, he made the journey with his two lovers, Salai and Melzi in tow. While in France the trio resided in the villa of Cloux at Amboise, and da Vinci continued his life's work, drawing and sketching his inventions and ideas.

Da Vinci died in France on May 2, 1519, at the age of sixty-four. After his death, Francisco Melzi wrote a letter to one of Leonardo's half brothers. It is one of the most famous professions of Renaissance gay love. In the letter he proclaimed, "As long as my body holds together, I shall feel perpetual unhappiness, and rightly so, for he showed me daily a very warm and complete love. The loss of such a man is a sorrow to everyone, for nature will not be able to create his equal again."

Like so many geniuses in time, da Vinci's brilliance was not appreciated until years and years after his death. Although he was known for his painting skills and the mastery of his sketches, it was not known how clever and intuitive he truly was. He also questioned the logic of the Bible. One of his greatest paintings, *The Last Supper*, supposedly positioned Mary Magdalene at that event, as one of the disciples of Christ.

This tipped off the great theories that Mary Magdalene was not a prostitute at all, but that she was originally one of the apostles, who wrote her own "Gospel according to Mary Magdalene." The theory is that it was the jealous disciple, Paul, who decided to slander her, dismiss her, and call her a "whore." It is suspected that this was merely an act of misogyny. These theories about Mary Magdalene were the basis for Dan Brown's huge bestseller, *The Da Vinci Code*.

RANDY: "Whether or not you believe the theories talked about in *The Da Vinci Code*, what I liked the most was the fact that over 500 years later, we are still talking about Leonardo da Vinci."

MARK: "I know how your mind works. You are wondering whether or not 500 years from now people will be listening to 'Y.M.C.A.'"

RANDY: "How did you know?"

MARK: "I simply know how your mind works. Maybe you should write a book called *The Village People Code*."

RANDY: "Okay, I will make a note of that. Now let's move on to the creation of the most famous gay statue of all: Michelangelo's *David*."

If the only homosexual event of his entire life was carving the internationally famous statue, *David*, Michelangelo would still merit mention in this book. Although there is some conjecture about this talented artist's gay life, there is enough conclusive evidence to support this claim.

Although he was born, on March 6, 1475, as Michelangelo di Lodovico Buonarroti Simoni, he has been forever been known and recognized by his singular first name. As one of the true artistic masters of the Italian Renaissance, Michelangelo was an accomplished painter, sculptor, architect, poet, and even an engineer. Similar to da Vinci, he was one of the most sought-after artisans of his day.

He demonstrated his incredible artistry as a sculptor and artist at an early age, and by the time he was thirty years old, he had already produced two of his undeniable marble masterpieces: *David* and the *Pietà*. Even at the time of the sixteenth century Italian Renaissance, when the nude male figure of *David* was created, it was controversial for the erotic feelings that it inspired. With it, Michelangelo demonstrated his obvious love and appreciation of the male body.

This was also reflected in his feelings for a young nobleman in 1532 by the name of Tommaso dei Cavalieri (circa 1509–87) whom he had met while working in Rome. His correspondence and his famous sonnets written about Cavalieri reveal an emotional and physical love for the boy. Never married, Michelangelo once wrote about his bachelorhood: "Already I have a wife who is too much for me, one who keeps me unceasingly struggling on. It is my art, and my works are my children."

While much of the famed artist's letters and writings exist, the prime recipient of Michelangelo's love was evidently Tommaso dei Cavalieri. The young man was twenty-three years old when Michelangelo met him in 1532. At the time the artist was fifty-seven.

Later that year he returned to Rome, expressly to visit Cavalieri. He returned to Florence, and then in 1534 he permanently moved to Rome. He wrote several sonnets, or love poems, to Cavalieri proclaiming his fascination with his physical beauty.

Cavalieri was conclusively open to the older man's affection, and in one letter he wrote to Michelangelo, "I swear to return your love. Never have I loved a man more than I love you, never have I wished for a friendship more than I wish for yours." Cavalieri was to remain devoted to Michelangelo until his own death.

In addition to his brilliant skills as a sculptor, Michelangelo was commissioned to create two of the most influential works in the history of Western art: the fresco scenes in the Sistine Chapel in Rome: the painted depiction of *Genesis* on the ceiling and dynamic the *Last Judgement*, which is painted on the altar wall.

With regard to the *David* statue, an amusing Michelangelo story exists. *David* was commissioned by the government officials in the city of Florence. The chief executive of Florence, Pietro Soderini, complained that he did not like the nose on the eighteen-foot-tall statue. So, Michelangelo got his mallet and chisel and climbed onto the scaffolding to make some alterations according to this request. What Soderini did not know was that in one hand the artist concealed a handful of marble dust. While Soderini looked on, Michelangelo reached the statue's face, aimed the chisel at *David's* nose, and made a requisite amount of noise, releasing a cloud of the concealed marble dust. In reality the chisel never touched the statue. Looking downward he asked Soderini how he liked it with this supposed alteration. "I like it better now," the man answered with a smile, "You have given it life." (1)

Only Michelangelo knew the truth of his actions. He was not about to let some idiot politician tell him what to do. With *David*, the sculpting master had created the most famous gay male statue in history. Michaelangelo's life came to an end on February 18, 1564.

RANDY: "If Michaelangelo only knew how many gay bars and gay saunas would feature a plaster of Paris knock-off version of the *David* statue, I wonder if he would have carved it to begin with?"

MARK: "Are you kidding? Now that's what I call longevity for your art."

RANDY: "If only your book *The Captain & Tennille* would continue to have that kind of longevity."

MARK: "Hey, it's still for sale on eBay!"

RANDY: "That's because you keep bidding the price up."
MARK: "Let's get back to our history lesson."
RANDY: "I like historical figures who shake things up and make the general public ask questions about what's going on."
MARK: "Yeah, had the *National Enquirer* been around back then, we would have known much more about Michelangelo's private life. Instead, we now know more about Britney Spears' life than we ever wanted to know."
RANDY: "Well, Miss Britney sure knows how to work a headline."
MARK: "Well, it sounds like Britney has some issues with parental authority."
RANDY: "Speaking about rebelling against parental authority, now we come to Frederick the Great."

Although he is primarily famous for his later-life feats of military strategy and for uniting many sections of land in the area of his own native Prussia, Frederick the Great is also known for possessing one of the most tragic gay love stories in European history. He was born on January 24, 1712. Since his father was King Frederick William I, younger Frederick grew up in a position of wealth and privilege. He was also well educated and had a taste for the arts and the finer things in life. In other words, he was a sensitive boy, and he was also very homosexual.

When Frederick II was only thirteen years old, his father passed a law in Prussia for that "all gypises found within the borders of his kingdom were to be strangled, while sodomites [gay men] would be burned alive." (2) Talk about a bad time to be gay!

Frederick had a page in his court by the name of Peter Christoph Keith. When the young Prince Frederick was sixteen years old, he became friendly with Keith, who was a year older than he. Reportedly, Keith became a devoted friend of the Prince. As young Frederick's sister Wilhelmine was to write, "[Frederick and Peter Christoph Keith] soon became inseparable. Keith was intelligent, but without education. He served my brother from feelings of real devotion, and kept him informed of all the King's actions." However, she was also to note, "Though I had noticed that he was on more familiar terms with this page than was proper in his position, I did not know how intimate the friendship was." (3)

When Frederick's father, the King, got wind of this, he promptly sent Keith into exile, and that was the end of that. To avoid such homosexual carryings on, the King appointed a more proper companion to the young Prince, to make him more of a man. He chose a

Lieutenant Borcke to be his son's new masculine "buddy." Unfortunately for the King, this plan backfired too, and soon the Prince was writing love letters to Lieutenant Borcke.

When Prince Frederick realized that this love affair with Borcke was not going to work out, he turned his desires toward the son of a Prussian General. The young man, Hans Hermann von Katte, was six years older than the Prince, was a music lover, and he favored French literature. His official title was as the Prince's protector and confidante. So devoted was Katte that he would even stand guard while the Prince received his flute lessons.

It wasn't long before this relationship had grown into a full-fledged love affair. When the King took to humiliating his son in public, Prince Frederick decided he had enough of this routine and plotted an escape with his boyfriend to England. The plan almost worked. Sadly, when Prince Frederick and his lover Katte reached the border of Prussia, they were both arrested as treasonous deserters. When the matter came up before the courts, Katte was sentenced with life imprisonment, and they refused to judge the Prince, as he was destined to become their next leader.

Well, King Frederick I was not amused by this leniency of the sentence; he condemned Katte to death and had the Prince imprisoned. One November morning in 1728, the Prince was awakened in his cell and ordered to look out of his window. His boyfriend was dragged out into the courtyard, and horrified, the Prince called out, "My dear Katte, a thousand pardons."

"My Prince, there is nothing to apologize for," Katte shouted back at him. (3) With that he was forced to kneel over, and was promptly beheaded while his royal gay lover looked on in horror. As the sword came down the Prince fainted as he watched the man he loved killed in front of him.

The Prince was released from prison in 1731. As he went out into the world, he did so with two new male friends who were to remain loyal to him for years. One was Dietrick Lieutenant Count von Keyserling, who became a lifelong friend of the Prince's. It was widely suspected that they were lovers as well. The other soldier he befriended was Michael Gabriel Fredersdorf, a private in the Prussian army. It is also suspected that he and the Prince were lovers.

When he came out of incarceration, he found that he was to marry a woman he had "zero" interest in. It was a marriage of alliance, which his father had arranged. It was Elizabeth Christine of Brunswick-Bevern he was forced to wed. After his father's death, and his ascension to the crown, he gave his wife her own palace in Berlin, sent her off to it, and made a habit of seeing her only once a year.

As the King of Prussia, Frederick proved a beloved and effective ruler. Part of King Frederick II of Prussia's legacy were his strong military plans and his ability to consistently remain victorious over his enemies.

Since he had no physical interest in his wife, they had no children or heirs. In fact, there are many who claim that once he became King, he had no interest in relationships with either sex. He is credited with annexing many of the territories that became the nineteenth-century united Germany, and many of his commissioned buildings still stand in Berlin, as well as his summer palace, Sanssouci, in Pottsdam.

RANDY: "Well, I have to say, Frederick the Great's daddy sounded worse than Joan Crawford came across in *Mommie, Dearest*."

MARK: "Yeah, instead of 'No wire hangers,' Fredrick's father was more like, 'No gay lovers.'"

RANDY: "Like Faye Dunaway as Joan Crawford said: 'Leave it to you to know where to find the booze and the boys.'"

MARK: "On that note, now let's jump back to some more of the famous authors in history."

Forceful women in history who are both successful and powerful—especially pre-1900 AD—are few and far between. Most of them were rulers whose rise to power had to do with the fact that they were next in line to take the throne of their countries like Elizabeth I [England], Czarina Catherine the Great [Russia], or Empress Maria Theresa [Austria]. Those who had the opportunity to become both famous and forceful by merit of their own wits is an even smaller list. And, those who had legendary lesbian affairs on the side are even more rare. Authoress, writer, and political critic Madame de Staël is one French aristocrat who leads the list.

She was born in 1766, the daughter of Swiss statesman Jacques Necker and Suzanne Curchord Necker, who was the hostess of a prominent literary salon in Paris. Her father at one point was the Minister of Finance to French King Louis XVI. Anne Louise Germaine Necker was definitely destined for an interesting life. She published several of books during her lifetime, had a comfortable marriage of convenience, and pissed off Napoleon to the point where she had to leave the country for her own safety. In an era where a woman was not supposed to be outspoken, she was VERY outspoken.

When Germaine Necker was only sixteen years old, her parents began to make arrangements for a marriage for her, which was the socially accepted thing of the day to do for one's daughter. Their first target was William Pitt the Younger of England. However, Germaine protested. She could not see herself living in England. Instead a marriage was arranged for her with a Swedish ambassador to France, living in Paris. This was more to her liking, even though Baron Erik de Staël-Holstein was a full seventeen years older. The formal arrangements took all of three years to negotiate and ultimately involved the King of Sweden as well as the French court.

The whole event was more for the benefit of Germaine's father's career than for her happiness. Once married, Germaine had no interest in Erik, although she bore him three children. The marriage dissolved in 1797, and she had all the prestige of her title as a one-time Baroness, and none of the headache of a husband to go along with it.

During the infamous 1793–94 Reign of Terror, in which King Louis XVI and his wife, Queen Marie Antoinette, were both deposed and then beheaded, de Staël fled to England. In doing so, she saved her own life. Next, Napoleon Bonaparte came to power in France, and de Staël returned to her homeland.

In 1798, when Germaine became acquainted with another woman of social standing, Juliette Récamier, she heard fireworks go off, and the duo became an inseparable pair in Paris society. Like so many men and women of her day, it is Germaine's correspondence that is the most revealing of her personal life. De Staël wrote to Récamier: "I clasp you to my heart with more devotion than any lover . . . I love you with a love surpassing that of friendship. I go down on my knees to embrace you with all my heart." (1)

Récamier recalls their first meeting and Germaine gazing toward her "[with] great eyes . . . and paid me compliments upon my figure which might have seemed exaggerated and too direct." However, those comments certainly got her attention.

De Staël was to later write of her female lover, "I have loved you for three years. It is sacred, is it not? I shall die thinking of it." (1)

In addition to her love letters, de Staël became quite famous for her books, including *Letters on the Works and Character of Jean-Jacques Rousseau* (1788), and *A Treatise on the Influence of the Passions Upon the Happiness of Individuals and of Nations* (1796). She became outspoken about her dislike of Napoleon. Having met him in 1796 she claimed "no emotion of the heart could act upon him . . . for him nothing exists but himself; all other creatures are ciphers."

In 1800 she really let loose with her criticisms of Napoleon, claiming, "Bonaparte is not a man only ... but a system; and if he were right, the human species would no longer be what God has made it."

Napoleon blasted back at her, "Tell her she must never stand in my way. If she does, I'll smash her. I'll break her." Furthermore, he banished her to stay outside a forty-mile radius of Paris. She simply left the country and continued her campaign against him. She moved to Germany and later through Russia and into Sweden, where he could not touch her.

However, she always kept her female lover in her heart. She wrote to Récamier, "You are a heavenly creature; had I lived beside you, I would have been very happy. Fate bears me away. Adieu."

After Napoleon's downfall, de Staël returned to France and launched a literary salon, where she encouraged viewpoints other than just the French ones that had been imposed under Bonaparte's reign. When a stroke partially paralyzed her, Récamier came to visit her at Coppet, her father's chalet on Lake Geneva, shortly before her death in 1817. The last words that de Staël said to Récamier, "I embrace you with all that remains to me." (1)

RANDY: "I think if Madame de Staël was around nowadays, she would be best buddies with Rosie O'Donnell."
MARK: "She was one outspoken gal, that's for sure."
RANDY: "Napoleon ran her out of Paris to shut her up! It seems to me, that throughout history, it was the men who got to do what they wanted more than the women."
MARK: "That's for sure."
RANDY: "And, it's obvious to me that the artists and writers traditionally had more of a free hand to do what they wanted to do, and get away with it.
MARK: "Well, history sure attests to that fact!"

Herman Melville is revered as one of the ten greatest American authors of this country's first two centuries. While his first novels were bestsellers in their day, his career suddenly lost favor with the public. When he died, he was nearly obscure, and his longest and grandest novel, *Moby Dick*, had literally sunk his career. Like the painter Vincent van Gogh, Herman Melville's real success came after his death. When *Moby Dick* was rediscovered by a twentieth-century audience, it was heralded as a masterpiece of world literature.

Herman was born on August 1, 1819, in New York City into a colorful Boston family. His father, Allan Melvill, was an importer of

French dry goods. For most of Herman's childhood, the family was quite well-to-do. However, the financial strain of three boys in school soon overwhelmed Allan. Unable to control his financial problems, he decided to move his family to Albany in 1830, where he began working in the fur business. However, the career change was disastrous and caused him untold mental stress, causing his death from a sudden illness. He left his family in sheer poverty. After Allan died, his mother added an "e" to the end of the family name to distance herself and her children from her late husband's karma. Forced to turn to her own family for financial support, she found herself and her children treated poorly for her stupid life choices.

Young Herman Melville struck out on his own, finding work as a property surveyor on the Erie Canal in upstate New York. When he failed to earn enough money, his brother aided him in landing a job as a cabin boy on a ship leaving New York City headed for Liverpool, England. Keeping a log of his life on that ship became the basis for his 1849 book, *Redburn: His First Voyage*.

On New Year's Day 1841, Herman set sail from Fairhaven, Massachusetts, on the whaler *Acushnet*, which was heading for the Pacific Ocean. Much of what he wrote in his epic, *Moby Dick*, was learned on his 18-month voyage on the *Acushnet*. When the ship reached the Marquesas Islands, Melville decided to get off and live with the natives for several weeks. While there he chronicled his experiences in his *Typee* and the sequel *Omoo*. He then sailed to the Society Islands, and then to Hawaii.

Many theories abound about the action in his most famous works. They seem to heavily center on the sexually charged male bonding that takes place aboard ships. There were usually dark-skinned cabin boys, who were slightly feminine, with delicate features, who become the soul mates of a big burly sailor. It is a common theme in his books.

In *Typee*, Melville wrote of his character Tom's sudden attraction to the youth, Marnoo. In the story, Marnoo slights Tom, and the incident is described in what we can't help but now recognize as a fairly homosexual manner: "Had the belle of the season, in the pride of her beauty and power, been cut in a place of public resort by some supercilious exquisite, she could not have felt greater indignation than I did at this unexpected slight."

In *Billy Budd*, the main character is without a doubt a gay martyr/ victim. When Captain Vere fantasizes about Billy he proclaims, "[Billy] in the nude might have posed for a statue of young Adam before the Fall."

There were clearly times in Melville's life that he struggled with his sexuality. Although in his personal life he married Elizabeth Shaw in 1847, and they had three children, he clearly was not happy.

In 1850, Herman Melville moved from New York City to western Massachusetts, in the Berkshire Mountains. There he found camaraderie with other writers including Fanny Kemble, Oliver Wendell Holmes, and Nathaniel Hawthorne. When thirty-one-year-old Melville met forty-six-year-old Hawthorne, Herman fell in love with him. He even dedicated *Moby Dick* to Hawthorne as an expression of his love. Although they remained friends, Melville was disheartened when Hawthorne rejected him. He used the pain of this rejection as an inspiration for his novel, *Pierre*.

While *Moby Dick* received mixed reviews, when *Pierre* was released, it was savaged by the critics. After that he began to have trouble selling his writing. When Harper & Brothers turned down his next manuscript, *The Isle of the Cross*, Melville was crushed, and *The Isle of the Cross* was lost forever.

From 1857 to 1860, Melville went out on the lecture circuit, mainly speaking of his travels in the South Pacific. When the Civil War ended he wrote over seventy poems that were published as *Battle Pieces* in 1866. Again, the critics slaughtered him. The Melvilles came close to separating at this point, but in 1867, when their oldest son, Malcolm, committed suicide, they found a bond in their grief.

His writing career was no longer supporting him, so he took a job as a customs inspector, working for the City of New York. Herman Melville held that post for nineteen years. Ironically, the Customs House he worked in was located on Gansevoort Street in lower Manhattan, which had been so named for his mother's wealthy and powerful family. He died in New York City, of illness, on the morning of September 28, 1891, at the age of seventy-two. His controversial and very gay novella, *Billy Budd*, was not published until years after his death.

Never fully appreciated during his life, Herman Melville left behind a great literary legacy. In reality, he was ahead of his time. His *Benito Cereno* is a one of the rare nineteenth-century works to really confront the trauma of race relations in the United States. And, his *The Paradise of Bachelors and the Tartarus of Maids* and *Billy Budd* have been popular works for scholars to cite and analyze for their homoerotic themes.

MARK: "It's really interesting to note that Herman Melville took off for the sea to begin with, to hang out with all the boys."

RANDY: "Hey, it's just like the character of Samantha on *Sex and the
            City* proclaimed, her favorite week of the year is Fleet Week,
            when all of the sailors come to New York City."
MARK: "This sounds like the lead-in to a Village People song."
RANDY: "'In the Navy' anyone?"
MARK: "It sounds like Herman Melville got on board a hundred years
            before you recorded that song."
RANDY: "You got that right. Okay, let's talk about one of my favorite
            writers, Walt Whitman."
MARK: "He was 'earth friendly' a century before Al Gore started talk-
            ing about global warming."
RANDY: "Good call!"

For all of his life, Walt Whitman was an independent thinker. He
was very much into ecological matters, living in harmony with the
universe and having the freedom to express himself as a gay man. His
Leaves of Grass, which was considered controversial at the time of its
first publication, is now heralded as his masterpiece of lyrical poetry.
The odds of his achieving such notoriety in his life was not a given.

Walt was born on May 31, 1819, in West Hills, Long Island. Educated in public schools, young Whitman's family moved to Brooklyn.
His mother preached to him about valuing his family ties, and he
was to remain devoted to his parents throughout his life. His parents'
Quaker teachings instantly put him on the path of pacifism and living harmoniously with God and the universe.

Living in New York City put him in proximity of several famous
and influential people in parades and other public gatherings. He
personally saw President Andrew Jackson and was very impressed.
He also saw the French statesman and Revolutionary War hero, the
Marquis de Lafayette. Spying the smiling six-year-old Whitman
caused Lafayette to pick him up and in arms and carry him around.
That event became a pivotal happening in the young man's life. He
felt that he had been touched by greatness, and he suddenly felt that
he too aspired to a life of accomplishment.

His *Leaves of Grass* was at first something that was self-published
and not very well received. The original 1855 edition of it contained
a mere thirty-two poems. However, he kept adding to it. In 1860,
Leaves of Grass included 124 new poems, and was a full 456 pages
long. By 1865, after *Leaves of Grass* was purchased for publication
by a mainstream American publishing house, Whitman soon found
himself virtually world famous in literary circles. Many of his poems
contained graphic depictions of the human body, and the book

was not heralded by the Victorians in the United States. However, it was instantly a hit in the more progressive European markets. The French in particular loved Whitman's writing from the very start.

During that decade there was much upheaval in the country because of the Civil War. His brother George was captured by the Confederacy following a battle. By January 1865 Whitman moved to Washington, DC and took a job with the Indian Affairs Department. He later worked for the Department of the Interior. It was that same year that Walt had his most notable, enduring, and memorable homosexual affair.

It was a stormy night in DC, and Walt Whitman found himself the last passenger on a streetcar in town. The eighteen-year-old conductor, Peter Doyle, struck up a conversation, and it was a matter of love at first sight. Whitman was to write, "It was a lonely night, and so I thought I would go and talk to him. Something in me made me do it and something in him drew me that way. He used to say there was something in me had the same effect on him. Anyway . . . we were familiar at once— I put my hand on his knee—we understood. He did not get out at the end of the trip—in fact went all the way back with me." (1)

Doyle had been a soldier for the Confederacy, but now that the war was over, he had moved to Washington, DC, as well. Whitman was deeply smitten with Peter Doyle. He sent his friend bouquets and love notes, and they would take long walks together in Washington, and across the river in Alexandria, Virginia.

Walt Whitman continued to live openly, celebrating man-to-man sexuality and harmony, and the human body. One of his most notorious poetic passages was written about his own penis.

When a series of strokes made it unable to hold a regular job, Whitman continued to work at home on his poetry. He had his continuing relationship with Doyle to rest upon. He told Doyle, "I don't know what I should do if I hadn't you to think of and look forward to."

However, in 1873, Doyle assumed the job of brakeman for the Baltimore & Potomac Railroad, and they grew apart. Whitman replaced Peter in his life with a series of other young men, including Harry Stafford, an errand boy in Camden, New Jersey, who was staying with Walt's brother George. And then there was a twenty-five-year-old farmhand by the name of Edward Cattal, whom Whitman wrote of in his personal diary. They would have romantic rendezvous in the moonlight.

Whitman was to spend the rest of his life in Camden, New Jersey. Up to the very end of his life he kept making additions to his evolving *Leaves of Grass* anthology. When another famous writer,

Britain's famed Oscar Wilde, came to America on a lecturing tour, he insisted upon meeting the great Walt Whitman.

When Whitman was at the very end of his life he was still making revisions to the final version of *Leaves of Grass*, which is known as the "deathbed edition." He died on March 26, 1892. Walt Whitman was an inspiringly independent voice in the changing times of his century, who continues to be looked upon as a patron saint of the nonconformists of society, especially the gay nonconformists.

RANDY: "Well, we have covered a lot of territory here."
MARK: "Alexander the Great and his longtime lover, Sappho and her girls, Christopher Marlowe questioning authority ..."
RANDY: "And Herman Melville chasing sailors."
MARK: "And all of this took place before the 1800s were over."
RANDY: "Now we come to more modern history: important gay people whose lives were at least partially lived into the 1900s."

As the twentieth century approached, social mores and morals began to change. Along with that, the way in which society viewed homosexuality changed as well. For some of the luminaries who we are about to discuss, it ruined their lives, particularly Oscar Wilde and Alan Turing. For others, it became a cause of defiance and self-expression, like Frida Kahlo and James Baldwin. And, for others, their brushes with homosexuality defined the material they wrote, like Colette. And for some, like Japanese writer Yukio Mishima, it led to a tragic end. Wanting to leave this world dramatically, in 1970 he committed hara-kiri with his own sword.

It was the literati who tended to experiment the most with exploring their gay side. The writers of each era were the ones who made a living out of pondering life, love, and motivation. More often it was they who also broke away from traditional society and went off to march to their own drummer. This was certainly true of Gertrude Stein, E. M. Forster, Virginia Woolf, T. E. Lawrence, and Jean Cocteau. After all, one's sexual life is the height of their self-expression, and their individuality.

In the late 1800s, at the height of the culture of Victorian England, Oscar Wilde became a huge celebrity. Known for his wit and his writing, he became the toast of society. He became so famous that he once sailed to the United States for a speaking engagement. When Oscar Wilde got off the ship in America the customs officer asked him what he had "to declare?" Without missing a beat Wilde replied, "Nothing but my genius."

Born on October 16, 1854, in Ireland to an aristocratic family, Oscar was educated at home until he was nine years old. From 1871 to 1874, he studied at Trinity College in Dublin, where he was an outstanding student, and there he won the Berkeley Gold Medal, which was the highest award there was for students of the classics at Trinity. Magdalen College, in Oxford, England, granted him a scholarship, and he studied there from 1874 until his graduation in November of 1878.

He returned to Dublin after college, and fell in love with a woman by the name of Florence Balcombe. When she announced her engagement to *Dracula* author Bram Stoker, a heartbroken Wilde announced that he was leaving Ireland forever. With the exception of two brief visits to the Emerald Isle, he basically kept his promise. The next six years were spent in London, Paris, and the United States.

Oscar started teaching classes in aesthetic values in London, where he wrote the massively successful novel *The Picture of Dorian Gray*, and in 1882 he went on a lecture tour in the United States and Canada. Publicly, he became well known for his foppish ways and penchant for dressing like a dandy. While he dressed like a Victorian Boy George, his plays, especially *The Importance of Being Earnest*, won him fame and acclaim.

While he was in England he met Constance Lloyd, whose father was the wealthy Queen's Counselman, Horace Lloyd. Wilde proposed marriage to her, and they were wed on May 29, 1884, in Paddington, London. Since her father was rich, Constance was on an allowance of £250, which provided the Wilde's with an existence of luxury. They had two sons, Cyril (born 1885) and Vyvyan (born 1886).

However, more often than not, it was Oscar's wild life—pun intended—and his gay social circle that really made him legendary. His biographers claim that his first same-sex affair came the year after his marriage, when he met seventeen-year-old Robert Baldwin Ross. Not long afterward he began to frequent the gay bars and brothels of London.

It was during the early summer of 1891 that a poet, Lionel Johnson, introduced twenty-two-year-old Lord Alfred Douglas to Oscar Wilde. This became the love affair that was to be his undoing. At the time Douglas was an undergraduate student at Oxford University.

Douglas was to write late in his life, "From the second time he [Oscar] saw me, when he gave me a copy of *Dorian Gray*, which I took with me to Oxford, he made overtures to me. It was not till

I had known him for at least six months and after I had seen him over and over again and he had twice stayed with me in Oxford, that I gave in to him." (4)

When Lord Alfred's father, John Sholto Douglas, Marquess of Queensberry, got wind of what his son was up to, he was convinced that he was being corrupted by Wilde, against his will. He was determined to publicly insult and demean Wilde in any way he could. When it was learned that he was going to attend the London opening night performance of Wilde's play *The Importance of Being Earnest*, with the intention of throwing a bouquet of turnips onto the stage as a visual slur, he was banned from the theater.

Oscar took off for a vacation in Monte Carlo with young Lord Alfred, whom he nicknamed "Bosie." While there, the Marquess of Queensberry left a calling card at the club Wilde's family belonged to. On it was handwritten, "For Oscar Wilde posing Somdomite [sic]."

Wilde accused him of libel, and Queensberry was arrested. However, that opened a whole can of worms. Queensberry was released and Wilde was slanderously written about in the London newspapers. Before long, Wilde found himself in court defending his gay lifestyle. When it came to light that Wilde kept company with a series of "rent boys," cross dressers, and other homosexuals, his trial became the scandal of the day.

It is from the 1895 Wilde trial that his words for homosexuality: "the love that dares not speak its name," became famous. When he was asked in court to define what this love is, according to the court records from the trial, Wilde replied: "'The love that dares not speak its name' in this century is such a great affection of an elder for a younger man as there was between David and Jonathan, such as Plato made the very basis of his philosophy, and such as you find in the sonnets of Michelangelo and Shakespeare. It is that deep spiritual affection that is as pure as it is perfect." (5)

After a lengthy trial, Wilde was found guilty of "gross indecency" under Section 11 of the Criminal Law Amendment Act of 1885. Wilde was subsequently imprisoned for two years at Holloway. While there he was visited daily by his young lover, Lord Alfred Douglas.

Following his two years of incarceration, Wilde moved to Paris, where he was free to live out the final three years of his life in self-imposed exile and a reported sea of absinthe. He lived the last chapters of his life in the Hôtel d'Alsace, [currently known as L'Hôtel] in Paris, free to carry on his gay lifestyle.

Oscar Wilde succumbed to cerebral meningitis on November 30, 1900. Originally, Wilde was buried in the Cimetière de Bagneux, which is located outside Paris. Later his body was moved to Père Lachaise Cemetery in Paris. By now he was a legendary literary figure, and his elaborate tomb in Père Lachaise was designed by acclaimed sculptor Sir Jacob Epstein.

His boyfriend at the time, Robert Ross, requested that his own ashes be interred there as well. That wish was complied with in 1950. On the carved relief of Oscar Wilde's tomb was an angel. And appropriately so, the angel had male genitals. The genitals were removed when people claimed they were "obscene." The genitals reportedly were used for years as a paperweight at the office of the Père Lachaise Cemetery groundskeepers. Although they later disappeared, the legend of Oscar Wilde has never vanished.

A compelling film was done of his life in 1997, called *Wilde*. Starring Stephen Fry as Oscar and Jude Law as "Bosie," the supporting cast includes Vanessa Redgrave and Tom Wilkinson. Wilde's most famous film adaptation is still the Oscar-winning [Best Cinematography] 1941 movie, *The Picture of Dorian Gray*, starring Hurd Hatfield, Donna Reed, and Angela Lansbury.

RANDY: "What a Wilde boy he was!"
MARK: "You can say that again."
RANDY: "He really should have left England before he was arrested; it would have made more sense."
MARK: "Hey, as Martha & The Vandellas proclaim, 'Love Makes Me Do Foolish Things.'"
RANDY: "We are getting ahead of ourselves."
MARK: "Right you are."
RANDY: "Before we go off on a tangent of famous Motown songs, let's talk about one of our favorite twentieth-century woman-who-loved-women: Frida Kahlo. I know that you have a special place in your heart for painters."
MARK: "You know me so well. And one of my favorites is Frida Khalo."
RANDY: "She is as famous for her 'unibrow' eyebrows as she is her great self-portraits."
MARK: "And I loved Selma Hayek in the *Frida* movie!"
RANDY: "Especially her scenes with Ashley Judd."

Known for her realist paintings of herself in all sorts of odd get-ups and situations, openly bisexual Frida Kahlo has become revered as being the most celebrated female painter in the history of Mexico. She was married to Diego Rivera, who was a huge star in the art world and throughout his life. Together, they were both colorful and creative entities.

It is interesting to note that many people we today consider to be "famous" were not necessarily stars in their own lifetime. Vincent van Gogh certainly falls into this category. He never sold a painting during his life. A similar fate was Frida Kahlo's. While she was alive, she was primarily of note for being the wife of Diego Rivera.

It was not until the early 1980s that the work of Kahlo first came to international light. Amidst the 1980s Neomexicanismo art movement, Frida's incredibly distinctive self-portraits were publicized, exploited, and at long last: celebrated.

When she was once asked why she was her own primary model, she replied, "I paint myself because I am often alone and I am the subject I know best." (6)

The union of Diego Rivera and Frida Kahlo was a notoriously fiery and tempestuous one. He drank a lot and had affairs with women. Not to be outdone, so did Frida.

She was born Magdalena Carmen Frida Kahlo y Calderón on July 6, 1907. Her mother gave birth to her in the family house, which was called *La Casa Azul* (The Blue House), in Coyoacán, which at the time was outside of sprawling Mexico City. Her father was born Carl Wilhelm Kahlo in Pforzheim, Germany. And, his father was a painter and goldsmith.

Frida was three years old when the Mexican Revolution began in 1910. At the age of six she contracted polio. Since the polio left her right leg thinner than the left, she took to wearing long skirts to hide her deformity. In September 1925, she was riding a bus when it hit a trolley car on a busy street seriously injuring her. One of the trolley car's iron handrails impaled her in the abdomen, injuring her uterus. During her life she underwent thirty-five operations, many due to the polio and the trolley accident.

It was while she was confined to her bed that her mother got her an easel, oil paints, and brushes, so she could pass the time. In her lifetime Frida Kahlo did over 143 paintings; fifty-five of them were her dramatic self-portraits.

She married Diego Rivera in 1929. They had an unconventional marriage that raised eyebrows but that did not phase the couple. Diego didn't mind the fact that Frida had affairs with women, but what he did disapprove of were her affairs with men. Known as Communist sympathizers, they befriended Leon Trotsky, who was granted political sanctuary when Stalin took over the Soviet Union. Trotsky came to live with Rivera and his wife, and he and Frida had a notorious affair. Trotsky was later assassinated, after he had moved out of Frida and Diego's house.

Frida Kahlo lived a colorful life and died on July 13, 1954. It was not until after her death that Diego finally and fully appreciated Frida. Just like her artwork, her life was not celebrated as fully as it was postmortem.

RANDY: "Now we come to one of my favorite gay historical figures, Alan Turing."

MARK: "He was such a brilliant man, and yet he was persecuted for his lifestyle choices."

RANDY: "So many of the people in this chapter were truly born before their time. Alan Turning was one of them."

MARK: "The term 'tortured genius' certainly comes to mind."

RANDY: "You got that right."

Alan Turing is the English mathematician, logician, and cryptographer who broke the Nazi's notorious Enigma Code, which helped win World War II. He was also a tortured genius who was tormented for his homosexual affairs. His torment drove him to commit one of the most imaginative suicides on record [we kid you not]: by poison apple. Take that, Sleeping Beauty!

Born on June 23, 1912, Alan Turing was somewhat of a genius geek in his day, and he is looked upon as the father of modern computer science. Having worked on developing the Manchester Mark I, he envisioned a future where machines could hold and retrieve data. The laptop computers we are now so dependent upon go back to the concepts set forth, largely, by Turing.

He was reportedly a befuddled genius at school; he dabbled both in mathematics and in homosexuality. At the age of fourteen he attended Sherborne School in Dorset. Although it was recognized that he did have "genius" potential, he also had no interest in literature or studying the classics. It was only mathematics and science that held his attention.

When he was sixteen years old, in 1928, he embraced the work of Albert Einstein and was able to draw questions about it. Turing also fell in love with one of his schoolmates, Christopher Morcom. Unfortunately, the desire to have a physical love affair was not

returned. It ended tragically when Morcom suddenly died only
weeks before their final term at Sherborne. The cause of death was
deemed the effects of bovine tuberculosis, which Christopher had
contracted as a boy, when he drank the milk of an infected cow. The
sudden death of the boy he loved profoundly saddened Alan.

Turing attended King's College in Cambridge from 1931 to 1934
and graduated. He wrote a momentous paper "On Computable Numbers, With an Application to the Entscheidungsproblem," dated May
26, 1936, laying out the plans for a Turing machine that could calcu-
late numbers.

After Germany declared war on England in 1939, Turing went to
work with the British government to crack the code of the German
Enigma machine. It took Turing only weeks at offices at Bletchley
Park to devise an electromechanical machine that was capable of
breaking the Enigma. Turing called his deciphering machine "the
bombe."

In November 1942, Turing went to the United States, where he
worked with the U.S. Navy cryptanalysts on Naval Enigma and
assisted in "bombe" construction in Washington. After the war was
over, in 1945 Turing was awarded the officer of the Order of the
British Empire (OBE) for his wartime efforts.

Reportedly, Turing did little to hide the fact that he was gay. He
didn't think that it was a matter of criminal knowledge, and he
would often comment about a handsome man he encountered while
accompanied by his colleagues. In 1952 Turing's home was robbed,
and he filed a routine police report. While giving the facts about the
robbery, he mentioned to the police that he thought the burglar
might be one of his former male lovers. That was all they had to
hear. It wasn't long before they drew up a police case against him as
a suspect for the crime of "gross indecency."

Turing pleaded "guilty" at his trial and faced either two years in
prison, or the new "therapy" to cure homosexuality: "chemical cas-
tration" via hormone injections. Opting for the hormone injections,
Turing was left psychologically and physically scarred by this ordeal. It may have complied with the law, but it reportedly did nothing to deter his gay desires.

On June 7, 1954, tormented by the humiliating ordeal he had gone
through, he plotted his own suicide. He dipped an apple in cyanide,
took a bite of it, and lay down on his bed. A misunderstood genius,
Alan Turing died for what he believed in: especially his homosexual
lifestyle.

MARK: "Wow, that is one tragic end."

RANDY: "You got that right. The poison apple was a dramatic touch."

MARK: "Very Sleeping Beauty."

RANDY: "Well, we have certainly laid the groundwork for showing the various roles that gay men and women have played in various cultures throughout history."

MARK: "We have also spanned a lot of time in this chapter. But I think that unless you can see where the world's view of homosexuality has been in the past, you cannot fully appreciate how it has evolved."

RANDY: "Well, that is our history lesson. Now it's time to get down to the heart of this book, gay men and women in the arts, and especially in modern pop culture."

Chapter 2

That's Showbiz ... and the Kid Does Stay in the Picture!

Traditionally, actors and actresses were not just considered to be Bohemians or nonconformists, they were labeled "undesirables," one rung above "circus performers" on the ladder of society. In 1920s Hollywood, boarding houses would place signs in the windows declaring a "Vacancy" and below it would be a sign reading "No Actors." Times have changed!

It was only after 1920s silent film stars Gloria Swanson and Rudolf Valentino were elevated to the status of being American royalty that things began to change. The power of celebrityhood certainly erases all sorts of objectionable behavior. It was also amongst the show business set that homosexuality first became acceptable.

Although homosexuality was permissible in the inner circle of Hollywood, it has traditionally been a place where homosexuality also had to be masqueraded to the general public. This was especially true from 1920 to 1970, and beyond.

Masquerade marriages, planned appearances with a member of the opposite sex, and publicity departments working overtime to squelch "gay" rumors have long been staples of closeted movie stars. Charles Laughton and Elsa Lanchester were the perfect example of the 1930s Hollywood arranged marriage. He liked boys, and she didn't care. However, when he once confessed to her that he had sex with a young man on their living room sofa, she insisted he purchase her a new sofa. He gladly complied, not wanting to enrage Elsa—the famed star of *The Bride of Frankenstein*.

Gay people who worked behind-the-scenes had it the best. The general public didn't care what writer Noel Coward was doing in his spare time, nor did they think to delve into director George Cukor's bedroom activities, or wonder whether Adrian the costume designer secretly liked boys. They were not in front of the movie cameras.

Musicians were another story, too. They could often get away with much more latitude in their lives than film actors. No one seemed to care who broke Bessie Smith's heart. All her fans knew was that she could sure sing the blues about it.

Being a movie star was a whole different animal. The fan magazines were all fed stories about the latest male dates that Tallulah Bankhead had; or how Rock Hudson, Montgomery Clift, or Tab Hunter were about to marry some blonde beauty. However, behind the scenes, it was often a whole different story.

RANDY   "One of the best, bawdiest, and most dramatic early singers was Bessie Smith."

MARK   "She clearly had her own style. Any woman who can sing a song like 'I Ain't Gonna Play No Second Fiddle,' is clearly someone who knows what she wants."

RANDY   "She also did a song called the 'Sing Sing Prison Blues.'"

MARK   "Bake that gal a cake with a saw and file in it. She's bustin' out of Sing Sing!"

RANDY   "You got that right."

MARK   "And, there is a direct line between Bessie Smith and you."

RANDY   "What do you mean? I never sang the blues."

MARK   "Ain't that the truth? However, if we are going to play a round of 'Six Degrees of Randy Jones,' now is the time. The last person to produce Bessie Smith recordings was a young man by the name of John Hammond."

RANDY   "And, it was John Hammond who originally signed me to my first solo recording contract in 1982."

MARK   "Exactly! And, since you appointed me your production assistant on that project, you introduced me to Hammond in the studio one afternoon."

RANDY   "As per usual, you and I are in the middle of everything."

MARK   "Well now, that's the perfect intro to catapult us into the middle of Bessie Smith's story."

Although there is some conjecture whether Bessie Smith was born in 1892 or 1894, there is no doubt that she was one of the most talented and beloved blues singer of the 1920s and 1930s. Her singing was so expressive that she was one of the main influences on Billie Holiday, Dinah Washington, Nina Simone, and Janis Joplin.

Her songs were rough and tough blues numbers like: "Give Me a Pigfoot and a Bottle of Beer," "Me and My Gin," "I've Been Mistreated and

I Don't Like It," "I Ain't Gonna Play Second Fiddle," "Send Me to the 'Lectric Chair," and "Nobody Can Bake a Sweet Jelly Roll Like Mine."

Bessie's sincerely sung and heartfelt songs—many of which she wrote—were often metaphors for sex. In one song, "Empty Bed Blues," she sings of her man slipping his "bacon" in her "pot." She also had a song called "Need a Little Sugar in My Bowl" in which she claimed that she needed a little "hot dog" in her "roll."

Her signature song was "T'ain't Nobody's Business If I Do," and that was how she ran her life. She was a rough and tough woman of the streets, who cussed like a sailor and could fight with her fists when she was threatened. She was into hard liquor, wild parties, and she spoke in coarse language. In fact, the way she talked was so expletive-laced that "Bessie Smith" became a slang expression. "Why, I've never heard such 'Bessie Smith,'" someone would say to describe a nasty statement. She was also unabashedly bisexual and clearly preferred female lovers instead of men, so the sugar she got in her bowl was mainly of the lesbian variety.

In her native Chattanooga, Tennessee, Bessie was born one of seven children. Her father was a part-time Baptist preacher. Shortly after Bessie's birth he died, and when she was only eight years old, her mother died as well. The Smith children were left in the care of their older sister, Viola. By the time she was nine she was singing on street corners for nickels and dimes. Her brother Andrew would play the guitar, and little Bessie would sing. The location that they preferred was right outside of the White Elephant Saloon at Thirteenth and Elm Streets.

Her oldest brother, Clarence, left home to join a performing troupe that was owned by a man named Moses Stokes, in 1904. Bessie stayed in Chattanooga with the family and continued polishing her distinctive singing style. In 1912, Clarence came back to Chattanooga, where the Stokes troupe was booked to perform. He arranged for Bessie to audition for the Stokes troupe managers, Lonnie and Cora Fisher. They liked young Bessie and hired her to be a dancer.

The troupe was presenting a vaudeville style show with lots of different performers. One of the star performers was blues singer Ma Rainey. Known as "Mother of the Blues," she was a notorious lesbian, and she was also a huge star at this point in her career. She took young Bessie under her wing and showed her how to be a professional singer.

Ma recognized that her new protégée wasn't lacking in musical talent, but she did need some help in developing "stage presence," which is the ability to hold the audience's attention, both vocally and visually. Bessie was an eager student, and by 1913 she launched her own act, which debuted in Atlanta, Georgia, at the "81" Theatre. Touring up and down the eastern seaboard and the South, by 1920 Bessie Smith had developed a strong reputation as a masterful and expressive blues singer.

At the height of the heady Jazz Age that blossomed in "the Roaring Twenties," people started buying blues records. The success of a singer by the name of Mamie Smith at Okeh Records caused other labels to seek out new talent to record. Columbia Records decided that they were going to release a series of "race records" and sent out talent scouts to find new vocalists. What they came back with were glowing reports about Bessie Smith.

Bessie was signed to Columbia Records in 1923 and her first two-sided release, "Gulf Coast Blues" on one side, and "Down Hearted Blues" on the other side, was an immediate hit. Both songs were composed by a singer who was signed to Paramount Records, Alberta Hunter.

Bessie was signed to the Theater Owners' Booking Association (TOBA), and they proceeded to book her in clubs and theaters all over the country. She proved to be a mesmerizing performer, and her personal appearances started to sell records. Suddenly her career was in full swing. She was reputed to be the highest paid black entertainer of the era.

Bessie Smith never owned a house, nor maintained an address, anywhere. She had adopted the life of a show business gypsy, and she preferred to live in hotels and dressing rooms as she moved around the country, singing the blues for her eager audiences.

Although this should have spelled wealth, Bessie was unfortunately signed to contracts that didn't pay her a lot. Like so many performers, she was signed to bad deals that paid her managers and handlers more money than she often saw. Performers on the circuit would joke that the TOBA actually stood for: "Tough On Black Artists."

Regardless, Bessie Smith was a star. In fact, Columbia Records for a short time heralded her in the press as "The Queen of the Blues," but before long they elevated that moniker to "Empress of the Blues." That she truly was, and she was also a unique original product of her own self-creation.

In fact, she lived up to the title "Empress of the Blues," as dozens of her songs had the word "blues" in the title. These include: "Jail-House Blues," "Empty Bed Blues," "Backwater Blues," "Weeping Willow Blues," and even the "Dying Gambler's Blues."

In 1922, Bessie met a man by the name of Jack Gee, who was a good-looking night watchman. They married the following year, and he tried to bring some stability to Bessie's life. She, however, was not interested in that, and continued to have affairs with both women and men. Jack would often walk in on Bessie, to find her in the arms of a lesbian lover.

As Bessie's riches rose, she traveled around in her own private railroad car, which could be hitched up and taken from town to town on the rails. She made 160 recordings with Columbia, and her accompanying musicians included the likes of Louis Armstrong, James P. Johnson, Joe Smith, Charlie Green, and Fletcher Henderson.

In 1929, Bessie was one of the stars of the film short, *St. Louis Blues*, in which she sang the title song. It was produced by W.C. Handy, whose composition "St. Louis Blues" was the basis for the sixteen-minute movie. The film was shot at the Astoria Studios, in Queens, New York. She was accompanied by musicians from Fletcher Henderson's orchestra, with the addition of the Hall Johnson Choir, and pianist James P. Johnson. That same year she appeared in a Broadway show called *Pansy*. It only ran for three days, but Bessie got a lot of publicity out of her appearance.

In 1929, the American stock market crashed, and so began the Great Depression. These were not good years for Bessie, especially when Columbia Records did not renew her contract. In 1933, John Hammond caught Bessie singing in a small nightclub in Philadelphia and invited her to record four "sides" for the Okeh Records label. She agreed and was paid $37.50 each for these songs. The songs, recorded on November 24, 1933, constitute the final studio recordings of her career.

These four "sides" featured several hot new musicians who were from the emerging Swing Era of music, including trombone player Jack Teagarden, trumpeter Frankie Newton, tenor saxophone man Chu Berry, pianist Buck Washington, guitarist Bobby Johnson, and bass player Billy Taylor. During the session Benny Goodman dropped in, because he was in the studio next door recording with Ethel Waters. Goodman is heard on Bessie's recordings of "Take Me for a Buggy Ride" and "Gimme a Pigfoot," where he is part of the musical ensemble.

Unfortunately, Bessie Smith met a tragic ending. She was in a horrible car crash the night of September 26, 1937. The car was driven by her latest boyfriend, Richard Morgan, a Chicago bootlegger. As they were driving down U.S. Route 61 between Memphis, Tennessee, and Clarksdale, Mississippi, the car struck a Nabisco truck, which was parked without its lights on, approximately seventy miles out of Memphis. There are several stories about what happened after the collision of the car and the truck. And there is even an Edward Albee play based on the incident, called *The Death of Bessie Smith*.

The prevailing story is that she was refused admittance to an all-white hospital in Mississippi, which wasted precious time. Taken to a black hospital, she had her right arm amputated, but never regained consciousness. She died that morning, the cause of death attributed to hemorrhaging.

She was later immortalized in song, in recording reissues, and in several books. Bessie Smith attained legendary status in the decades that followed her death. Dinah Washington recorded one whole album of Bessie Smith songs in 1957 on Verve Records called *The Bessie Smith Songbook*. The rock group The Band wrote and recorded a song tribute to her called "Bessie Smith." Bette Midler recorded Bessie's "Empty Bed Blues" in 1977 on her *Broken Blossom* album.

However, the greatest tribute of all came from Janis Joplin. It seems that Bessie was originally buried without a proper gravestone. It was Janis Joplin who paid to have one made, and in doing so, she paid ultimate tribute to "The Empress of the Blues."

RANDY: "While we are on the subject of the most famous lesbians of the twentieth century, we have to discuss one of my all-time favorites: Tallulah Bankhead."

MARK: "What a trip she was!"

RANDY: "She was campy, vampy, and one witty Southern gal. I think that she is the one broad who gave 'the Roaring Twenties' their 'roar!'"

MARK: "You got that right. Unfortunately, only one of her movies was a critical success, but what a movie it was."

RANDY: "Who can forget her in Alfred Hitchcock's *Lifeboat*?"

MARK: "I sure can't."

RANDY: "That's just because she got her typewriter thrown off that damn lifeboat."

MARK: "As a writer, that woulda taken the wind out of my sails!"

RANDY: "Well, let me tell you, nobody ever took the wind out of Tallulah's sails."

MARK: "Definitely not. Nothing ever stopped Tallulah!"

Tallulah Bankhead was one of the most celebrated stage and screen actresses of the twentieth century. Born on January 31, 1902, she was not only born ahead of her time, she was also an incredible example of divine self-creation. Although she was the toast of Broadway and London's West End, the most outrageous role she ever played was that of Tallulah Bankhead. She was by far larger than life, totally outlandish, and a bisexual as well. She once quipped about her substance abuse and sexual habits, "My father warned me about men and booze, but he never said anything about women and cocaine." (7)

She lived a fast life, and was known as being a party girl. She once said of herself, "If I had my life to live again, I'd make the same mistakes, only sooner." (7)

Tallulah was one of a kind. She admitted, "Nobody can be exactly like me. Sometimes even I have trouble doing it."

She also had a low and distinctively gravelly voice. When she was once asked why she called everyone "Dahling" she replied, "Because all my life I've been terrible at remembering people's names. Once I introduced a friend of mine as 'Martini.' Her name was actually 'Olive.'" (7)

After becoming an award-winning stage actress, she tried her hand at films in the 1930s, but her first six big screen-starring roles fell flat. While she was perfect on stage, she was simply too over-the-top for film.

Finally, in 1944 she was cast in the properly juicy role she longed for. She turned it into her most highly acclaimed film performance. Starring in Alfred Hitchcock's *Lifeboat* presented her with a role that was tailor-made. She portrayed a woman trapped in a lifeboat in World War II, in the middle of the Atlantic Ocean. As a spoiled chain-smoking journalist, wrapped in a mink coat, and toting a typewriter, she won the film acclaim that she had so longed for. The film was so good that Hitchcock was nominated for an Academy Award as Best Director. Now Tallulah was finally a bona fide movie star!

Tallulah was born in Huntsville, Alabama, into an affluent Southern family. In fact, both her father, William Brockman Bankhead, and her uncle, Senator John H. Bankhead II, were U.S. congressmen, and her grandfather was a U.S. senator. She received her unique first name as a tribute to her maternal grandmother.

She was educated and groomed to be a proper Southern belle. However, she wanted none of that. When she was fifteen years old, Tallulah entered a movie magazine beauty contest, and she persuaded her parents to let her go to New York City. She quickly landed supporting roles in plays, and she became a regular member of the famed Round Table at the Algonquin Hotel. Around this same time she started experimenting with marijuana and cocaine. She soon had a reputation as a wild party girl around town.

After gaining acclaim in several productions, her friends had begun spreading the word that Tallulah was a great actress. She went to a party in the winter of 1922 and met a British producer by the name of Charles Cochran. He thought Bankhead was beautiful and might be perfect for a part that he was going to cast in London. Several weeks later, Tallulah received a telegram asking whether she could come across the Atlantic to portray the part of the American girl in his next play.

She agreed, and by the time she was done, she was the toast of London. Tallulah made her debut on the London stage in 1923, and over the next eight years she was to appear in over a dozen plays. One of her biggest hits was *The Dancers*. She was an acknowledged star when in 1924 she played Amy the waitress in Sydney Howard's *They Knew What They Wanted*. The play was a huge hit and won the 1925 Pulitzer Prize.

In her personal life, she swung back and forth between male and female lovers. Her longest relationship during this era was with an Italian businessman named Anthony de Bosdari. Their affair lasted just over one year.

In the 1930s, Hollywood beckoned. She had an offer to do six films for Paramount Pictures, for $50,000 each. It was an offer that was irresistible, so off to the orange groves of California Tallulah went. In two years Bankhead starred in half a dozen feature films at Paramount: *Tarnished Lady* (1931), *My Sin* with Frederick March (1931), *The Cheat* (1931), *Thunder Below* with Paul Lucas (1932), *Devil and the Deep* with Cary Grant and Gary Cooper (1932), and *Faithless* with Robert Montgomery (1932). However, none of them became hits at the box office.

She later proclaimed, "The only reason I went to Hollywood was to fuck that divine Gary Cooper." (8) In 1938, Tallulah was in the running for the role of Scarlett O'Hara in *Gone with the Wind*, and at one point producer David O. Selznick considered her his first choice. However, the role eventually went to Vivian Leigh.

Tallulah simply went back to the stage, on Broadway. She drew raves by starring in such classics as Lillian Hellman's *The Little Foxes* (1939), and playing Sabrina in Thornton Wilder's *The Skin of Our Teeth* (1942).

When Alfred Hitchcock's *Lifeboat* was released, her role as cynical journalist, Constance Porter, won her the New York Film Critics

Circle Award. With unbridled immodesty, a beaming Tallulah accepted her trophy and exclaimed, "*Dahlings*, I was wonderful!" (8)

In her personal life, she continued to be wildly promiscuous, seemingly bedding anyone who crossed her path and looked interesting. According to her, "I've tried several varieties of sex. The conventional position makes me claustrophobic. And the others give me either stiff neck or lockjaw." (8)

She was briefly married to actor John Emery from 1937 and 1941. She was also rumored to have had affairs with several other famous women in the show business world including Greta Garbo, Marlene Dietrich, screenwriter Eva Le Gallienne, Hattie McDaniel, Alla Nazimova, writer Mercedes de Acosta, and singer Billie Holiday. Comedy actress Patsy Kelly claimed that she too had a long-term affair with Tallulah.

She was so famous that she even played The Sands in Las Vegas. As part of her Vegas nightclub act Tallulah told the audience, "Now listen, *dahlings*. I want to correct the impression that this is my first time in a nightclub. I've spent half my life in saloons. But this is the first time I've ever been paid for it." (9)

She played Blanche DuBois in the Broadway production of Tennessee Williams' *A Streetcar Named Desire* in 1956. One of her most memorable performances in the 1950s was her December 3, 1957, television appearance on *The Lucille Ball-Desi Arnaz Hour*. Bankhead portrayed herself in the episode titled "The Celebrity Next Door."

Her final film was the campy horror classic *Die! Die! My Darling!* costarring Stephanie Powers. Tallulah's last acting role in March 1967 was as the villainess Black Widow, on the popular television show *Batman*.

On May 14, 1968, Tallulah was one of the guests on *The Tonight Show*. Johnny Carson was not there that night, so Joe Garagiola was filling in. Also on the show were Beatles John Lennon and Paul McCartney. They went on the show to announce the debut of their new Apple Records. Tallulah, who had been drinking before the show, told John and Paul that she would love to go to India to meditate with the Maharishi like they had in February of that year. She never made it however. She died at the age of sixty-six on December 12, 1968.

Tallulah Bankhead will always be remembered, not only for her career achievements, and her bisexual affairs, but by her own pronouncements about herself. She always admitted to her famous foibles throughout her life. "I'm as pure as the driven slush," she once said about herself. (7)

She was not at all shy about her substance abuses either. According to Tallulah, "Cocaine, habit forming? Of course not, I ought to know, I've been doing it for years." (7)

When she was asked if she kept a diary, she replied, "It's the good girls who keep the diaries. The bad girls never have the time." (7)

RANDY: "Now we come to a decade where pop history really came into being: the 1950s."

MARK: "That's where you and I truly came into the picture."

RANDY: "Ain't that the truth! And what a decade it was. It marked the emergence of Elvis Presley, Marilyn Monroe, and the birth of rock & roll."

MARK: "It was also a decade where two of our next gay icons emerged: Liberace and Rock Hudson."

RANDY: "I remember watching Liberace on television and thinking to myself, 'I have never seen a performer or anyone ever like him before.'"

MARK: "In 1950s television, he was sure a long way from Saturday morning fare like *Sky King* and his niece Penny."

RANDY: "You can say that again. If it wasn't for Liberace, there might never have been an Elton John!"

In the 1950s, Liberace was without a doubt one of the most flamboyant male stars to grace television, movies, and concerts. A wild trailblazing character of a man, Liberace took the image of an elegant Mozart-like pianist and blended it with the wardrobe of a Las Vegas showgirl. A scandalous dandy in velvet and satin suits and wearing too much jewelry, Liberace became one of the most indelible images of the postwar decade.

Born Wladziu Valentino Liberace, on May 16, 1919, in West Allis, Wisconsin, he was to become known around the world as "Liberace," yet to his friends he was just "Lee." His mother, Frances Zuchowski, was Polish/American; and his father, Salvatore Liberace, was an Italian immigrant from the city of Formia.

Although he was classically trained, "Lee" found that audiences liked classical music much better if there was a bit of pop music and some flourishes blended with it. In the mid-1940s Liberace made a living playing music in dinner clubs and nightclubs around the country. In 1943, he had to opportunity to film a couple of "soundies." These were short films to be shown as filler in between movies in theaters. They were essentially the precursor to modern music videos.

Starting on July 1, 1952, *The Liberace Show* debuted as a network television show, with the original piano man performing music with panache on an elaborate baby grand. Liberace would be dressed in some sort of lush outfit. Usually there would be an enormous chandelier on the piano top. Each of his broadcasts would end with his signature song "I'll Be Seeing You."

Although he was about as gay as a pink French poodle, somehow American audiences bought his lavishly over-the-top style as "class" and tuned in to his program weekly. Before long, he was one of the most popular and high-profile stars of the decade of the 1950s. In 1955, he starred in his own big budget Hollywood film, which was called *Sincerely Yours* and costarred Dorothy Malone.

Also in 1955, Liberace took his flamboyant performing style to Las Vegas. Booked at the Rivera Hotel, he made $50,000 per week. He had in excess of 160 official fan clubs, to which a quarter of a million members belonged. In 1960, he was given his own star on the Hollywood Walk of Fame, on Hollywood Boulevard, for his glittering presence on the television.

According to Angela Bowie, "In the 1950s United States, Liberace, Little Richard, and Johnny Ray were closeted gay men with enormous followings. Live shows, record sales, and television exposure ignited the charisma of these stars among young people. Even Hollywood jumped on the bandwagon, and all three of them had their time basking in the glory of mainstream cinema: Liberace, (*Sincerely Yours*/1955), Little Richard (*The Girl Can't Help It*/1956), and Johnny Ray (*There's No Business Like Show Business*/1954). No one ever pointed out in the 1950s that all three of them were gay peacocks, strutting in full regalia. My understanding of homosexuality began with Liberace, although nothing was ever said about his sexuality. Back in the 1950s, on his weekly television show, he was unbelievably fabulous, decked out and looking as tasty-as-a-biscuit in beautiful jackets, complete with that outlandish candelabra on the piano." (10)

Liberace became famous just for being his over-the-top self. In 1965, he appeared in a small part in the movie *When the Boys Meet the Girls*, which starred Connie Francis. He had a critically acclaimed part in the black comedy *The Loved One* (1966), playing a casket salesman. In the mid-1960s he did a cameo role on the series *The Monkees*, at an art gallery, as himself. He also appeared as the villain, Chandell and his evil brother Harry, on the camp television series *Batman*.

In the early 1970s, when Glam Rock was the big and glittering craze in rock & roll, whom did David Bowie most want to meet?

Why, Liberace, of course. Angela Bowie recalls, "I was happy to have the opportunity to meet him in person in the 1970s. The second I saw him, I was dazzled. He came into our stateroom to meet David and I. He wore a beautiful emerald green jacket with silver and black beadwork on the collar and lapels, looking like a matador. He had a soft way of speaking that just enthralled me. Liberace did not disappoint us one bit: he was absolutely bigger than life." (10)

Along the way, Liberace had his share of sex scandals. In the London newspaper, *The Daily Mirror*, columnist Cassandra [pen name of William Connor] made fun of Liberace, calling him: "the summit of sex—the pinnacle of masculine, feminine, and neuter. Everything that he, she, and it can ever want ... a deadly, winking, sniggering, snuggling, chromium-plated, scent-impregnated, luminous, quivering, giggling, fruit-flavored, mincing, ice-covered heap of mother love." (11)

Liberace sued the publication for libel. When he testified in a British court, he claimed that he was neither a homosexual nor had performed any homosexual acts in his life. He won the suit, and an £8,000 ($22,400) settlement in damages.

Three decades later, the charges were harder to deny. In 1982, one-time Liberace live-in boyfriend, Scott Thorson, sued him for $113 million in palimony after an acrimonious split-up of their five-year relationship. Publicly, Liberace continued to deny that he was gay. Two years later, the majority of Thorson's legal claim was dismissed in court. However, Liberace paid him $95,000 to basically drop the charge and go quietly away.

During the 1970s and 1980s, Liberace maintained his fame and earning power in Las Vegas. He commanded $300,000 a week playing at the Las Vegas Hilton and in Lake Tahoe. His outfits simply became more and more outrageous with time, and his jewelry and rings got bigger and even more diamond encrusted.

On November 2, 1986, Liberace gave his final stage performance, at Radio City Music Hall in New York City. He was looking thin and weak lately, but he maintained his image as a grand and flamboyant piano player right up to the very end. He died on February 4, 1987, in his house in Palm Springs, California; still denying that he was HIV positive, had AIDS, or that he was gay. His body was entombed in Forest Lawn–Hollywood Hills Cemetery in Los Angeles.

All of his life, Liberace wanted to be bigger than life. In death, he has become exactly that. Today, the Liberace Museum in Las Vegas, Nevada, proudly displays the outlandish stage costumes, the designer cars, the insanely large jewelry, and all of his lushly decorated pianos.

RANDY: "While Liberace was someone who wore his flamboyance on his sleeve, at the same time, Rock Hudson was presenting just the opposite image."

MARK: "That's right; in 1950s Hollywood, Rock was someone who seemed to personify the all-American hero image."

RANDY: "Yes, but much of Hollywood's film industry was aware that Rock was gay. He was such a well thought of man that there were very few if any who truly wanted to rock the boat and disrupt his life and career."

MARK: "Rock Hudson's life story is all the more fascinating because of that."

RANDY: "You ought to be quite an expert on that, after all Rock Hudson provided you with one of your most successful books."

MARK: "You got that right! When my book, *Rock Hudson: Public and Private*, came out in 1986, it was the first book about his life that told the whole story."

RANDY: "And, as I recall, you sold half a million of them."

MARK: "What can I say? Timing IS everything in this business!"

RANDY: "That's right! What time is it?"

Without a doubt, Rock Hudson had one of the most important and impressive careers in show business. For more than thirty years, Rock embodied the personable, handsome, and virile movie star. His six-foot, four-inch frame, his clean-cut all-American good looks, and his appealing manner made him one of the most idolized stars of the century. But throughout his career, he, his manager, and his movie studio, all did their best to keep his personal life on the "down low."

Born on November 17, 1925, in Winnetka, Illinois, Rock Hudson hit the pinnacle of his film career in 1956, when he starred opposite Elizabeth Taylor in *Giant*, a role that established his reputation as a pillar of masculine power and that would earn him a "Best Actor" Oscar nomination. His subsequent teaming with Doris Day for three pictures in the late 1950s and early 1960s set a new style in sexy sophistication, and made him the romantic idol of millions of female moviegoers.

More than twenty years later, in 1985, Rock Hudson proved that he could still cast his movie star spell when he starred opposite Linda Evans on the hit television series *Dynasty*. That same year the world was stunned by the news that he was dying of AIDS. His last-minute public admission of his homosexuality was made after years of scandals and denials.

For the first couple of years since the HIV virus and AIDS were defined by the medical profession, the general public still thought that it was something that would never touch their lives in any way. However, when Rock Hudson made the public admission, in the last months of his life, suddenly someone who everyone knew and liked—via his film and television appearances—was dying of a disease that most people did not fully understand.

Born Roy Harold Scherer on November 17, 1925, Rock Hudson fell in love with the idea of becoming a film star when he saw John Hall rescuing Dorothy Lamour in the 1937 film called *The Hurricane*. He worked as a Navy aircraft mechanic in World War II, and when the war ended, he decided to move to California and attempt to fulfill his dreams of breaking into the movies.

Rock was discovered by an agent named Henry Willson. At the time, the young actor was supporting himself by driving a truck. Willson decided to take him under his wing and created a heroic macho image for Roy by giving him a name that would signify power and strength. Borrowing from the Rock of Gibraltar and the Hudson River, Rock Hudson was born.

Making his film debut in the 1948 production of *Fighter Squadron*, Rock Hudson appeared in twenty-six films over the next six years, including adventure dramas like *Undertow* (1949), *One Way Street* (1950), *Winchester '73* (1950), *Desert Hawk* (1950), *Air Cadet* (1951), *Bend in the River* (1952), and *Sea Devils* (1953).

It was in 1954 that Rock's star image gelled when he appeared with Jane Wyman in the remake of *The Magnificent Obsession*. It was during this same period that the popular 1950s scandal sheet *Confidential* contacted Rock's studio, announcing that it had conclusive evidence that Hudson was homosexual, and that it planned to publish the story. In an effort to keep the allegations of Rock's homosexuality from appearing in print, the studio urged the magazine to run instead a story about a lesser-known gay actor, George Nader.

Hastily, a "fixed" marriage for Rock Hudson was arranged as a publicity ploy by Henry Willson, who hoped that a wedding would forever quell allegations of Hudson's homosexuality. In 1955, Rock eloped with Willson's long-time secretary, Phyllis Gates. The marriage lasted less than three years, but it effectively created a smoke screen around Rock's private life. In 1956, Rock Hudson made the film *Giant*, and suddenly he was a bona fide superstar and America's top male sex symbol. For the next fifteen years, rumors about his homosexuality were again dismissed as slanderous Hollywood gossip.

In a career move that made him America's top male box-office draw, Rock turned from adventure films and drama to sparkling comedies opposite Doris Day. Day was destined to become linked with him as his most famous leading lady. Their three romantic farces—*Pillow Talk* (1959), *Lover Come Back* (1961), and *Send Me No Flowers* (1964)—defined the moral values and humor of the early 1960s "New Frontier" America. The films in which Doris Day appeared as the bubbly contemporary career woman and Rock Hudson appeared as the suave, smooth, and sexy bachelor made them the most famous cinema couple of the era.

As the decade changed, so did Rock's screen persona. In a cinematic era of spies and espionage, Hudson portrayed a series of macho adventurers in such films as *Blindfold* (1966), *Seconds* (1966), *Tobruk* (1967), *Ice Station Zebra* (1967), *The Undefeated* (1969), and *Hornet's Nest* (1969). His rugged hero image remained intact as he began his third decade as a screen idol and the dream lover of millions of women.

Even for a dashing forty-five-year-old screen star, however, the opportunities to play romantic leads were dwindling. The late 1960s counterculture ushered in a whole new brand of younger leading men like Peter Fonda and Jack Nicholson. Rock found himself in need of a new vehicle. In 1971, with the debut of the television series *McMillian & Wife*, he found one. The show costarred Susan Saint James and Nancy Walker. It ran through 1977 and maintained great ratings. Suddenly his rugged and familiar face was right in middle-America's living rooms.

It was during this era that Rock's name again came up in gossip columns. A slanderous item claimed that Rock had "married" television actor Jim Nabors in a private gay wedding ceremony. The public dismissed the story as ridiculous, but people in the industry weren't so amused. Nabors' CBS-TV variety show was promptly canceled. According to Nabors, although he and Rock were just casual friends, they could never be seen together in public again.

When *McMillian & Wife* concluded production in 1977, Rock accepted other television offers, appearing in three mini-series: *Wheels* (1978), *The Martian Chronicles* (1980), and *The Star Maker* (1981). In 1980, Rock reunited with his *Giant* costar, Elizabeth Taylor, for the tongue-in-cheek Agatha Christie whodunit *The Mirror Crack'd*. Hudson appeared in the made-for-television production *World War III* and a short-lived television adventure series called *The Devlin Connection* in 1982. Throughout this period Rock maintained his solid and appealing leading-man image.

In 1984, after a two-year absence from television and movie screens, it was announced that Rock had signed to appear in ten episodes of the top-rated television series *Dynasty*. Millions of *Dynasty* fans were thrilled by the prospect of seeing the legendary Rock as the stars of the glossiest, most publicized soap opera in television history. The Rock that his fans saw in the first episode was a mere ghost of the virile Rock Hudson of twenty, ten, or even two years before. He was thin and pale, and his eyes lacked the sparkle they had always projected. "Did you see Rock Hudson on *Dynasty*!?" people gasped all over America, immediately speculating that Rock had fallen ill to the plague that was killing thousands of male homosexuals: AIDS. Statements were issued claiming that Rock had been dieting and never felt better. But the hollow cheeks and sunken eyes that *Dynasty* viewers glimpsed only increased the speculation that Rock Hudson was indeed dying of AIDS.

Ironically, it was at a press conference with his close friend and former costar Doris Day that the whole tragic scandal began to explode. It was early in July 1985, and Rock was making his first public appearance since his last *Dynasty* episode. In the two months following the last *Dynasty* filming, Rock seemed to have aged fifteen more years. On Tuesday, July 23, it was front-page news that Rock had collapsed on his way to the American Hospital in Paris, where new AIDS cures were being experimentally tested.

Rock Hudson's subsequent admission of both his battle against a terminal case of AIDS and his homosexual lifestyle was perhaps the most magnanimous gesture the dying actor could have possibly made. Suddenly the sexually transmitted disease wasn't just an affliction striking members of society's underworld—it was an illness that could strike the most highly respected and beloved of national heroes. For four decades Rock Hudson had stood for clean-cut all-American values, and in his final act, he opened the door to his long-secret private life in an effort to save the lives of others.

In his final public statement, read aloud by Burt Lancaster at a gala AIDS fundraising benefit in Los Angeles on September 19, 1985, Rock Hudson stated, "I am not happy that I am sick. I am not happy that I have AIDS, but if that is helping others, I can, at least, know that my misfortune has had some positive worth." (12)

In the months after Rock's death, millions of dollars poured into discovering a cure for AIDS. Prior to Rock's own tragic illness, AIDS was considered an affliction that was unspeakable. Even Rock's Hollywood friend President Ronald Reagan would not discuss the topic or AIDS publicly, nor would he support efforts to procure sufficient governmental funds toward its cure. On October 2, 1985, however, the day that Rock died, the House of Representatives voted to provide $189.7 million for AIDS research and prevention awareness. Rock Hudson will always be thought of as being the kind of all-American hero and likeable guy he portrayed on the silver screen. He is also the most famous gay actor Hollywood has ever produced.

Chapter 3

Stonewall, the 1970s, and Bisexual Chic

As the decade of the 1970s was about to dawn, several very important events occurred. It was like pieces of society's evolving jigsaw puzzle suddenly fell into place, and new doors were forced open for the first time in modern history. And, after these doors were suddenly open, there was no going backwards.

The 1970s was to be the decade of "gay liberation," the disco movement, EST (Erhard Seminar Training), glitter rock, retro fashion, bell-bottom pants, platform shoes, recreational drugs, and a purveying sense of self-absorption that caused social historians to label it "the 'Me' decade." It was the decade where the futile Vietnam War ended, Nixon was forced out of office, and sexual taboos were shattered.

RANDY: "Now we come to the events that made Greenwich Village such a epicenter for the gay movement."

MARK: "How can you have Village People, without Greenwich Village?"

RANDY: "Precisely. And, you can't discuss the Gay Liberation Movement of the 1960s and 1970s, without mentioning the Stonewall Riots."

MARK: "Fasten your seatbelts. It's gonna be a bumpy night!"

In the early morning hours of June 28, 1969, police clashed with the patrons of a gay bar in Greenwich Village's Sheridan Square, called the Stonewall Inn. It was commonplace for there to be police raids in gay bars in New York City, and every other city in America. However, on this particular night, the homosexual patrons of this particular liquor-serving establishment stood up for their rights and effectively changed history forever. This night is credited as the beginning of the Gay Liberation Movement.

By the late 1960s, the youth of America was used to standing up to authority and questioning the decisions and motives of both the government and law enforcement. The Vietnam War had tipped off a revolution from within society. Protest marches and disruptive public demonstrations had suddenly become woven into the current climate of America. Black people had protested in the summer of 1967 in Detroit and Newark. Students had recently protested the Vietnam War at Kent State and countless college campuses across the United States. By 1969, gays and lesbians in New York City stood up for their rights and forced a highly publicized flashpoint that became the Stonewall Riots.

Like so many bars and clubs in Manhattan, the Stonewall Inn had reputed mob ties, and operated without the benefit of an active liquor license. It did mainly a cash business, so that it could be run without tracing the ins and outs of its cash flow. There were also reported kickbacks to the police.

There were many reputed reasons for the raid on the Stonewall Inn that particular June morning. An urban myth claims that the resistance of the patrons had something to do with the death and New York City funeral of gay icon, Judy Garland (June 10, 1922–June 22, 1969). The funeral had taken place on June 27 at the Frank E. Campbell Funeral Home on the Upper East Side of town, so there seems to be very little actual correlation between the two events.

For whatever reason, things reached a boiling point when, at 1:20 A.M., a police inspector and seven uniformed officers entered the nightspot, issuing a warrant for serving drinks without a liquor license. Apparently, it was quite a mixed crowd that evening, including transsexuals and lesbians. According to reports of the actual details of the riots and protest that ensued, it seems that the police officers attempted to take several of the gay bar's patrons into custody when one of them resisted being arrested. The next thing the police knew they were being pelted with stones and bottles by a gathering crowd outside the bar. At one point someone started a fire in an attempt to cause mayhem and confusion, and soon police reinforcements had to be brought in. Because it was a Friday night, there were crowds of people in Greenwich Village, and soon the crowd mushroomed into an unruly mob. Thirteen people were arrested, and four police officers, as well as several protesters, were injured. Two rioters were reportedly beaten severely. Amidst shouts from the crowd, calling for "Gay Power!" it wasn't long before the crowd grew to well over 2,000 citizens and 400 police officers.

Author and activist Elliot Tiber was there that night. He recalls, "Several of us jumped on top of car hoods and roofs and started chanting for the mayor to get down there now, or else this was going to get ugly. We were ready to take over Greenwich Village. I jumped off the cop car and screamed at the top of my lungs, 'Gay power!' Elation rose from my stomach and into my heart. For the first time in my life, I was proud to be gay." (6)

The protesting continued for several nights. Saturday night drew more crowds, as word spread of the previous night's incident. After the weekend, the battle still raged. Five days after the riot, on Wednesday night, there were another 1,000 people protesting and causing property damage in front of the Stonewall Inn. Ultimately, these riots and clashes with the police also tipped off a series of legal battles involving the city's infringement on people's civil rights. The 1969 raid on the Stonewall Inn is now looked upon as the official beginning of global gay liberation.

In several cities around the world, the Stonewall Riots are annually commemorated the last weekend in June with Gay Pride Marches. New York City's parade down Fifth Avenue is among the largest, and it all stems back to Stonewall. Other cities to annually hold such June events include Los Angeles, California; Sydney, Australia; Cologne, Germany; San Francisco, California; Anchorage, Alaska; Detroit, Michigan; Philadelphia, Pennsylvania; Boston, Massachusetts; Washington, DC; and Phoenix, Arizona. In other cities, the commemoration takes place at different times of the year. For instance, in Tucson, Arizona, the annual "Gay Pride Picnic" had to be moved to October because of an alarming number of cases of "heat stroke" that were caused by the late-June 100+ degree desert temperatures. Likewise, Dallas, Texas, and Palm Springs, California, also hold their events in months other than June.

After the riots in 1969, the Stonewall Inn was closed for the majority of the 1970s and '80s. It received its first renovation in the early 1990s and reopened. A second renovation took place in the late 1990s to capitalize on the club's historic significance, including a new multifloor layout. The club experienced a resurgence, but then lost its lease in 2006. The bar's newest incarnation began under new management in February 2007.

The effects of the Stonewall Inn and the infamous Stonewall Riots continue to resonate with the themes of "gay liberation" and gay history. To commemorate the Stonewall Riots, in 2006 the country of Iceland adopted a law to grant same-sex couples the same legal rights given to heterosexual couples.

RANDY: "I distinctly remember that it was around the same time that you and I both moved to New York City, that the whole Glam Rock phase was underway."

MARK: "We were both still in college when I remember reading about the New York Dolls and the club called Max's Kansas City. It made me want to move to Manhattan immediately."

RANDY: "And let's not forget the contributions to stage make-up that Alice Cooper provided."

MARK: "We also can't forget Tim Curry in *The Rocky Horror Picture Show*. That was glam rock taken to Broadway and Hollywood."

RANDY: "It just goes to show you the kind of miracles that can be done with a pair of fishnet stockings ..."

MARK: "... and a transvestite from transsexual Transylvania!"

Clearly, as the 1970s were dawning, there were all sorts of signs pointing to the liberalization of sexual mores in the United States. This was reflected in the media's coverage of sexual matters, including reports that "swinging," homosexuality, lesbianism, and bisexuality were all on the rise. Instead of gay issues remaining a scandalous secret, like in Victorian times, they were increasingly reported in the media, from intellectual properties like newspapers and magazines, to inclusion in mainstream movies and popular music.

In the March 19, 1973, issue of *Time* magazine, in an article entitled "Switch Partners," the publication spoke of two New York Yankee pitchers, Mike Kekich and Fritz Peterson, who "swapped wives," and publicly spoke about it. In the Winter 1974 issue of *College* magazine, distributed to American university campuses, an article entitled "Growing Up Gay" spoke frankly about homosexuality as a viable lifestyle option in the 1970s, unlike in any previous decade. And, the September 8, 1975, issue of *Time* magazine ran the cover story "I Am a Homosexual: A Gay Drive For Acceptance" on U.S. Air Force Sgt. Leonard Matlovich and his public admission of his lifestyle. That particular article, which surveyed the changing sexual landscape in America, shockingly proclaimed, "Homosexuals in the U.S. face an array of penalties more severe than in any Western nation outside the Communist bloc. Sodomy between consenting adults is still illegal in 38 states and may result in sentences of up to 21 years and conceivably life." (13)

Still, it also noted how the social acceptance of homosexuality was on the rise, and that the liberalization of the country post-Stonewall was underway. The same issue of *Time* magazine's interior coverage, headlined: "Gays On The March," reported of "jolting evidence of the spread of unabashed homosexuality once thought to be confined to the worlds of theater, dance, fashion, etc. Similarly jolting have been public announcements of their homosexuality by a variety of people who could be anybody's neighbor." (13)

It also reported when the famed establishment personal-help columnist calling herself "Dear Abby" [Abgail Van Buren] had recently [1975] addressed a distraught parent whose daughter announced that she was a lesbian. When the seeker confided that the girl was going to "ruin" her life, "Dear Abby" calmly responded, "Why do you assume that her sexual preference will necessarily 'ruin her life?'" (13)

While this was going on, assuredly, nothing signaled a change in sexual behavior, tolerance, and a loosening of taboos more than the whole glitter rock and glam rock movement in the early 1970s. The new wave of rock stars out for a bit of flamboyant gender-bending included Alice Cooper, Gary Glitter, Elton John, Lou Reed, Iggy Pop, the New York Dolls, Queen, and David Bowie. They performed in make-up and boas and women's dresses, or covered in glitter and feathers. They wore black fingernail polish, and "tarted" themselves up in a way that 1960s rock stars never thought of, all pushing the boundaries of gender identification. Even bona fide lesbian rockers were coming into the fashion, including Joan Armatrading, Fanny, Janis Ian, Isis, and Deadly Nightshade.

RANDY: "This brings us to one of the most revolutionary married couples of the gay and bisexual movement."

MARK: "How can we discuss gender-bending and bisexuality without discussing the controversial marriage of Angela and David Bowie?"

RANDY: "When the whole glitter rock movement of the 1970s started, they were the darlings of the whole movement."

MARK: "Not to mention the fact that Angela Bowie is one our dearest friends."

RANDY: "Miss Angie, truly is 'one of a kind!'"

Without a doubt, together and separately, the most intriguing and revolutionary couple of the "Me Decade" were Angela Bowie and David Bowie. That a married couple could do more for gay rights

than any pair of homosexuals could ever accomplish is only part of
the drama. They truly had the most unique union of the entire era,
and their guilt-free pronouncements about their lives and their attitudes resonated throughout the world.

It was David Bowie who is credited with taking sexual androgyny
to new heights. And it was his first wife, Angela, who was the mastermind behind the vision of his career and his image. When David
started launching his recording career, a manager told him that there
were too many "David Joneses" in show business—including Davy
Jones of the Monkees—and that he should pick a new last name, so
he chose Bowie. According to him, he took it from the legendary fron-
tiersman Jim Bowie, who is the namesake of the Bowie knife.

Angela Barnett was born the daughter of a mining business owner
and his wife on the Mediterranean island of Cyprus. She was educated in a girl's school in Switzerland, and in the mid-1960s she
attended the Connecticut College for Women. While she was there,
she found herself oddly attracted to one of her female classmates.

Angie wrote of the girl, Lorraine, in her fascinating book *Free
Spirit*, "When we gazed into one another's eyes, a strange feeling
came over me. I felt an irresistible urge to kiss her. I couldn't begin
to understand why and I had to stop my thoughts from running
away. I could find no logical explanation." (14)

As a teenage girl, Angela confesses, "Lesbianism was not really a
subject at which I had any expertise, nor was sex." (10) She claims
that she had no regrets when she began having sex with Lorraine.
She found it a natural human response to attraction.

When news of their physical affair quickly spread throughout the
school, it spelled potential disaster. As she today explains it, "In
1966 I was politely asked to leave Connecticut College for Women
for having an affair with a fellow student. The shocking revelation
was that I was asked to leave from anywhere, threw me in a tailspin.
How could I justify my behavior and the same to my family? Then I
started thinking, 'My family is not judgmental and my father would
not tolerate folks being persecuted for their identity.' So, I figured
that I was off the hook and fortunately, I was. Not so for my girlfriend, who was placed in therapy for four years. By the time I went
to Kingston Polytechnic in September of 1967, I was 17, so I figured
I would find a solution in the future to my sexuality." (10)

Speaking of David's early life, Angela was later to speak of his
first experimentations with bisexuality, and publicly wearing make-
up and women's clothes. "David never told me he'd sold either end

of himself for money, and I have no reason to suppose he did; all he told me in those early days was that he was bisexual and had had 'boyfriends,'" she explained. "But the club-trolling of queens was certainly an important factor in his rise from obscurity, and so was the mod ethos of intense narcissism, fashion competition, and all-around gender-bending. In David's teenage scene, the boys often knew more than girls about eyeliner, lipstick, and the creation of a good bouffant. So, ten years later, when David made his legendary first public appearance in a dress and shocked the hell out of establishment England (and most of pop America, for that matter), I'm sure it was no big deal in more than a few London households. I can just see your typical ex-mod sitting at the kitchen table in his under-shirt, the wife frying up the Walls pork sausages, he trying to ignore the kids and gazing at David swishing proudly in the *News of the World*, his mind drifting happily back . . ." (15)

Angela Barnett met David Jones in 1969, through a mutual friend, Calvin Mark Lee. According to David, "When we met, we were both laying the same bloke." Since they had become acquainted by sleeping with the same man, where could it lead from there? Well, sleeping with the same woman as well: journalist Mary Finnegan. When Angela's British visa was about to run out, and she would be forced to return to Cyprus, she quickly married David. From 1970 to 1975, Angela and David Bowie made international headlines as the most famous bisexual couple on the planet.

The reason for David Bowie's fame was not his sex life; it was his image and his cutting-edge music. He has had a career full of dramatic image reinventions. With make-up and scant female clothes, he became the Glam Rock culture's darling. And as his alter ego, Ziggy Stardust, he became a bona fide international star.

Having come from working-class Bromley, England, his early life would not suggest such dramatic behavior. He released his first album in 1969 on Mercury Records, *Man of Words, Man of Music*, with its outer space masterpiece, "Space Oddity." The song about the fictional Major Tom floating through space in his astronautical tin can became a huge hit in England, and later, an FM radio favorite track in America. His subsequent albums included gender-bending songs like "Oh, You Pretty Things," "Queen Bitch," "Suffragette City," and "Rebel Rebel," featuring lyric lines about drag queens, and swishing boys. The song that he wrote and produced for the group Mott the Hoople, "All the Young Dudes" in 1972, became something of a theme song for the pan-sexual lifestyle he came to personify. Likewise, by producing Lou Reed's biggest hit, "Walk on the Wild Side," he furthered his influence as the king of glam rock.

On stage David had taken to performing simulated fellatio on his guitar player Mick Ronson's guitar-bearing crotch mid-show. When he created his revolutionary concert character, Ziggy Stardust, and the album *Ziggy Stardust and the Spiders from Mars*, Bowie began to branch out into the mainstream music world. The Ziggy character was a bisexual, androgynous space alien, and it was somewhat how his critics saw Bowie himself. Subsequent albums *Aladdin Sane* (1973), *Pin-Ups* (1973), *Diamond Dogs* (1974), and *David Live* (1974) all furthered his fame, and turned him into an international sensation. He reached a new pinnacle with he released his 1975 *Young American* album. With it he attained the kind of success in America that he had always longed to achieve.

While all of this was going on, both David and Angela were, separately and together, having sex with others. The two of them were very intertwined during the early 1970s, seen arriving at movie premiers and media events, or being photographed together in unisexual clothes. There is a famous series of photos of the two of them together, seemingly dressed as each other, with similar haircuts.

As though it was a case of *The Emperor's New Clothes*, for a long time journalists stayed away from questions about his sexuality. Finally, one brave journalist for *Melody Maker*, Mick Watts, fired off point-blank: "Are you gay?"

Without missing a beat, David replied, "I'm gay and always have been, even when I was David Jones." (16)

Looking back on this event, Angela recalls, "David was being David. He was being honest. When a *Melody Maker* reporter asked him if he was gay he replied, 'Yes, I am.' My husband could not have possibly envisioned the impact his simple statement was to have on public opinion. Social ethics and structures started to change. Gay people breathed more easily with fear of recrimination. Newspapers and magazines took up the theme. People were actually speaking about a subject that in the past had remained strictly taboo. Naturally, I was asked to express my opinion. 'Was I shocked by David's admission?' I wasn't going to backpedal. Not now. 'We are both free spirits,' I said. We decided to make a stand on the subject as a matter of policy. Gay people came to thank us personally for the exposure we gave to the subject." (14)

It was the "swinging '70s," and the most cutting-edge couple were definitely the Bowies. Not even the birth of their son, Zowie Bowie,

in 1971, cooled down their white-hot multimedia cache as rock &
roll's most trend-setting duo. Looking back on this era, Angela says
with conviction, "I am bisexual, in some circles famously so. My
open marriage with David Bowie, the stances he and I took, the philosophies we embraced and championed—these are matters of
record in the history of the modern struggle for sexual liberation.
David and I may in fact have been the best-known bisexual couple
ever. We are currently the most famous couple ever to admit and
celebrate our bisexuality so publicly. So if you didn't know before,
now you do." (15)

Brilliantly sharp, and always in control, Angela had her own distinctive design for living. According to her, "Monogamy wouldn't
have appealed to me in the first place; I myself was anything but a
one-man-or-woman woman. As long as we held true to each other
and respected the love between us, then, David and I were perfectly
free to romp and dally with whoever else might tickle our fancy ...
We were young and free and it was London, ground zero for the
bold, beautiful, brave new world; free love was natural, and simply
what we did." (15)

It was around the time that Mick Jagger was writing The Rolling
Stones' song "Angie" for and about Angela, that she found him
passed out and nude in bed with her husband, David Bowie. According to her, "When I walked into that room and found Mick and
David together; I felt absolutely dead certain that they'd been screwing. It was so obvious, in fact, that I never even considered the possi-
bility that they hadn't been screwing. The way they'd been running
around together and the way David made a virtual religion of slipping the Lance of Love [his penis] into almost everyone around him,
and then the fact that Mick had a perfectly good bed of his own just
three hundred yards away from where he was passed out naked
with David—it all added up inescapably in my head as well as my
gut. I didn't have to look around for open jars of K-Y Jelly. Maybe I
should have, because then my eyes would have seen the proof of
what I knew in my heart." (15)

By 1976, Angela and David divorced and went their separate
ways. Also that same year David made his film debut in Nicolas
Roeg's The Man Who Fell to Earth, fulfilling another career goal:
becoming a movie star. For a couple more years Bowie continued his
passion for dressing in drag in his videos and performances, finally
changing his persona for another self-imagined character, this time
a slim masculine one: The Thin White Duke. David went on to even

greater recording success with his 1983 *Let's Dance*, and its title hit plus "China Girl" and "Modern Love," produced by Nile Rodgers of Chic.

David Bowie continues to record and act in films, and he's married to model Iman. Angela is an author, singer, and songwriter, and lives in Tucson, Arizona. Neither of them has spoken to each other in years; however, they both continue to separately create. David's glam rock years and Angela and David's relationship were the "inspiration" for the central plot of the successful 1998 film *Velvet Goldmine*.

Although they have both gone on to other lives since the early 1970s, Angela and David Bowie did more to break down social barriers, just by living out the lives they fashioned for each other. While David no longer talks about his wilder times to the press, Angela is as effervescently outspoken as ever.

MARK: "I will never forget the first time I heard Lou Reed's song 'Walk on the Wild Side.'"
RANDY: "It truly defined an era."
MARK: "And, what was truly amazing was how mainstream radio programmers embraced it. Who could have predicted that this song about transvestites could become such a hit in Middle America?"
RANDY: "I guess it just goes to show you . . ."
MARK: "Goes to show you, what?"
RANDY: "You simply cannot keep a good drag queen down!"

Lou Reed has had a very creative and extensive career. He still continues to write and record groundbreaking material, yet in a mainstream sense, he will always be remembered by his biggest-selling hit, 1972's "Walk on the Wild Side." Never before had a song about hustlers, transvestites, transsexuals, and drag queens been in the Top Ten, and it was due to the collaboration of having David Bowie and Mick Ronson as the song's producers, and Lou Reed's perfectly sung version of his lyric monologue about Little Joe, Holly, Jackie, Candy, and the Sugar Plum Fairy.

In reality, all of these characters were part of the 1970s Andy Warhol circuit, who hung out at The Factory, and Max's Kansas City. In fact, Lou Reed was also a member of this elite circle. In the lyrics of the song, Little Joe is Warhol actor Joe Dallesandra, Holly is drag queen Holly Woodlawn, Jackie is drag queen Jackie Curtis, Candy is transvestite and Warhol actress Candy Darling, and the Sugar Plum Fairy is Warhol actor Joe Campbell.

Lou Reed's personal journey is a fascinating one as well. He was born Lewis Rabiowitz in Brooklyn, New York, in 1942. He showed musical aptitude at an early age, and his first singing group was as a member of The Shades, who sang doo-wop music.

When, as a teenager, Reed revealed that he had homosexual feelings, his parents had him see a psychologist. It was the psychologist who recommended an extensive series of electroshock treatments to discourage the homosexual cravings he was having. The process, which he went through at Creedmore State Psychiatric Hospital in 1959, caused him to lose his memory and to suffer from lethargy. It was an experience that he was to write about in the lyrics of his 1974 song "Kill Your Sons."

Lou attended Syracuse University and befriended poet Delmore Schwartz, who was to become something of a mentor to Reed. In 1963, he moved to New York City and landed a job as an in-house songwriter for Pickwick Records. While there he wrote and recorded a song called "The Ostrich," which became a minor hit with the band The Primitives. In The Primitives was a guitar player by the name of John Cale, and Cale and Reed began a lifelong friendship. Together they formed the band The Velvet Underground, which caught the attention of avant-garde artist and filmmaker Andy Warhol.

Warhol teamed the Velvet Underground with a European former model by the name of Nico. They performed at Max's Kansas City and recorded one legendary flop of an album together. However, the album 1967's *The Velvet Underground and Nico* has gone on to become something of a cult classic, in retrospect. At one point, *Rolling Stone* magazine listed it as Number 13 on their list of Best Rock Albums of All-Time.

Lou quit The Velvet Underground in August of 1970. After a brief stint working at his dad's tax accounting firm, he returned to the music business. In 1971, he signed a recording contract with RCA Records and created his debut solo album, *Lou Reed*. He went to England to record it with musicians culled from the group Yes—including Rick Wakeman, and members of Elton John's band. Released in 1972, it only made it up to Number 189 on the U.S. album chart. It was comprised of leftover compositions from The Velvet Underground.

However, it was his *Transformer* album that same year that made him a star. Coproduced by David Bowie and Mick Ronson, it contained the song "Walk on the Wild Side," which made it to Number 29 in the United States, and Number 10 in England. Lou became an instant cult figure in the rock world. He followed *Transformer* with a pair of successful albums, *Berlin* (1973), which made it to Number Seven in the United Kingdom, and Number 98 in the United States. The following year, his *Sally Can't Dance* album made it to Number 10 in America.

Lou reportedly continued to live a bisexual lifestyle, proving conclusively the folly of using electroshock treatments to "cure" homosexuality. His other hit albums since that time have included the "live" albums *Rock 'n' Roll Animal* (1974) [U.S. Number 45—certified gold, and U.K. Number 26], and *Lou Reed Live* (1975) [U.S. Number 62] and his studio sets *Coney Island Baby* (1976) [U.S. Number 41, U.K. Number 52], *Rock and Roll Heart* (1976) [U.S. Number 64], and *Magic and Loss* (1992) [U.S. Number 80, U.K. Number Six.] In 1990, he and John Cale reunited for the first time since their Velvet Underground career together, on an album salute to Andy Warhol called *Songs for 'Drella*. The name "'Drella" was Lou Reed's favorite nickname for Warhol, as it is a combination of the names of two of Andy's favorite fictional characters: Dracula and Cinderella. Lou Reed and David Bowie collaborated on Lou's 2003 album tribute to Edgar Allen Poe, *The Raven*.

RANDY: "Whenever I think of either pop culture, or pop art, I always think of Andy Warhol."
MARK: "It's hard not to think of him, he was such a fixture on the party circuit that you and I were on. We would constantly run into him at Studio 54, or any of the other events we went to."
RANDY: "He truly made being a pop icon, a business."
MARK: "And he made it a business to become a pop icon!"

As one of the most memorable and influential artists of the twentieth century, Andy Warhol's importance and stature in the art world has only grown in the two decades since his death. Although he is as famous as a marketer of art as he is a creator of artistic images, he is looked upon as a pop culture icon.

Born on August 6, 1928, in Pittsburgh, like so many people in the pop art field, Andy was a multi-media artist. He was not only a painter; he was a filmmaker, a record producer, an author, and the absolute focal point of so many other artists. He also had a great sense of humor about his art, and about the whole art scene in general. Warhol fully understood the ironic reality that art is a perceived commodity. In other words: one man's "junk" is another man's "art." Who else could take something as commonplace as a can of Campbell's soup, blow it up, silk screen it, and sell it for hundreds of thousands of dollars? Only Warhol.

His influence on other singers, actors, artists, and avant-garde performers represents an all-encompassing sea of people. This list includes artists like Keith Haring (May 4, 1958–February 16, 1990), Jean Michel Basquiat (December 22, 1960–August 12, 1988), and Mark Kostabi (born 1960). Composers and singers who benefited from their association with Warhol include The Velvet Underground, Nico, David Bowie, Lou Reed, Jackson Browne, and The Rolling Stones.

Andy was fascinated with the elusive cult of "celebrity." He loved the way the media can create and finish off the careers of so-called "stars," all in lightning-fast order. His quote about how "in the future, everyone will be famous for 15 minutes," is without a doubt one of the top ten pop culture quotes of the entire twentieth century. And never truer words were spoken. His famed 1970s and 1980s star portraits were colorful silk screen prints of such undeniable icons as Elizabeth Taylor, Liza Minnelli, Michael Jackson, Aretha Franklin, Mick Jagger, Marilyn Monroe, Judy Garland, Elvis Presley, and Queen Elizabeth II. He also saw the artistic merit in commercial objects and trademarks like his *Mammy*, *Life Savers*, and the television star puppet *Howdy Doody*.

He was famous for breaking down his portraits into shapes and colors, altering the colors of the ink amidst the print run. His bold and dramatic style, especially in his images from the 1980s, are instantly recognizable, and often stylistically usurped and copied.

Warhol was also fascinated with gay erotica and homosexual images. His films were filled with drag queens and transsexuals like Jackie Curtis, Holly Woodlawn, and Candy Darling. His art glorified many gay male themes, including his famous 1978 *Sex Parts* series, which were a series of prints comprised of close-ups of men's genitalia and depictions of real or implied man-to-man sex [including images of fellatio and anal intercourse].

The artist's fascination with pop culture and show business dates back to his working-class background in Pittsburgh, Pennsylvania, where he was born Andrew Warhola. His parents, Andrej [Andrew] Warhola [originally Varchola] and Julia Warhola, née Ulja [Julia] Justyna Zavacka, were immigrants from Miková, which at the time was located in Austria-Hungary. [Because the borders have since been redrawn, that area is currently part of northeast Slovakia.]

Young Andy's strange paleness came from a bout with a disease of the nervous system known as St. Vitus' dance, which is related to scarlet fever. It made him a sickly and often bedridden child, who grew up to be a hypochondriac who feared hospitals and doctors.

Warhol historians often argue about Andy's sex life. He was clearly one of the first in a series of American artists to admit that he was gay; however, some of his biographers claim that Andy was more of a voyeur than an active participant. He had no problem devoting whole films to homoerotic topics such as *Blow Job* (1963), *My Hustler* (1965), *Taylor Mead's Ass* (1965), and *Lonesome Cowboys* (1968). As he was starting out in the business, gallery owners often shunned him because his homoerotic drawings of male nudes were deemed too pornographic for general audiences.

Instead of waiting for the art world to catch up with his own sensibilities, he simply created a world and a mystique of his own, about himself. He did his best to stir up controversy about himself, and soon the art world was flocking to see what he would come up with next. When he did his *Campbell's Soup* in 1964, as part of an exhibit at Paul Bianchini's Upper East Side Gallery, one of his paintings of the red and white soup can sold for $1,500. And, actual Campbell's Soup cans autographed by Warhol were priced at $6.00 each.

There were many ironies about Andy Warhol. In the early 1960s, he did a series of silkscreens on the subject of the John F. Kennedy assassination. On June 3, 1968, a disgruntled playwright by the name of Valerie Solanas showed up at Warhol's gallery in Union Square, The Factory, and shot him with a pistol. The artist who made a famous series about an assassination had a would-be assassin of his own.

He went on to survive the attack, even more famous than ever before. When the disco era and Studio 54 were in full blossom, Warhol sightings were frequent. If there was a media event to be "seen" at, Andy was sure to make the scene.

Furthermore, his lifelong fear of doctors and hospitals came into play at the most ironic end of his life. In February 1987, Andy Warhol was at New York Hospital recuperating from what seemed to be routine gall bladder surgery. Suddenly, and without warning, at 6:32 A.M. on February 22, 1987, Warhol died. Perhaps his frightened perception of the medical community was more of a premonition of doom than an irrational fear.

As with many artists, news of Andy's sudden death made his artistic stock rise even further than the high watermark it was at during his life. There were several of his prints due to be released in 1987, including his *Beethoven* prints, which he never lived long enough to sign. However, these, and the monetary value of all of his works have only accrued innumerably in the meantime.

During his life Andy Warhol made an art and a science out of exploiting the many images of pop culture. This list includes his many gay and homoerotic artworks. These films and this artwork earn Andy an honorable spot on our list of influential gay artists and film directors whose groundbreaking body of work is indelibly woven into the fabric of our culture. While, like his prediction, all of the rest of us will each get our own "15 minutes of fame," Warhol cleverly orchestrated his own form of artistic immortality through his life and his art.

Chapter 4

It Takes a Village ... and a Cowboy and an Indian ... and the Navy and the Y.M.C.A.!

One can better realize the significance of Village People with an awareness of the place they were christened to salute, New York's Greenwich Village. The same is true for another locale, Fire Island. What made a beach resort the inspiration for a song on the group's very first album? What is the widespread American (and more pointedly homoerotic) enchantment with cowboys and American Indians? How about all the mysterious fascination with sailors in the Navy and the close-quarter possibilities of all that military male camaraderie? And what is it about staying at the YMCA that makes it supposedly so much fun to hang out with all of the boys?

This chapter will take some of the mystery out of these top five Village People references. A basic knowledge of this information makes it much easier to understand what made the group so unique, and why it has become so broadly embraced internationally by the culture in general and specifically by the growing gay movement.

Greenwich Village is historically a hotbed of liberal thinking that has traditionally been home to writers, actors, and artists, but it has also been the center of New York City's gay scene. Located in the lower part of Manhattan Island, it was supposedly named after Greenwich, England, after the British took control from the Dutch.

The actual part of the island that is known as "Greenwich Village" is a very specific area. It borders Broadway to the East, 14th Street and Chelsea to the North, SoHo to the south, and the Hudson River on the West. What is now known as the East Village was once considered a part of Lower East Side and was informally named the

"East Village" in the 1960s to capitalize on the cache that Greenwich Village has always possessed. What is known as the West Village is the part of Greenwich Village to the west of Sixth Avenue.

Part of Greenwich Village and the East Village is on the formal numbered grid system of streets that was set forth by the Manhattan Commissioner's Plan of 1811, whereas everything west of Greenwich Avenue is part of an older system of street layouts, which at times don't seem to make any sense compared with the rest of the city.

Dutch settlers turned the marshland that eventually became Greenwich Village into a pasture in the 1630s. Much of the Village is comprised of the Bouwerie, the personal farm of New Amsterdam's original Dutch Governor, Peter Stuyvesant. In 1766, Bernard Ratzer made a map for Henry Moore, the Royal Governor of New York, and placed Greenwich a full two miles from the city of New York, which at the time was only the tip of Manhattan, now known as The Battery, and the Wall Street area.

In 1822, there was a yellow fever epidemic in New York City, and several people fled to Greenwich Village to get away from the disease that was spreading rapidly. This led to more growth for the Village, and street patterns were later drawn up around the haphazardly placed settlements that sprang up in the area. In 1876, Washington Square Arch was erected at the end of Fifth Avenue to commemorate the 100th anniversary of the inauguration of the country's first president, George Washington.

Even at the early phases of its existence, Greenwich Village was characterized by its Bohemian culture, complete with artists, activists, writers, and free thinkers. By the beginning of the twentieth century, Greenwich Village had certainly acquired a reputation for being an area of New York that did not conform to the rest of the city. Already printing presses, art galleries, and theaters featuring experimental entertainment were flourishing there.

Right after 1900, several creative people were Greenwich Village residents, including dancer Isadora Duncan and playwright Eugene O'Neill. The Village was also a neighborhood that appealed to several political and social rebels such as Max Eastman, Emma Goldman, John Reed, and Margaret Sanger. As the rest of Manhattan grew around it, soon 14th Street became the chicest east/west street in the city. It was the heart of shopping and culture. Even the city's main opera house was on 14th Street, as was Luchow's restaurant, where Diamond Jim Brady once took Lily Langtree. And, incidentally, nearly eighty years later, Randy Jones performed a solo New Year's Eve concert in the very same Luchow's /Palace venue.

The first gay gathering spots were operated as "speakeasys" in order to avoid raids by the police. In the 1920s and 1930s, there were two well-known eateries that were known spots for gay men to gather, both located on Christopher Street right in Sheridan Square. One was called Stewarts, and the other was the Life Cafeteria. The 1939 *WPA Guide to New York City* wrote about the Life Cafeteria, calling it "a cafeteria, [at Sheridan Square], curiously enough, is one of the few obviously Bohemian spots [left] in the Village, and evenings the most conventional [patrons] occupy tables in one section of the room and watch the 'show' of the eccentrics on the other side." (17)

After World War II, Greenwich Village continued to attract free thinkers, artists, and musicians. On Christmas Day of 1949, The Weavers performed at the Village Vanguard and started off a folk music scene there. In the 1950s, while fleeing from repressive social conformity, the Beat Generation found its center in Greenwich Village amidst the abundance of welcoming coffeehouses, bars, theaters and nightclubs.

Radically different writers like Jack Kerouac, Allen Ginsberg, William S. Burroughs, and Dylan Thomas all frequented Greenwich Village in the 1950s. At the same time painters like Jackson Pollock were hanging out in the Cedar Tavern. In the 1960s, the hippies were there. Three members of the quartet The Mamas & the Papas met in the Village. Barbra Streisand and Bob Dylan launched their careers there, as did Joni Mitchell. Peter, Paul, and Mary, Simon and Garfunkel, Joan Baez, Phil Ochs, and Nina Simone all got their start by singing in small clubs in Greenwich Village, including Gerde's Folk City, which is a very special place for Randy Jones, as we shall soon see.

It was also in Greenwich Village where several of the city's bars catering to alternative clientele were located, particularly in the Christopher Street area. Two establishments, Julius' and the Stonewall Inn, are especially significant in the modern struggle for gay equal rights. Julius', located at 159 West Tenth Street, was the site of the April 21, 1966, lesser-known "Sip-In" staged by members of the New York Chapter of the Mattachine Society. At that time, the NY State Liquor Authority had a rule that ordered bars not to serve liquor to the "disorderly." This was concurrent with a period in which all homosexuals were considered "disorderly" and therefore could be refused service, evicted from the premises, or ordered by bartenders to not face other customers to avoid "cruising." On that April day in 1966, the Mattachine Society's president, Dick Leitsch, John Timmons, and Craig Rodwell walked into Julius' directly up to the bar, and proceeded to order cocktails. The bartender began to prepare the drinks, but then upon hearing the well dressed men self identify as homosexuals, put his hand over the glass, stopping short of serving the drink, which was photographed. *The New York Times* published a story April 22, 1966, headlined, "3 Deviates Invite Exclusion by Bars." The Mattachine Society utilized this incident, armed with *The New York Times* story and photograph, to challenge the NY State Liquor Authority rule in court, and winning a favorable ruling that gays had the right to assemble peacefully and be served. Julius' has held the claim as New York's oldest "gay" bar ever since. The location is prominent in the 1970 film, *Boys in the Band* and was a favorite haunt for Tennessee Williams, Rudolph Nureyev, Truman Capote, and others, according to framed newspaper articles on its walls. Just around the corner and up the block on Christopher Street is where the Stonewall Inn is located, and Greenwich Village was fittingly the site of the Stonewall Riots, which have come to symbolize the birth of the gay liberation movement in the United States. The Stonewall event is perhaps considered preeminent in leading to the modern movement for gay and lesbian issues. However, one must never forget the import of being able to freely walk into an establishment, place an order for and receive a cocktail of one's choosing!

Although it is formally known as Greenwich Village, it is also fondly referred to as "The Village." While the rest of Manhattan has a distinctive style of its own, the Village has a unique flair about it as well. There could be no more fitting place and namesake for a musical group who prided itself on singing songs of passion and liberation. Hence, the group with the deepest and longest lasting impact on pop/dance music and culture from the period, and taking at least in part its inspiration from popular cultural male images embraced heartily by the burgeoning gay movement, was named: Village People.

MARK: "Another one of your landmark songs, was 'Fire Island.'"

RANDY: "Yep. In our concerts we used 'Fire Island' as the opener and it usually got the audience going ... with an unrelenting beat, landmark names like the Pines, the Grove, the Boatel, Ice Palace, the Sandpiper, and of course our warning of 'Don't go in the bushes, don't go! Something might grab ya, something might grab ya!'"

MARK: "While many of your songs have double entendre meanings, and are written to be tongue-in-cheek, there is no question that 'Fire Island' is a song about the gay resort area."

RANDY: "That, perhaps, is the essence of the success of Village People. For our hits, we recorded expertly crafted, immediately accessible 'G' rated pop songs with irresistible hooks and a captivating beat. However, each listener, whether one be man, woman, black, white, young, old, gay, straight, or whatever, could hear his or her own individual interpretation of the lyrics according to one's particular familiarity, experience or background."

MARK: "Well, let's pack the steamer trunks for Fire Island."

RANDY: "Did you say 'steamer trunks,' or 'streaming drunks'?"

MARK: "In this case, either would do."

RANDY: "I'll drink to that!"

The sandbar-like island that runs parallel to Long Island, New York, is known as Fire Island. In geographic terms, it is technically a barrier island, which is approximately 31 miles long, and its width varies between 0.1 miles to 0.5 miles. There are less than 500 permanent residents who live on Fire Island, according to the year 2000 census. However, in the summer, the population swells into the thousands, as summer vacationers flock to the beaches and tiny communities along the island.

Ever since Manhattan's theatrical personalities began journeying to Fire Island in the 1930s, it has been an attraction for untold numbers of celebrities, artists, and Bohemians. One has to reach the island by boat, and no privately owned automobiles are allowed on the island between Memorial Day and Labor Day. Personal travel is by foot or by bicycle.

The communities on Fire Island are, in reality, unincorporated hamlets. Two of these small communities, the Fire Island Pines and Cherry Grove, have a long history as being popular destinations for thousands of lesbian, gay and gay-friendly vacationers. There are also hotels, shops, clubs, and restaurants there to cater to the eclectic community.

Because of this reputation, "Fire Island" was one of the perfect geographical tribute songs to be recorded by Village People. Henri Belolo and Jacques Morali, the producers of the group, wanted to glorify these destinations which were riding the wave of social and sexual progressiveness, including San Francisco, Key West, and Hollywood. It was the liberated atmosphere of Fire Island that inspired the Village People song, and it is an atmosphere that continues to exist on Fire Island today.

RANDY: "Let's face it, there wouldn't be the group Village People, as we've come to know it, without the male fantasy images already being in place in history and in pop culture. The Hollywood film industry had already done the heavy lifting for us as a group by creating and spreading around the world a familiarity with the six images that we grew to represent. A full 75 years before we began, the movies, both silent and sound, had laid the groundwork for us by disseminating and marketing a myriad of characters that we reflected in the Cop, the Construction Worker, the Biker, the Sailor/Soldier, not to mention the whole Cowboy and Indian thang!"

MARK: "You've got that right. Many of the great Western films that have been made throughout the twentieth century highlighted a certain homoeroticism that was linked with cowboys."

RANDY: "Listen, I grew up on Roy Rogers, Davy Crockett, Gene Autry, Clint Walker, 'The Cisco Kid', 'Maverick,' 'The Rifleman,' 'Have Gun, Will Travel' and 'Gunsmoke.' I am familiar with the 'cowboy' genre! As I recall upon my first meeting with the producers of Village People, I was dressed in my regular fashion: 501 Levis, Tony Lama boots, western shirt, etc. Hence my image was my contribution to the overall look of the group. And as I said when asked about what could be the possibilities for two cowboys out for months at a time by themselves as Heath Ledger and Jake Gyllenhall were in *Brokeback Mountain*, I had to remark that given the right conditions, the thought certainly would have to go through the mind of even the straightest of cowboys! But I do not know what was up with Tonto and The Lone Ranger!"

MARK: "Hmmmm, that is a good question, indeed."

What is it about cowboys and Indians that strikes a chord with boys and men and even more so with gay boys and men? Well, part of it is undoubtedly because the whole cowboy movement in the 1800s in the western part of the United States was largely an all-male society. The so-called "Wild West" was given that moniker owing to the fact that the territories west of the Mississippi River were mainly untamed, rough, and relatively female-free.

According to several books supporting this theory, there was a singular form of male bonding and male intimacy that existed in the West. One of them, *Queer Cowboys: And Other Erotic Male Friendships in Nineteenth-Century American Literature*, written by Chris Packard in 2005, claims that correspondence and literature from the 1800s confirm the unique male relationships that existed and flourished out on the range.

Even the writings from such classic authors of western literature, including James Fenimore Cooper, Mark Twain, and Owen Wister, feature examples of adult relationships where men often preferred the company of a male companion to the more traditional marriages that were prevalent in the eastern United States. Cowboys, Indians, journalists, miners, and explorers had their own males-only clubs. This was still a period when women were not equal citizens, could not vote in national elections, and were considered little more than chattel in a marriage.

When the California Gold Rush took place in 1849, there was a settlement in Placerville, where a museum now stands. In the museum are early photographs depicting the male miners and cowboys in each other's arms, dancing with each other at a celebration. Wild West indeed!

And, what would cowboys and the legend of the West be without their testosterone charged counterparts: American Indians? Think of the Lone Ranger and his loyal companion, Tonto. The mind reels at the spectrum of the male-bonding possibilities that they perhaps experienced!

So, once again, as testified to previously, over one hundred years of Western films, full of cowboys and Indians, are responsible for turning true-life experiences into history and history into fascinating folklore. When it came time to populate Village People, the images of the "Cowboy" and the "Indian" were undeniably perfect!

RANDY: "Continuing a discussion of Village People is difficult without exploring the myth and folklore surrounding our song, 'In the Navy.' One of my favorite 'Navy' memories involves the one and only Bob Hope. Bob, along with many of our other 'god-uncles' in the business, like Merv Griffin, Dick Clark, and Hugh Hefner, tendered tremendous support by having us on their television programs innumerable times and involving us repeatedly in their events, both charitable and private. They understood what we were really about and realized the broader ultimate entertainment value of our act. Without their incredible enthusiasm at the beginning and throughout the early days, we would not have happened in such a big way. That being said, Bob always had a finely pointed sense of humor. As we were preparing to appear with him on one of his USO specials aboard the USS *Intrepid* in NY Harbor, the brouhaha about 'In the Navy' was beginning to make a rumble in the press. Rumors of the Department of Navy threatening to withdraw use of the *Intrepid* for the show if we were allowed to perform swirled around in the papers. So Bob made a statement in which he said if the Navy yanked permission to use the ship, he would call a press conference and personally embarrass every highly placed Navy official of which he had any scandalous knowledge. He said, 'The boys in Village People are a great bunch of guys, some of the most professional I've ever worked with. And besides, they're not going to spend the night on the boat!' We proceeded to perform 'In the Navy' on the *Intrepid* for the Bob Hope USO special. And the rest is history!"

MARK: "Well, hello sailor!"

RANDY: "We've already had some discussion of sailors and the possibilities of the exploration of intimate experiences on some very long voyages in our section about Herman Melville, but ... are you willing to dive a little deeper?"

MARK: "All right, let's get down to the docks and examine this topic."

RANDY: "Or in the words of Admiral David Farragut 'Damn the torpedoes! Full speed ahead!'"

What is it about sailors which gives them the reputation for being excessively "randy" when they are on "leave" in a port? One only need to try being cooped up on a ship for months at a time, and it won't be long before any man who suddenly finds himself on shore leave for twenty-four hours wants to go and "sow more than a few wild oats." Just rent a copy of the MGM movie musical, *On the Town* and observe the less-than-kinky trio of U.S. sailors, Gene Kelly, Frank Sinatra, and Jules Munshin to have the point illustrated.

Coming off a long voyage, sailors arriving at one of Manhattan's numerous docks were saddled with this reputation of "randiness," along with that of just being a man and ready for action. According to the book *Gay New York—Gender, Urban Culture, and the Making of the Gay Male World 1890–1940*, by George Chauncey, when horny men of the ocean suddenly hit town, they were looking for sex, booze, and entertainment. Not really too different from most men anywhere. Posed with limited time to find a sexual partner, there were few options. One could hire a female prostitute, or search out a more-than-willing same-sex partner. The book cites a court report about an investigation into activity surrounding the Brooklyn Navy Yard in 1917. According to one piece of testimony in the court transcripts, "The streets and corners were crowded with the sailors all of whom were on a sharp lookout for girls ... It seemed to me that the sailors were sex mad. A number of these sailors were with other men walking arm in arm and on one dark street I saw a sailor and a man kissing each other ... It looked like an exhibition of mail [sic] perversion. Some of the sailors told me that they might be able to get a girl if they went 'up-town' but it was too far up and they were too drunk to go way up there." (18)

"Cruising" down 42nd Street, or a visit to Bryant Park, or Central Park, were three frequent meeting places in which a guy on a man-to-man sexual mission could go, starting in the 1930s. Battery Park was another notorious place in New York City where men tradition-ally went to pick up sailors.

There were some specific places for Navy men to go for refuge and entertainment. One of these organizations was the Seaman's Church Institute. The area surrounding Seaman's Church Institute was another notorious place to pick up a horny sailor.

Go West was the fourth album released by Village People. The first single, was "Go West," an uplifting, near cinematic anthem to hope, the future, and the possibilities to come. But *In the Navy,* the album's second single, was the chart buster, reaching the Number Two position on the *Billboard* singles charts in America. It was the kind of catchy, well crafted pop song that spoke of traveling the world, getting an educa-tion, camaraderie between men, saving the motherland, etc., complete with yet another irresistible beat and easy to emulate rhythmic hand-claps. And it also was replete with double entendre lyrics, depending once again on the listener's experience, familiarity, and background. The little kid who sang along and could always chime in on the chorus, "In the Na-a-vy," heard the song one way, while the sailor who may have had a brief liason with another lonely sailor while at sea listened with a completely different set of ears. Again, Village People had recorded another seemingly bland silly pop song, while simultaneously straddling a very fine line of controversy. The U.S. Dept. of the Navy allowed the group to utilize the fast frigate USS *Reasoner* in San Diego Harbor, complete with 200 U.S. sailors in dress blues and whites, to shoot the music video for "In the Navy," including footage of the Navy's own Blue Angels flight demonstration squadron in exchange for per-mission to use the song as a recruiting tool.

RANDY: "The Dept. of the Navy actually awarded each of us in Village People with a citation worded that we were 'officially declared

ITHACA COLLEGE LIBRARY

to be Honorary United States Seamen with all of the rights and privileges, but none of the duties and obligations.' I've got mine hanging right over my toilet. Everyone gets a huge guffaw from reading it! But I was and still am very honored."

After the video was completed, all was copacetic until someone in a higher command got cold feet and plans to use the song to replace "Into the Wild Blue Yonder" were shelved due to the "protests" over the use of taxpayers' money to make the music video of a, by that time, controversial singing group.

MARK: "Now we come to the origins of the most important song that Village People ever recorded."

RANDY: "Could you be speaking of 'Y.M.C.A.'?"

MARK: "Precisely. After all, it was your group who first proclaimed what fun it was to stay there."

RANDY: "If there was ever a double-entendre laden song, that came from out of left field, this song has to take the prize! Actually it's taken several prizes and given me more than a few gold and platinum records!"

MARK: "Remember the tour we went on a couple of years ago, to see the new expanded YMCA?"

RANDY: "I sure do. That was the new location for the McBurney branch, one of the oldest in New York City. It was the first gym I joined upon moving to live in the Village in New York. Incidentally, I think I'm the only original member of the group to actually live in the Village, where I've continued to live to this day. The YMCA of Greater New York is an incredible organization that benefits thousands of families and young people in Manhattan and beyond. In fact, that same McBurney branch of the Y was where I took Jacques Morali, our composer-producer, to work out several times right after I became part of Village People. He was fascinated by a place where a guy could play basketball, work out with weights, take classes, swim, have a meal, and get a room for the night. Jacques was gay, and since I had a lot of friends that I worked out with who were in the adult-film industry, he was very impressed by being introduced to the same people he had seen in films and magazines. Those visits to the Y with me, I think planted the germ of an idea in his head, and that's how he got the idea for 'Y.M.C.A.'—by literally going to the YMCA!"

MARK: "Okay, now I think that it's time for us to take a look at this organization and its long history."

What would the legend of Village People be without the song "Y.M.C.A."? Something would simply be missing from the equation.

But what is it that makes a place as innocent as the Young Man's Christian Association something of a "gay" reference point?

According to the aforementioned source book, *Gay New York— Gender, Urban Culture, and the Making of the Gay Male World 1890– 1940*, the all-male YMCAs (note the organization has no punctuation in its title) were originally established as havens for young single men who found themselves in the big city, alone and with no afford- able place to stay. With their common bathrooms and large common showers, they became known as places where like-minded men could conveniently meet.

When Village People recorded the song "Y.M.C.A.," it was the per- fect establishment to spotlight. Yes, on one hand it is a Christian association, formed to keep young men who are alone in the city, off the streets, away from female prostitutes, and in a wholesome all- male environment. However, on the other hand, hanging out with all the boys can conjure up all sorts of other sensual possibilities, in a similar manner to which the English Public School system has an associated homoerotic tradition. After all, the YMCA was founded in London, England in 1844, by a young man named George Williams.

And just how did those hand movements for "Y.M.C.A." come about? Randy explains it all: "And, for the record, the letter-forming dance that is associated with this song was not a formal part of Vil- lage People choreography at all. We created the original choreogra- phy while we were flying up from South America to do 'Uncle' Dick Clark's *American Bandstand* show in LA. We worked on the chor- eography on the airplane, right in the aisles—handclaps, turning, marching in place, stuff like that. Well the audience at this particular taping of *Bandstand* was a bunch of kids bused in from a cheerlead- ing camp. The first time we got to the chorus, we were clapping our hands above our heads. The kids thought it looked like we were making a 'Y'. So they automatically did the letters. We saw this and started doing the letters with them. It was organic and purely audience-generated, which is probably one of the reasons why it's still so popular today. To this day every weekend at weddings, birthday parties, bar mitzvahs, high school reunions, sporting events (like every Yankees home game!) and retirement parties, people are dancing to 'Y.M.C.A.' It has indeed become deeply imbedded in pop culture and is the best known of all the Village People songs. And I am personally proud to be part of its legacy!" (19)

Chapter 5

The Birth of Disco and the Formation of Village People

By the mid-1970s, the phenomenon that is disco had transformed the landscape of New York City's nightlife, and ultimately that of the world. Ground zero for all the weekend euphoria typified in *Saturday Night Fever* was originally a nightclub opened in Paris 1958 by one Belgian-born Regina Zylberberg, but forever known as "Regine." This Gallic location holds the claim as being the first night-spot where recordings were used to replace live performances of music. The path from Regine's in 1958 to the supreme signifier of the movement, Studio 54 in 1977, had stopovers in places such as Sybil Burton's The Arthur, Ondine's, The Cheetah, Le Club, and The Peppermint Lounge in New York City. However, the surge to the zenith of the movement is one that is indelibly influenced by brilliant R&B pop music and its embrace by the burgeoning gay liberation movement of the late '60s and early '70s.

It could be said that the Ice Palace on Fire Island was the first gay disco. But the notorious Sanctuary, which opened in 1969, certainly epitomizes the post-Stonewall era when gay men had won the right to drink and dance together in a completely uninhibited manner without being harassed by the police. The Sanctuary is forever immortalized as the club where Oscar winner Jane Fonda hangs out as "Bree Daniels" in the 1971 film, *Klute*. As the '70s progressed, other primarily gay, black, and Latino underground locales sprang up including Dave Mancuso's The Loft, The Tenth Floor, Flamingo, The Gallery, and The Anvil, among many others. 1973-74 signaled an evolution somewhat with the opening and popularity of John Addison and Maurice Brahms' Le Jardin in the basement of New York's Hotel Diplomat. It had a central clientele of gay men, but was

unique in its ever-growing quota of beautiful women and fashionable straights. This harbinger of things to come was a heady mix of
gay sensibility, beauty, fashion, and music meant to be danced to
and was an undeniable trend that would sweep the globe. Le Jardin
was the site where, on March 3, 1975, Gloria Gaynor was crowned
the Queen of Disco. From the early '70s to the present, the whole
world has been dancing to a disco beat.

In Manhattan alone, dance clubs began opening at a hastening
pace, and the disco craze brought with it new fashions, new music,
and a spotlight on nightlife that hadn't been as evident or as focused
in years. It was the era of chic discotheques like Hurrah, Studio 54,
Xenon, Ice Palace 57, and Regine's. Before it was over, discos sprang
up in every major city, including La Palace in Paris, Heaven in
London, The I-Beam and Trocadero Transfer in San Francisco,
Menjo's in Detroit, The Second Story in Philadelphia, and Studio One
in Los Angeles.

It all started with a sound that was part danceable R&B, part pure
pop, and always upbeat. In 1973, when The O'Jays' "Love Train"
reached Number One on *Billboard*'s Hot 100 charts, the ball was certainly hustling towards a disco beat. The first real hit song that was
initially embraced by the dancing denizens of disco and signaled the
beginning of the disco era was the song "Rock the Boat" by a Los
Angeles trio called The Hues Corporation. It followed close on the
heels of "Love's Theme," an instrumental hit in February 1974.
"Love's Theme" was a huge influence on the coming "disco" sound
and was recorded by Barry White's Love Unlimited Orchestra. However, "Rock the Boat," released in May 1974, fully embodied the
essence of disco and by July, 1974, managed the journey all the way
to Number One on the *Billboard* charts in America. All of a sudden,
the midwives could stand aside and disco could step onto the dance
floor to strut its stuff! Interestingly enough, that same year more and
more records, which were very danceable, started appearing on the
charts with greater frequency. The next big Number One disco hit of
1974 was George MacCrea's "Rock Your Baby." That autumn Gloria
Gaynor had her first disco-oriented hit with her danceable remake
of the Jackson Five's "Never Can Say Goodbye."

The following year, in 1975, it was Van McCoy's "The Hustle," and
the Silver Convention's "Fly Robin Fly," and suddenly the sounds of
disco and dance music were all over the airwaves. In the same year,
Neil Bogart's Casablanca Records released Donna Summer's 17-
minute "Love to Love You Baby" bringing disco—and Casablanca—

their first bona fide disco superstar. Casablanca Records, which formerly had been known for its acts like KISS and George Clinton's Parliament, was suddenly the premiere label for disco acts.

In this era Motown Records got involved in recording danceable music as well. In 1974, the Jackson 5 released "Dancing Machine"; the following year The Miracles hit the charts with "Love Machine," and in 1976 The Supremes recorded their Number One dance hit "I'm Gonna Let My Heart Do the Walking." It was also that same year that Dr. Buzzard's Original Savannah Band released their phenomenal debut album, with "Cherchez La Femme" on it, and it became such a huge hit that suddenly recording artists were not just putting one or two disco songs on their albums, whole LPs full of nonstop dance music were being released. Suddenly everyone in the business was jumping on the disco bandwagon.

Meanwhile, as all of these great songs were galloping up the record charts, there had to be a place in which all of this uplifting music could be listened to, danced to, and celebrated. This is where the discotheques provided the perfect fit. At the core of this whole phenomenon were the New York City gay and underground discos, where a whole new generation of homosexual men, newly liberated from the shackles of police interference, could meet, groove, and dance all night long.

Trends and events of the sixties and early seventies provided fertile ground for the disco phenomenon to proceed and flourish. There were the Stonewall Riots in 1969, preceded of course, in April 1966, by the ground-breaking "Sip-In" at Julius' and the Compton's Cafeteria Riots (August, 1966) in San Francisco's Tenderloin district, which was the first recorded transgender riot in United States history. After these particular events, it was much easier for gay people to gather in their own public establishments without fear from the police in Manhattan, San Francisco, and Los Angeles

Following San Francisco's "Summer of Love" in 1967 and the 1968 Be-In in NYC's Central Park, there was another specific event that took place in the summer of 1969. It was the Woodstock music festival, which was the embodiment and the answer to the idealistic '60s dream-like question: "Can everyone PLEASE just get along?" At Woodstock, half a million people came together at Yazgar's Farm in Bethel, New York, because of the music, the love, and "the happening" itself. White, black, and brown people, hippies, rock & rollers, bikers, gays, and straights were all there peaceably coexisting with incredible music playing over the loudspeakers.

Not one particular event, but bridging the '60s and '70s was the velvet underground/glam rock movement, where bisexuality, homosexuality, provocative cross-dressing, and the entire "free love" concept was hatched. In the 1970s, with acts like Queen, T-Rex, Marc Bolan, David Bowie, Lou Reed, and The New York Dolls, the sight of boys in make-up dancing together was suddenly accepted as another kind of "not just for Halloween, but year round," gender-bending aspect to an ever growing panoply of eye-popping lifestyles.

A generation that was bred on the civil rights struggles of the Fifties and Sixties (including blacks, women and gays) and the free-love, "if it feels good do it as long as it doesn't hurt anyone else" philosophy of the hippies and the infamous 1968 "Summer of Love" in San Francisco, found itself coming of age. Yes, this population, the "baby boomers," found themselves of age and able to vote, to drink (at least in many urban areas), and to enjoy a coming decade that with the end of the Vietnam War was relatively free of social strife. It was the 1970s, and the "Me Decade" felt it was the generation which was truly free to love whom they wanted, be whom they wanted to be, to dress the way they wanted, and to party and go out to dance on any night of the week.

As America was adapting and navigating its way through these complex social changes, and listening to "Rock the Boat" and "Dancing Machine," by 1974, a new revolution was taking root. It was the disco era, a distinct time period when people of every color and sexual persuasion, could come together, dance together, and live out their dance floor fantasies.

Mentioned previously, Le Jardin was one of the early New York City discotheques catering to a fashionable mixed-gender, mixed-sexual orientation, mixed-racial crowd. Another was a small two-story restaurant located on Fifth Avenue between 12th and 13th Streets called Ashley's. It was a chic place to trip on drugs, drink, have dinner, and dance, in the heart of Greenwich Village. At these places, one would not want to show up on a Saturday night in jeans and sneakers. The crowd would dress up for the night; suddenly there was a sense of theatricality and costuming one's self for a night on the town. Disco music and an elaborate night of dancing suddenly needed disco fashion. One would also want to come fully accessorized, with boas, scarves, and flowing dresses for the women; suits with open-fronted jackets, shirts with flashy gold chains, and trendy bell-bottoms for the guys; and ludicrously high platform shoes for everyone.

Then, there were the decidedly different gay discotheques of Manhattan, including Twelve West, Flamingo, and Paradise Garage. These clubs were 99% for-men-only. And how did they get away with that? They would do it mainly by licensing themselves as "private clubs," so that they could be selective about the clientele. On the other side of the coin, there was also an exclusive women-only disco as well, on the Upper East Side, called Sahara. If there were members of the opposite sex in any of these clubs, they were either in the record business, VIPs, or friends of the owners.

Since the start of the 1970s, there were all sorts of inroads made into defining a new sound for the decade. The aforementioned glam rock movement was certainly one of many directions that music took. There was also the R&B music to go along with the fresh wave of 1970s "cops and pimps and robbers" films like *Superfly* (Curtis Mayfield soundtrack), *Shaft* (Isaac Hayes soundtrack), and *Willie Dynamite* (Martha Reeves theme song). Pop music also established several new easy-listening stars including, the Carpenters, Roberta Flack, the Captain & Tennille, John Denver, and the totally unique and "Divine Miss M": Bette Midler!

During this time, record companies were busy chasing the trends. When disco proved to be a viable new format, ripe for developing, every record label soon created whole new departments to handle the booming dance format that was sweeping the business. The recording industry early on became aware of the burgeoning gay audience. Without a doubt, it proved to be a embracing market that was perfect for tapping. The gay male crowd frequented the discos, promoted the music, and faithfully purchased vinyl copies of the albums, as well as the new 12-inch disco "remixes" and "extended" versions of the hits.

Two very clever music producers from France, Henri Belolo and Jacques Morali, perceived what was going on in the music business and what was going on in American culture. Tumultuous events like the Compton's Cafeteria Riots of 1966 and the Stonewall Riots of 1969, were led by some mighty powerful personalities. One in particular was Sylvia Rivera, a transgender activist. That night her actions proved that a man may choose to wear a dress, but if angered sufficiently, he can still rip a parking meter out of the sidewalk and smash a cop's car with it. As transvestism was a widely accepted stereotype of gay men, to counter it there was a growing visibility among gay men in reclaiming the hyper masculine images of the American male, i.e., the Cowboy, the leather-clad Biker, the

Uniformed Services, etc. Upon coming to New York City, it was not ususual that Belolo and Morali observed gay men proudly strutting about Greenwich Village in such displays. Morali was gay, Belolo is not, but having many gay friends, Belolo was interested in their musical tastes, their interests, fantasies, and dreams. And after the successes with the Ritchie Family, his new American group and their successes "Brazil" and "The Best Disco in Town," he was looking to follow up with the next "Big Hit," as any smart businessman would be. On one of these strolls about the Village, the duo found themselves in one of the more infamous watering holes, The Anuil. Here they were, surrounded by all the costumed types that they had observed on the streets. And on the bar dancing in a headdress and bells was the image of an American Indian come to lusty life, with a cowboy watching intently. Then, as Belolo relates the story, he and Morali got the idea simultaneously. They began to think of what would be a collection of fantasy images that would trigger the attention of the gay community and at the same time appeal to the broader audience already familiar with the same stereotypes. Right there was the Cowboy. And dancing on the bar was the Indian. That sure seemed like a good start. With both Morali and Belolo fascinated by American culture, what could be more American than Cowboys and Indians?

The group known as Village People came together in a round about way. Armed with a idea for an album and a group, the two producers immediately went to work in the studio, producing four cuts, inspired by the locales that they had learned were known for having gay life: San Francisco, Hollywood, Fire Island, and the Village. With Victor Willis, recruited from the company of Broadway's *The Wiz*, to lend his soulful and unforgettable vocal talents as the lead and professional session singers to provide the backing vocals, the first incarnation (at least aurally!) was born. With a quick photo session of random Village types, none to actually become members of the group, except the Indian, the first Village People album came into being. That album became a success, albeit an underground success, thanks to the initial support of the community by which it was inspired.

With the first album, *Village People*, selling in excess of 100,000 copies over that first summer after its release, Henri Belolo along with his co-producer, Morali, knew they had a hit when Casablanca Records chief, and Neil Bogart congratulated them. They all concurred that Village People was an extraordinary idea and provocative idea for the time, but to continue and extend the success it was absolutely necessary to have the living, breathing, flesh and blood embodiment of the masculine images singing the music. There was a dire need to have six capable performers to breathe life into the fantasies of the music and to sing, promote, and bring the concept of Village People to television and the live performance onstage. That's when they rounded up the very UN-usual suspects: the inspirational bar-dancing Indian, Felipe Rose; a Brooklyn-Battery Tunnel worker, biker Glenn Hughes; Broadway chorus boy, David Hodo, as construction worker; a session singer from the debut album, Alex Briley; and of course the dynamic lead singer, Victor Willis. The soon-to-be cowboy Randy Jones, had been seen earlier while performing with Grace Jones, whom he had worked with as a fashion model and subsequently performed in and participated in creating her groundbreaking live act. Recalling his first meeting with Morali, after appearing on the runway and performing with Grace Jones at the 1977 *Billboard* Disco Awards, "Jacques approached me and complimented me on my moustache and said he liked the way that I moved. He then asked if I could sing, since he was forming a singing group. He said he was interested in hiring me. Of course I said, 'Yep, I can sing.' And I made sure that the next meeting place was in a formal office in the daylight! As I remember, I dressed as I always had, cowboy boots, jeans, a western shirt, so I was comfortable as I could have possibly been. When invited to join Village People, I jumped right in. It was and it is the best decision I've made in my professional life. I remember signing a contract and in less than a week we were in the studio recording a new album. Things moved very fast!"

Studio time was booked, and the record company was waiting for the follow-up album to *Village People*. There was no time to waste. Remembers Randy, "Henri and Jacques had a concept, and an incredibly strong idea as to what they envisioned. We breathed the life, the flesh, the blood, sweat, tears, and laughter into their concept making it a reality. All of a sudden, I was a member of Village People. That same week, there I was with the other five guys singing 'Macho Man' into a microphone, reading Victor's handwritten lyrics off of a piece of paper, which was complete with coffee and egg stains from breakfast all over it. Things happened that quickly!"

With a group like this, it would have been a disaster if the six members of the band did not get along well. Randy found that there was an immediate camaraderie between the six of them. As he explains it, "It was almost a brotherhood and certainly a baptism by fire because we went through three months of tough rehearsals for

not much money to begin with. Then we hit the road and began pro-
moting the first album where we were the official group." (19)

The songs on the *Macho Man* album all fit into the whole free-
for-all disco lifestyle that seemed to be emerging in every urban city
on the planet. "Macho Man" perfectly defined the character concept
of the group and gave all men, straight or gay, a chest-thumping anthem to work out to at their gym. The song "I Am What I Am" was a
gay liberation statement, aimed directly at gays and lesbians who
were standing up without apology for their lifestyle. The song "Key
West" was a salute to the Florida town that Ernest Hemingway and
Tennessee Williams, along with gay men and women, had made a
vacation destination. "Just a Gigolo" was an homage to the ever-
seductive gigolo. "I Ain't Got Nobody" was about looking for love.
And, the sixth and final track on the album, "Sodom and Gomorrah"
was about the Biblical city where an "anything goes" attitude spelled
"ruin" for it. The song subliminally thumbed its nose at those critics
who found that the disco and gay movements paralleled the downfall of those cities.

Mark Bego was a magazine writer in the 1970s when he was
invited by Marsha Stern to be the first press member ever to interview the newly formed Village People, on April 13, 1978. He recalls:

When I got to the offices of this company known as Can't Stop Productions,
five of the six members of the newly created group were there waiting for
me. I was informed that the sixth member, Biker Glenn Hughes, was on his
way to the interview, but was reportedly driving his motorcycle into Manhattan from Long Island, and he was stuck in traffic. We started the interview without him.

"How did the group come together?" I asked. "I know that some of the
band members were not on the first album, *Village People*."

Victor Willis explained, "The first album was done mainly in the studio.
And the second album, the group did, that is really our first album as a
group."

"If you can, can each of you tell me what you did before joining Village
People," I inquired.

"I was in a couple of Broadway shows," David said.

According to Victor, "Jacques and I had an open audition, announced in
the newspaper. Alex Briley was part of the group the longest."

Said Felipe, "Jacques saw me in the discotheques, dancing. He liked the
sense of freedom that I danced with. Then I went into the studio, and one
thing led to another, and here I am."

"How did you get interested in the bells and the Indian headdress?"
I asked him.

"I am part Indian; those are my roots. And I wanted to establish that identity."

"You were studying to be a professional dancer?"

"Yes, my head was going there."

"What were you doing before joining the group, Alex?" I asked.

"Just before I came into Village People," he said, "I was a back-up singer for Bobbi Humphrey. I had been traveling with her. And, besides that, I was directing a choir in my church. Basically, I've always been singing."

"Randy, what did you experience before the group?" I asked the group's cowboy.

"Before and since college I've been doing musical theater, modeling and some work in film and TV. I've danced with a few dance companies, the Pauline Koner Dance Consort, The Anna Sokolov Dance Company and the Agnes DeMille Heritage Dance Theatre. I've done a couple of things off-Broadway, and I did a few commercials, like BIG RED chewing gum. I've been a singer and a dancer since I was twelve . . . at least!" he replied.

"Professionally?"

"Well, I started studying when I was about eleven or twelve. I've been singing and dancing, performing professionally since 1970."

"Where are you from originally?"

"Raleigh, North Carolina."

"When did you come to New York?"

"Two and a half years ago," Randy said.

They talked about their hopes for the group, and how they saw their stage act evolving into a spectacle of a Broadway show scale. Randy also spoke of running into former First Lady, Lady Bird Johnson at the Plaza Hotel, while they were shooting a video for the *Macho Man* album. According to him, "We gave her a copy of the album, which had just come out. We told her we are Village People, and she smiled and said, 'I wondered who *y'all* boys were.'"

Glenn was the last one to arrive at the interview. He had trouble finding a midtown parking space for his huge motorcycle. He had dark hair and wore a leather vest and several chains around his neck. He also sported a handlebar mustache.

"I'm Mark Bego," I said, standing up to shake his hand.

"I'm Glenn Hughes," he said.

"Nice to meet you Glenn," I sincerely said.

"We were talking about what all of you guys did before joining the group. So you were a toll taker for the City of New York?"

"Yes, I did that for six years," he explained. "I had gone to a lot of auditions, and rarely followed through with them. You know, you have to work to support yourself in the meantime."

"Where are you from originally?"

"I was born on Long Island."

"How do you look upon all of the stuff that has happened to you since joining the group?"

"With awe!" he said with a big hearty laugh.

Well, I certainly was in awe of Village People. That was for sure. That was one of the most fun group interviews I had done to date. *Disco World* magazine never did publish my interview with the group, but I was very quickly able to get them in my new column in *Cue* magazine.

I reported in my "Night Beat" page in *Cue*, "Last month the six singers who are collectively Village People transposed their disco hits (including 'San Francisco') to Hurrah's stage with maximum success. Backed by a live band, the group added Motown choreography to accompany the hits like 'Macho Man.' VP member Randy Jones says he enjoys the casual set-up at Hurrah's—playing to an audience that has the freedom of dancing, standing or sitting on floor pillows."

However, it wasn't long before the small club dates they were originally booked in would not be big enough to accommodate their fans; they would soon be selling out huge auditoriums all over the world. This was the beginning of my lifelong relationship with each of the members of Village People. (20)

As per the intentions of the producers' concept for Village People, the images on the cover of the second Village People album, *Macho Man*, perfectly resonated in the eyes and ears of gay male disco record buyers. According to Randy, "The mid- to late-'70s was a time when the gay subculture was throwing off the shackles of Stonewall and that victim attitude, and taking possession of their masculinity." (19)

Once the *Macho Man* album was released, the next task was to promote it and the group at every discotheque and nightclub that Can't Stop Productions could book. Randy remembers, "We went around to every disco and music venue in the country and built a base for *Macho Man* and for Village People. The plan that our production company put together with the record label and promotion company was like a military strike operation. First we'd book the gig and then travel to the town where we had the date. After we had checked into the hotel, those of us that were skillful at doing radio and press interviews would launch out and cover those areas. If we'd been able to arrange an in-store record signing appearance, we'd all convene to do that. As a group we would do our soundcheck, then back to the hotel for a bite to eat and hopefully a bit of rest. And finally the reason we were in town, the show! And the show is what really put us over. It was a frothy combination of youthful enthusiasm, borderline naughty comedy, irresistible thumping music, great pop songs and six very healthy sexy examples of sweaty '70s manhood! And after the shows, some of us were more than willing to stay and hang in the club with the crowd and extend the audience development! After all, that's what the '70s was about—the party! And if we were nothing else, we were THE PARTY! The reception that we received was overwhelmingly positive. More likely than not, after we had been to a city with the big push, we were added to the local radio stations' play-list and added to the club DJ's play-list, not to mention the Village People albums were flying out of the stores! Before long, the whole Village People phenomenon began to grow and gain momentum at an astonishing rate. As the single version of 'Macho Man' took off on the music charts, and hit Number One on the *Billboard* Disco Chart, the excitement was building by the day."

Not only did the single do well on the Disco Chart, in America it hit Number 25 on the Pop Chart, and the *Macho Man* album made it to Number 24 and was certified platinum for sales in excess of 1,000,000 copies sold in the United States alone. Based on the success of that album, the *Village People* debut album was certified gold for 500,000 copies sold.

Randy recalls,

Those early days, at the height of our success as Village People, were the most breathtaking months of my life. We could easily find ourselves on three different continents in the space of five days. I remember a particular itinerary that included performing on *American Bandstand* in Los Angeles, flying to Rio de Janeiro for a massive soccer stadium gig in front of 100,000 people, and then taking the Concorde to Paris to work on a Jean Yanne-directed French film called *Jet te Tiens Par Le Barbiche*tte. We did all of this in less than a week! Once in a while I was able to pause and look around at the glorious madness swirling around us. On a rare free evening I went to the top of the Eiffel Tower for the first time and looked out at the beautiful City of Light, Paris and remembered that this was an experience that the majority of the people on this planet would love to have had, and most likely never will. I have always tried to make it a point to remember and to enjoy every moment that comes along. (19)

The demand for the third Village People album—*Cruisin'*—was so great that it was quickly recorded and released. Containing the songs "Y.M.C.A.," "The Women," "I'm a Cruiser," "Hot Cop," "My Roommate," and "Ups and Downs," it referenced more gay issues of the day. As previously mentioned, the YMCAs were long known as a location for like-minded men to gather. "The Women" dealt with famous women like Marilyn Monroe, Jean Harlow, Gina Lollobrigida, and

Sophia Loren, whom gay as well as straight men find fascinating. "I'm a Cruiser," with Glenn Hughes' distinctively low voice on the chorus, was about cruising the streets. "Hot Cop" was basically the theme song for Victor Willis's police officer character in the group, as well as heavily nodding towards the gay and straight fascination with uniformed law enforcement officers. "My Roommate" is about a roommate who lives to go to the disco. Could he be gay, could he be straight? And, "Ups and Downs" was an ode to taking so-called "recreational drugs" for a night on the town, very '70s style!

However, none of this material was presented in any sort of offensive "gay" fashion. While anyone who was actively gay or familiar with the '70s gay culture could perceive a subliminal text, the lyrics of the songs were actually free of any blatant sexual references whatsoever. The tongue-in-cheek brilliance of all of the Village People songs was that they would be construed as being sexy and sexual, but only in a double entendre fashion.

It was 1978, and the height of the disco world. All of a sudden the members of Village People were overnight superstars, not only in gay subculture, but their star shone much brighter in the realm of international pop stardom. With instant fame and notoriety came instant universal sex appeal. "For several years, beginning in the late '70s, life was a whirlwind of non-stop activity," says Cowboy Randy. "I didn't hear the word 'no' very often. Even before Village People, working as a model with Grace Jones and Janice Dickinson, there was a lot of craziness. It was a time when many people were very comfortable with casual sex: straight, gay, or bi. With success, everyone around you tends to say, 'Yes,' so it can be easy to lose perspective. Groupies are, by their nature, extremely enthusiastic and cooperative, and I've been blessed with plenty. The expression, 'Rock out with your cock out,' began at parties at places like Studio 54 in New York City and Le Palace in Paris. At least that's where I first remember hearing it. That period was nothing like today in the twenty-first century. Who knows if there will never be another period like it. The generation that came of age in the '70s had been bred on the philosophy of free love: 'If it feels good, do it.' We weren't aware of the health issues that people have to deal with today." (21)

The year 1979 was an even more successful year for Village People. For the entire year they were acknowledged as being among the Top Ten most recognizable superstars in the business. Furthermore, Casablanca Records was acknowledged as the most successful disco label in the business. When they signed pop diva Cher to a recording contract, she instantly scored a huge hit with her chart-topping song "Take Me Home." Together with Donna Summer, Village People were crowned royalty at Casablanca.

For the first three weeks of 1979 the song "Y.M.C.A." was Number One on the British music charts. The single sold a record-breaking 150,000 copies in one day. In England, the single set a high-water mark, selling over 1,300,000 copies. In the United States "Y.M.C.A." hit Number Two on the *Billboard* Pop Singles Chart for three weeks. On January 12, 1979, Village People won an American Music Award under the Favorite Disco Group category.

In less than two weeks, the single "Y.M.C.A." was certified platinum by the R.I.A.A. (Record Industry Association of America) for over a million copies sold in the United States. In March 1979, Casablanca Records released the song "In the Navy," which became an instant hit. Both that single, and the album it came from, *Go West*, were certified platinum million-sellers before they peaked on the American charts. "In the Navy" made it to Number Three on the Pop charts, and *Go West*, which was the first single released from the same titled album, peaked at Number Eight in the United States and Number 14 in the United Kingdom. Incidentally, the Pet Shop Boys would later in 1993, cover the single, "Go West" and have a international smash hit with it. Village People, as a group, would attain even greater universal fame when they were featured on the cover of *Rolling Stone* magazine, Vol. 289, April 19, 1979. They were at the absolute pinnacle of their success.

While Village People were on the road in the midst of a world tour, in 1979, the U.S. Navy was in negotiations to use the song "In the Navy" as promotion for their television and radio recruitment commercials. It appeared that "Anchors Aweigh" was getting a bit stale as a recruiting anthem, and on the horizon, nothing was hotter than Village People and "In the Navy." So seemingly someone positioned in senior management from the Department of the Navy got an idea to "spice" things up a bit! Representatives for the U.S. Navy contacted producer Henri Belolo, who decided to grant the rights gratis, on the condition that the Navy assist them in shooting the music video on one of their ships. Several weeks later, Village People arrived at the San Diego Naval Base where they were provided with a warship, the fast frigate USS *Reasoner*, several Phantom aircraft, and couple hundred Navy personnel, half dressed in uniform blues and half in uniform whites. For the day, the members of Village

People were declared honorary "members of the United States Navy with all the rights and privileges, but none of the duties or obligations." Randy comments: "They even gave us this framed official looking document and then took photos of us on the ship holding them. The photo of us on the ship is on my Myspace page, and the framed document hangs over my toilet. Everyone that sees it thinks it's hilarious and can't believe it! It's just another incredible artifact from the Village People part of my career."

A few weeks after the video began airing on television, according to Henri Belolo, the *New York Post* ran an article on the front page criticizing the Navy for using tax dollars to fund a music group's video. In addition there were rumors that the song was rife with subtle gay innuendo. It caused a big scandal and made the single even more popular on the radio, in discotheques, and in music shops around the world. Even the always good humored American showman Bob Hope weighed in when there was rumor that the Department of the Navy was going to withdraw permission to use the USS *Intrepid* anchored in New York Harbor as the location for Hope's upcoming USO television special on which Village People was scheduled to be featured guests and perform "In the Navy." Hope put out the word that if official Navy permission was withdrawn to use the *Intrepid* for his USO program, he would call a press conference to reveal any 'secrets' that he may have knowledge of in relation to any members of the Department of the Navy. "Besides," he wryly surmised, "the boys in Village People are some of the most talented and professional fellows I've ever worked with ... and they have no intention of overnighting onboard the ship!" (19)

Village People struck a cultural nerve not only in America, but around the world and bridged the gap between multi-cultural, multi-ethnic, and multi-sexual communities, entertaining audiences that had the group performing in venues as varied as discos like Studio 54 to sold-out houses at Madison Square Garden and massive crowds of 100,000 in Brazilian soccer stadiums. The group found itself featured on the covers of *Rolling Stone, People* magazine, along with most other major publications around the globe. Village People was spotlighted on programs internationally as varied as *Midnight Special* and *Don Kirshner's Rock Concert,* Germany's *Musik Laden,* Britain's *Top of the Pops, The Merv Griffin Show, The Tonight Show* and all of the top music television programs of the era.

Recalls Randy Jones, "Those years were a 'Baptism by Fire,' and it's a bond that we six original members will always share. We worked with a myriad of talented and skilled people to come up with our exciting stage act. From costume and set designers, to choreographers, to lyricists, musicians, and technicians, they all contributed to the final goal of making the six of us look and sound as good as humanly possible while out there performing as 'Village People.' We six individuals totally breathed life into and gave character and substance to those inspired images that had caught the eyes of Jacques Morali and Henri Belolo in that sensual landscape of Greenwich Village." (19)

There was also an interesting dynamic between Village People and the group's creator, Jacques Morali. As Randy explains it, "If Jacques could have had his way, it would have been he who was in the spotlight along with the group. But he had to let his creation get the lion's share of the glory. In a perfect world—in Jacques' world—he would have been a music superstar. He would have had a sexy mustache and been right there in the line with us. So, he could be very protective of us, and at times he attempted to be very manipulative of us as well." (19)

At times the Village People's schedules were so hectic that they could barely catch their breath, especially from 1978 to 1980. "We worked nonstop. We were pushed to the limit," Randy recalls. "A lot of the nightlife that people think we were so totally immersed in we only got a taste of since often we had to jump out of a limousine at 4 am in the morning, head into one club, only to be whisked out again 15 minutes later to travel to another promotional gig. But, as I learned, sometimes a taste is all one needs!" (19)

While *Go West* was one of the hottest albums of 1979, Village People were the toast of the music world. Suddenly they were hanging out with movie stars, film directors, established singing stars, and the crowned heads of Europe. There were few people on the planet who may have missed the impact of the Village People onslaught, regardless of their age, sex or ethnicity. However, the pressures, and the privileges of fame and instant wealth, began to affect the individual members of Village People.

Lead singer Victor Willis married a singer by the name of Phylicia Allen, the sister of singer/dancer Debbie Allen. She would later divorce him, marry and divorce Ahmad Rashad, a sports figure, and go on to become the costar of *The Cosby Show* on television, under her new name of Phylicia Rashad. During Victor and Phylicia's short marriage, from 1978-80, Phylicia actually recorded an album, *Josephine Superstar*, for which Village People contributed background vocals. She also was the opening act for several of the early Village People concerts. As previously mentioned, the pressures and privileges of fame and wealth can certainly affect the relationships within a pop group as well as the relationships with individual members' spouses. Historically, we've seen it happen with The Beatles, the Rolling Stones, ad infinitum. No one in Village People was immune. With the stress of his marriage collapsing and his own desire to forge his solo recording career, Victor managed to help create an environment within the group dynamic that was in mutual agreement to his departure prior to the filming of Village People's big Hollywood cinema push via Allan Carr, *Can't Stop the Music*.

Raymond Simpson, a background singer for his sister, Valerie Simpson and her husband, Nick Ashford, was tapped to cover Victor's place in the group. The change was relatively seamless. Simpson's vocal quality was definitely different from Willis', but the new material being written for *Can't Stop the Music* seemed to accommodate his abilities.

In a recent interview, Henri Belolo reveals that he (Belolo) and Morali had big plans for Victor to go solo. Victor also states that he did not care to participate in the group's big-budgeted Hollywood movie, *Can't Stop the Music*.

According to Randy, "Whatever was going on behind the scenes was between Henri, Jacques, and Victor. All of us in the group got on fine with Raymond, and suddenly we as a group could focus on the work we had before us, which was a world tour and a huge upcoming twenty-five million dollar Hollywood movie to make." (19)

The first Village People album to feature Raymond Simpson as the group's "Hot Cop" was 1979's *Live and Sleazy*. It combined one new studio album with a second disc of "live" versions of the group's greatest hits "Macho Man," "In the Navy," "Y.M.C.A.," "Fire Island," "San Francisco," and "In Hollywood." The new material included "Sleazy," "Rock & Roll Is Back Again," "Ready for the '80s," and "Save Me." The album peaked at Number 32 in the United States, and the single "Ready for the '80s" made it to Number 52.

The recent 1970s successes of musical films *Grease, Thank God It's Friday*, and *Saturday Night Fever* proved to movie and record producers that millions of dollars could be made on big screen movie musicals—which had previously seemed passé. Not only could they sell millions of tickets at the box office, they could sell millions of albums at the record stores as well. How far could the legacy of Village People be taken? To become movie stars, perhaps? Recalls

Randy, "Henri Belolo, a mastermind international businessman, who was orchestrating Village People's career moves, knew he had to strike while the iron was hot, and get as much for his artists as he could, so it was 'Hollywood here we came!'"

Into that marketplace, plans were put into place for Village People to star in the ultimate Busby-Berkeley-meets-disco inspired film: *Can't Stop the Music*. From 1979 to 1980, Village People worked on their one and only starring feature film. The group had actually appeared in a French film, *Je Te Tiens, Tu Me Tiens, Par La Barbichette* directed by the great Jean Yanne, which they filmed in 1978 in Paris. In this comedy, they performed a cut from their *Macho Man* album, "Hot Cop."

Film veteran and star comedienne, Nancy Walker, was signed to direct by Allan Carr, the film's producer. She had been a hit in the 1940s stage musical and Hollywood film *Best Foot Forward*, and most recently as Valerie Harper's mother on the hit 1970s television shows, *Rhoda* and *MacMillan & Wife*. Village People's costars included Oscar nominee Valerie Perrine, Steve Guttenberg, Olympic gold medalist Bruce Jenner, Tony Award winner Tammy Grimes, Marilyn Sokol, June Havoc, Altovese Davis, and female trio the Ritchie Family. It has become one of the most outrageous camp musical films ever made. From producer Alan Carr's rumored on-set excesses, to the nonstop party that was going on in front of the cameras, Hollywood has yet to see anything to compare to the likes of *Can't Stop the Music*. Randy Jones distinctly recalls:

Perhaps the most exciting time of my career with Village People was the filming of our movie *Can't Stop the Music*. How this came about was that we were shooting *Don Kirshner's Rock Concert*, as that week's hosts. We filmed the concert at the old David O. Selznick studios in Culver City—the ones where the front facade was used as the front veranda of Tara in *Gone with the Wind*.

Backstage, after the taping at the studio, and while still dripping wet from the stage, we were introduced to Jacqueline Bisset and her then-boyfriend Victor, by film producer Allan Carr. It was kind of appropriate that we were soaking wet when we met Jackie ... sort of an homage, since we all knew of her in that wet t-shirt from those great scenes and posters from *The Deep*. Once we toweled off and were shuttled into our limousines, we found ourselves being escorted into one of Hollywood's most famous nightspots, the restaurant Le Dome on Sunset Boulevard.

We gathered for dinner. "We" meaning not only the six members of Village People, but our producer and managers Jacques Morali and Henri

Belolo, Allan Carr, Jacqueline and Victor, along with at least another dozen friends, guests, and hangers-on. As was *de rigeur* for the era, it was difficult to determine who had an appetite and who didn't, since frequent visits to *les toilettes* more often than not had dinner guests returning with a case of the sniffles and no appetite for dessert. *Qu'est ce que c'est?*

Of course, Allan along with our producer/managers, had a very prominent place at the table along side Ms. Bisset. Managing to find a moment when everyone was at the table, he stood and tapped his spoon on his wine glass to get everybody's attention, to make an announcement. In his grandiose and effusive hyper-Hollywood manner, Allan announced, "After viewing the most incredible performance by this decade's and the next decade's outstanding musical artists at Don Kirshner's earlier this evening, I take pleasure in announcing that I—along with Henri and Jacques—will produce a new Hollywood film starring Jacqueline Bisset with Village People!" And that's how I found out we were "going Hollywood!"

Allan was fully prepared to make *Can't Stop the Music* as big as had been his incredibly successful film *Grease*. It was his intention to not only surpass *Grease*, but to make the first big movie musical of the '80s. At the time, Robert Stigwood was attempting to do the same thing by producing *Xanadu* with Olivia Newton-John and Gene Kelly. I have always had my suspicions that there was a huge competition between Carr and Stigwood.

When Allan began courting us to make the film, we had only been performing as a group for LESS than two years. We had been performing on the road NONSTOP, in the studio recording music, shooting videos and taping television programs that entire period. I guess you could say we just took it in stride that a huge Hollywood film was the next step. When Jacqueline pulled out of the project—because Allan would not cast her boyfriend Victor in the role that eventually went to Bruce Jenner—a parade of actresses were brought out on the road to our concerts for us to meet and review in person. Or maybe it was really the other way around! They included everyone from Olivia Newton-John (who opted to do *Xanadu*), to Cher, to Valerie Perrine. Eventually Valerie ended up with the gig of being in *Can't Stop the Music*. I gotta admit, Allan Carr was a nonstop promotion machine. In this same manner, after our concert at Madison Square Garden, this is the way in which we first met our beloved Nancy Walker, who was destined to become our director.

The script is a fictionalized, quasi-autobiographical account of the formation of Village People. The Alan Carr and Jacques Morali characters are pretty recognizable. In reality, I'm the only Village Person to actually LIVE in Greenwich Village. And I still live in the Village ... since 1975! All the other guys lived in other nearby boroughs, states, or neighborhoods. So I was accurately portrayed as a Village resident. Other than that I guess the story is a rather "Hollywood-ized" version of the events surrounding how Village People really got together. The script for *Can't Stop the Music* was created and written by the chemically fired-up minds of Allan Carr and Bronte Woodard. (Actually I've heard rumors that Bruce Vilanch was involved initially. Oh that he had stayed onboard and seen it thru!) Of course I'm not saying that those two divas were not very creative. Right up until the very last day of shooting, we were receiving new pages of dialogue, etc., each one a different color. I saved that script and it truly looks like a friggin' rainbow of colored pages. Considering the subject, I guess naturally so!

So how much of the story is true? Not much really, except that there indeed were SIX of us, Village People. But it was a real good excuse to meet and work with Valerie, Bruce, et al and burn through an estimated more than 25 million dollars of budget. Plus, whatever Allan Carr got out of the distribution deals for promotion, which was substantial!

Working on that film was truly an incredible experience. I mean, how many people can say that they have had the opportunity to portray "themselves" in a major Hollywood motion picture? I can't think of many ... maybe Audie Murphy in *To Hell and Back*. He portrayed himself in that film as America's most decorated war hero. Come to think of it, *To Hell and Back* might have been a better title for *Can't Stop the Music*!

Getting to know Allan Carr, Nancy Walker, Valerie Perrine, Bruce Jenner, Steve Guttenberg, Tammy Grimes, Marilyn Sokol, Barbara Rush, June Havoc (Gypsy Rose Lee's sister), director of photography Bill Butler, and all the rest of the great folks involved with that project was just part of the nonstop whirlwind that we found ourselves caught up in LESS than TWO years after we recorded our FIRST album as Village People.

In a short period of time, we went from recording our first album to shooting *Can't Stop the Music*, a major Hollywood film, budgeted at more than 25 million dollars, which was a helluva film budget in 1979 dollars. And we were surrounded by ALL the trappings that one would expect in a "Hollywood" scenario. The house in Beverly Hills, the cars, the parties, the groupies ... all of it happened so very quickly.

Make no mistake about it, the making of *Can't Stop the Music* was indeed a lot of work, but it was really a helluva lot of fun, too. It was an opportunity for the six of us from back east in NYC, to come out to LA and live a "Hollywood dream" for a couple of years. One of the places I lived while in LA shooting the film and after, was Joan Collins' house on Bowmont Drive up in Coldwater Canyon, while she was off in London shooting *The Bitch* or *The Stud*; I forget which role she played. Living in Beverly Hills more than lived up to everything I had ever heard about or seen in a film. Swimming pools! Movie stars! The only things missing were Jed, Elly May, and Granny! However, I distinctly think I remember Jethro being present. Uh-huh!

Of all of the film's production numbers, "The Milkshake" has a special place in my memory. We shot it on the same soundstage on which many of the Fred Astaire and Ginger Rogers musical numbers were filmed. That certainly was a magical and powerful experience to have. Especially for a kid like me who was raised up loving movie musicals. The all-white costumes for the number were designed by the great Theoni Aldredge at an estimated 15 to 20,000 dollars apiece. And there were back-up doubles of each! While we were shooting the number, which took five days, we couldn't sit or eat while wearing the costumes. We had to use the same leaning boards that had been used by some of the greats of Hollywood, like Ava Gardner, Joan Crawford, Clark Gable, and the like. When were off the dance floor set, we had to wear these boot/shoe covers that keep the bottoms of the boot from getting dirty, since the dance floor was black and reflective and so huge and had to be kept extremely clean. I think "The Milkshake" is one of the outstanding musical numbers in the film.

The infamous "Y.M.C.A." sequence of the film took the major part of a week to shoot as well. Of course all the effects that Allan added took who knows how long and how much money. We shot it at the Glendale, California YMCA. It was really large and beautiful. The place was very clean and seemed to sparkle with that hyper-clean scent of chlorine permeating the air. It just looked like a "movie" YMCA should look. And, jeez, it was peopled with some of the most incredibly attractive and endowed athletes I had ever seen gathered in one place, short of the Olympics. Prior to shooting the film, Allan had actually hired a photographer/model, Roger LeClaire, to spend nearly six months scouting around the US and Canada for some of the finest looking and most talented male athletes he could find. And there were certainly some exceptionally nice people that appeared in "Y.M.C.A." The most outstanding of the young men that he found ended up in the "Y.M.C.A." production number with us. Even while we were shooting it, we commented amongst ourselves how much the whole set-up reminded us of the Jane Russell/Marilyn Monroe production number with the shipboard athletes in *Gentlemen Prefer Blondes*.

For a week it was like a HUGE frat party. And well, it was clear who the "upper classmen" were! I met some of the nicest guys during that week. When looking back at that sequence now, it's almost like seeing a very expensive home movie of a bunch of your frat brothers from college. *Beaucoup des souvenirs!* Of course not everyone has home movies of your frat brothers completely NAKED in the showers. But we sure do.

If you look very closely during the musical number you'd be surprised at the young men you might recognize. Many have popped up in all kinds of places. Tom Hintnaus comes to mind, an Olympic-qualifying pole vaulter, who became one of the early Calvin Klein models. Unfortunately his Olympic hopes were dashed by the USA boycott of the Moscow Olympics. However, that shower scene in "Y.M.C.A." deserves special mention. Allan Carr spent two to three days just shooting all that locker room and shower scene stuff. This means there is a helluva lot more footage of those naked athletes in the shower than appears on-screen.

I know Allan Carr must have had some "entertaining" evenings showing the extra "footage" or should I say "yardage" (wink) that was left on the cutting room floor to some rather well-known Hollywood guests. To this day I wonder, "WHO got possession of THAT reel now that Allan has passed away?" Hmm . . .? Would someone call my attorney, please?!"

I think that *Can't Stop the Music* is the ONLY Hollywood film to ever receive a PG rating that contained not only Valerie Perrine's naked breasts, but also: FULL FRONTAL MALE NUDITY!!! I'm not sure how that happened. However, I've got suspicions. Either the MPAA rating guys were huge fans of Village People (and/or nude guys), or they were just high as a kite, or possibly BOTH! But somehow that shower scene remains in a PG-rated film. I'm sure there are lots of folks that are finally glad it's out now on DVD. There's something called frame-by-frame search and "freeze" with digital technology!

I think the musical sequences in the film are its strongest points. I still enjoy watching the final concert scene in San Francisco and "Liberation." The film itself is like a compressed time capsule of that period of American pop culture. You can put on the DVD when you have folks over, kick back with a cocktail and laugh at us, AND with us. That's what we were all about anyway. Our performances were always imbued with a wink, a wiggle, and a wave. We laughed at ourselves first, so the audience would know it was okay to laugh with us.

I am often asked, "Were there any divas on the set?" Let's see, hmm . . . how many people were in the cast? Just kidding. At that point in Village People's career, most people were falling over themselves to be about as charming and friendly to us as possible. If there was any hint of diva attitude or behavior—or as RuPaul might say "diva-ration,"—I guess Allan could have been the guilty party. After all, *Can't Stop the Music* was his ball of wax, being the producer and head pooh-bah. And by that time, he was REALLY playing the part of the big-time "Hollywood" producer.

Sometimes it was fun just to hang back and watch how he and Jacques would compete in "wearing" us as Village People to impress others. It has occurred to me that perhaps deep down inside, Allan or Jacques were a bit jealous and envious of us being the stars. I think they would have traded a testicle (albeit perhaps someone else's) in order to change places with us once in a while. They would have loved to have been an attractive young guy with tons of fans everywhere they went. Alas, they weren't us. But they sure did exercise a helluva lot of control over our musical careers. I don't really recall any of the actors being diva-like. Unless you count that one slip up during the filming of "Milkshake," when Valerie jokingly said to Alex one day on set, "Don't fuck up my close-up!" That comment was overheard and got plenty of ink in the gossip press. Tabloids tried to start rumors that Valerie Perrine and Village People had drawn battle lines and were in some sort of fierce throw down! According to the press, it was "VP vs. VP." But take my word for it—there was nothing of the sort!

Of course one day, amused by reading of our "feud" in the gossip columns, we decided to take matters in our own hands during lunch break.

There are large street-sized alleyways between the numerous and huge sound-stages on the old MGM lot where we shot in Hollywood. Squaring off on opposite ends of an alleyway—six Village People on one side, and one Valerie Perrine on the other—we proceeded to facedown ala Gary Cooper and the bad guys in *High Noon*. As the two sides drew closer and closer like gunslingers in the O.K. Corral, with eyes narrowed and hands on imaginary six-shooters, the atmosphere became thick enough to cut with a knife. And, as is the custom in the old West, the lady drew first. Before we knew it, we were surprised to see Valerie Perrine—star of the silver screen—turn around, lift her skirt, and hit us with a "full moon" shot. With dropped jaws, what could we do but retaliate with dropped "trou," returning fire with a six-pack of full moons!

From that day forward, even gossip in the press didn't cause any tensions between Village People and our female costar. Valerie is one of the loveliest ladies I have ever met, and I still love the doll to this very day. She's a fellow Virgo!

In the film, people have noted that Felipe seems to have the most lines and the most close-ups of all the Village People. Well, there's something "special" about Felipe's character. There were some odd things in the plot that I will never quite understand. I guess since Felipe's character was Samantha and Jack's neighbor he was intimate enough with them to come and go at will, comfortably entering their apartment from the fire escape without getting shot. For whatever reason, he was seen as more omnipresent in the film. As Samantha's friends, David and I were seen next most frequently and then the balance of Village People. But, as Mary J. Blige sings today, there were sooooo many "dramas" being played off camera that sometimes I swear I don't know how the director of photography, Bill Butler, knew where to point the camera to catch the correct action!

Decathlon. I've always been amazed that anyone could run, jump, throw a shot put, pole vault, throw a javelin, and God knows what the hell else, and win doing it. Win, like the great Olympic gold-medalist Bruce Jenner did in the 1976 Olympics. Now, speaking of Bruce Jenner, he was a terrific sport through and through. He was a real team player and genuinely enthusiastic from day one of filming *Can't Stop the Music*. And I believe he was absolutely at his peak during that period. I recall what an incredibly charming and attractive guy he was during the six months that were required for the rehearsals and the shooting schedule of the film.

His "good sport" amiability extended to being featured in a pair of severely trimmed thigh-high denim "cut offs," and a midriff revealing tee shirt previously seen ONLY on Christopher Street in Greenwich Village. The same shorts today are commonly known as "Daisy Dukes." And, I'm sure that Catherine Bach, costar of *Dukes of Hazzard*, is still looking for that missing pair to this day!

It is truly to his credit that throughout this experience, his abilities, his patience, and his tolerance were stretched to their limits through all the

Hollywood shenanigans going on around us. And there was certainly enough nonsense swirling around the set every day and night for all involved!

I still have the birthday gift that I received from Bruce that year, a great pair of Porsche Carrera Aviator sunglasses. And of course, how could ANY-ONE ever forget those fantastic, muscled furry thighs of his?! Not me.

Nancy Walker, who had an impressive career as an actress on Broadway and in film since the 1940s, had been chosen by Allan Carr to direct this innovative MGM-styled movie musical. After all, she too was an MGM musical star of such films as *Best Foot Forward*, *Girl Crazy*, and *Broadway Rhythm*.

Can't Stop the Music was to be Nancy's first outing as a director of a feature film. With the sterling career that she had behind her at that point, she certainly had been on enough sets to understand what the job of a director was and how to do it. But, of course Nancy, like the rest of us, was merely a piece of the whole megillah that the magical "wizard" Allan had assembled to create this MGM retro musical. Allan, ultimately was the "Grand Wizard." He loved having the final say on everything and having his finger in every "pie," so to speak. Well, Nancy Walker's job as director was absolutely no exception. I've got to hand it to Allan, he was exceedingly creative in his methods of interpolating his opinion and point of view into any area that he saw fit.

For example, dear Nancy would diligently rehearse a scene and get the actors prepared to go before the camera. Then, before the camera would roll, from someone else would ultimately come another piece of advice in an actor's ear to make some change to Nancy's direction. The advice would come in varying degrees from various sources: costume, make-up, director of photography, or anyone else in Allan's domain. It just seemed more often than not, Nancy appeared to be undermined nearly every step of the way through the making of the film. Perhaps it was done benignly and intended to be helpful, but it did in the final outcome, I believe, defeat her effort as a capable director. She always had the best attitude. I remember once when Nancy and I both had been the focus of one of Allan's huge blow-ups, and we were frustrated over a particular scene. She and I decided to have lunch in her trailer. She entertained me with incredible tales of her days in the movies, on Broadway, and as Rock Hudson's costar in television's *MacMillan & Wife*. Over lunch she told me something that has stuck in my mind ever since. According to her, "Honey, you just can't let any of it get you down. Just remember, movies are nothing but little pieces of shit snipped together to make something pretty to look at!"

Like our "rainbow"-colored shooting script, a gay subtext was unavoidable—given the screenplay's two authors, Allan Carr and Bronte Woodard, his coauthor on *Grease*. The film's dialogue was peppered throughout with double entendre, often walking the fine line between mainstream sensibility and a thinly veiled camp reading. Not surprisingly, this paralleled the same two-edged tongue-in-cheek, good-natured performance Village People's career personified up until this point.

I don't recall any particular instruction directing anyone to not play up any "gay" aspects. I think what there was of a script pretty much laid it out. With a female model living in NYC's Greenwich Village, who has a male roommate that composes music, she manages to collect together several guys from the neighborhood with some friends of friends to sing the music and make a demo. Now, given that simple plot in NYC, you've got to have something "gay" in the mix. Certainly with Allan Carr and Bronte Woodard working on the script, and Jacques Morali lending a hand in the kitchen, one couldn't help but come up with a frothy mix. And of course, anyone that lived through those times can testify to the gloriously heady feelings of freedom, liberation, and an "anything goes" atmosphere, especially in Hollywood and show business circles.

Allan, in keeping in step with his role as executive producer, head honcho—or as he was often referred to: "Caftans Courageous"—opted not to share the daily footage with us beyond the first day. I don't know what his logic was for not allowing us to see the "dailies." But, after all, he was writing the checks!

It's ALWAYS a shock to see yourself THAT big up on a huge screen. The first rough cut I saw was with Tammy Grimes out in LA. It was in a theater on the MGM lot. We had both been out on the West Coast to do some looping for a couple of scenes that were shot outdoors and the ambient sound had interfered with the dialogue. The day before Tammy was gonna leave town, Allan sent a car to bring us to MGM. Tammy and I had gotten on famously during the shooting, so hanging out with her was comfortable. During the ride to the studio we discussed who might possibly be joining us for the screening. I mentioned I hadn't run into anyone else doing looping, and neither had she. We were delivered to an incredible Hollywood screening theater at MGM with a massive screen. Upon entering the theater, we noticed we were the ONLY people present, other than the projectionist. All we heard as we took our seats was, "Welcome, Miss Grimes and Mr. Jones. My name's Pete. Just gimme the high sign when you're ready!" It was just like old Hollywood! Instead of regular theatre seats, there were large leather lounging chairs, with a small table in between.

After I settled back, I noticed that Tammy was VERY comfortable. She had brought several of the small single-size bottles of the booze selection from the mini-bar in the limo, and lined them up on the table. I proceeded to do the exact same thing with the ones that I had sneaked into the theater. We smiled very broadly at each other and settled back into the comfortable seats. So I guess you could say we enjoyed the first rough cut of the film. I think we made fun of ourselves and everyone else throughout the entire viewing. It's an experience I'll treasure forever. I mean Tammy Grimes is an actress that I have respected and admired since my childhood and there I was laughing and hooting with her at ourselves on a big movie screen on the same studio lot that Judy Garland and Clark Gable had worked on. I guess you could say I had a REALLY BIG SMILE on my face when I first saw the film.

When the film *Can't Stop the Music* was released, there was a huge red carpet premiere at the Ziegfeld Theater in New York City, and all sorts of excitement surrounding the event. The *Time Out London Movie Guide* claims, "The big joke in this disco-musical is having gay butch stereotypes of both sexes carry on as if they were straight. Six dopey members of the Village People, all with bursting flies, fall for Valerie Perrine (who has a just-platonic relationship with her male room-mate), while the Lesbian advertising agent swoons into the arms of a man. It follows that most of the dialogue is gay in-jokes, with the odd music biz joke for variety . . . Oh, and yes, there is fun in the showers in the 'Y.M.C.A.' number." (24)

Film critic Rex Reed wrote the most succinct review of the film's gay implications from a 1990s perspective. According to him in his *Guide to Movies on TV & Video*, "The kids reveled in the implications in everything the group (and the movie) stood for. They responded to the Village People the way they responded to Pee Wee Herman— as grownups who dress up in their fantasies the way children do at birthday parties . . . the movie is so bad, it's good." (25)

Yet, if the movie *Can't Stop the Music* did nothing else, it was to their credit that Village People helped bring positive "gay-friendly" images into more of a relaxed and mainstream fashion. For the first time ever, it looked like so-called "straight" society would embrace the gay community as part of a greater whole.

Randy recalls, "We did all kinds of press interviews and television appearances to promote *Can't Stop the Music*. Merv Griffin even devoted one of his entire programs to Village People, taped in Lincoln Center in New York City. As if to confirm our arrival in America's mainstream consciousness, Village People also became guest stars on TV's hit show, *The Love Boat*, with Allen Ludden, Bette White, Loni Anderson, and Robert Stack. As always, the fans loved it." (19)

The soundtrack album for *Can't Stop the Music* sold respectably well. It peaked at Number 47 in the United States, and Number 9 in the United Kingdom. The song "Can't Stop the Music" made it to Number 11 on the British singles chart.

The most unfortunate thing to happen in 1980 was the fact that the whole bottom seemed to just give way from the disco phenomenon.

This augured incredibly bad timing for the film *Can't Stop the Music*, and for Village People as well.

Popular music is a fickle business, as is show business in general. In 1978 and 1979, disco ruled the airwaves in the United States and the world. However, the music world is one that operates on the theory of finding out what "the next big thing" is, and in 1980 the musical taste of the world seriously shifted. Suddenly "disco" was out, and "New Wave" rock was in. Village People producers Jacques Morelli and Henri Belolo made the decision to make a clean break with the "'70s" Village People. They wanted to stylistically change the look and the sound of the group. They banked on a new craze that seemed to be sweeping Paris and London: "The New Romantic" fashion and music craze. It was a costumed look that took the fashions of the Renaissance era and mixed them with androgynous "glitter" make-up from the early 1970s.

It was Randy Jones who was not interested in this new look and sound for the group. Being a "cowboy" was one thing, but becoming a Renaissance "dandy" was one-step TOO GAY. Randy HATED the idea. He did not want to give up his identity as the Cowboy in Village People, and he was not going to wear leotards and a brocade jacket. And so, Jones quit the band, and was unceremoniously replaced by Jeff Olson in the group.

As Randy explains it, "In my mind, they were so terrified or disappointed by the lack of success of our film *Can't Stop the Music* that they thought they needed to do something drastic and new.... I thought I knew what was going on in Jacques' head. He thought: I'll take their images away and put paint and make-up on them so they can't be easily distinguished, and if anyone gives me a hard time: 'I'll just get rid of 'em.' I said I wouldn't do it [the Renaissance New Romantic look], and we ended my tenure at the end of that year.... The album [*Renaissance*] went right into the trash bin, did not work, did not sell, and the group limped along for another year or two after that." (23)

Village People released one single album with the "New Romantic" look in clothes and make-up on the cover. It turned out to be a huge bomb for the group. Through the early 1980s, the Randy-less Village People went from one European-only record label to another, unable to get a recording deal in the United States—which is undoubtedly the most fickle country on the planet. After *Renaissance* failed to ignite sparks on the charts for the group's new label, RCA Records, they were left without an American recording deal.

The group went on to record three more albums of music—*Sex Over the Phone, In the Street,* and *Fox On the Box*—but each of these albums was released in Europe only.

After that, Village People disbanded. Alex Briley, the G.I., ended up working in an office. Felipe, the Indian in the group, went through a series of odd jobs. David, the construction worker, became a bartender. Meanwhile, Randy recorded and released his first solo album, which was executive produced by the legendary John Hammond.

It was Randy Jones, who in the mid-1980s came up with the idea of a reunion of the group. He called up Ray Simpson, Alex Briley, Glenn Hughes, David Hodo, and Felipe Rose, and the six sat down together for the first time since 1980. Recalls Jones, "When I got the group back together in 1986, I wanted to get everyone in one place to see if we could all get along (first), and . . . I wanted to see how everybody looked!" (19)

"I remember that everyone was at the top of their game back then," recalls Mark Bego. "I ran into Glenn and Alex at The Bottom Line one night in March of 1988. I hadn't seen them in ages. Glenn and I became very close friends that year, and suddenly I found myself in the middle of Village People, just like it was back in the old disco days. At the time, the group had an offer from CBS Records in Australia. The company wanted Village People for a one-shot singles deal. If the song became a hit, it would lead to other recordings as well. Glenn had stopped over to my Greenwich Village apartment one night for a drink and he told me that about the record deal, which he hoped would lead to an eventual album. 'I would really like to find an old hit song that everyone loves, and record it with the group.' I got this funny look on my face, and I said to him, 'Would you believe I have just the song for you? Just the other day I was playing this record, and I thought it would be perfect for Village People. Besides, everyone could have a solo in the song.' 'What song is it?' Glenn asked. I proceeded to play The Temptations' 'Can't Get Next to You.' The next thing I knew, I was in a recording studio with the group, and they were recording it. It was a wonderful cut! Unfortunately, the Australian record company chose a song called 'Livin' In the Wildlife,' which was released as a 12" single. I still have a cassette copy of Village People's version of 'Can't Get Next to You' in my music collection, with Glenn, David, Ray, Felipe, Alex, and Randy each singing solo lines of lyrics, just like The Temptations' original track. Hopefully, one of these days, it will be publicly released." (20)

Unfortunately, in the early 1990s Jacques Morali died of complications from AIDS. It was a sad ending for a talented man. There was also a sense of sadness to his glory days. Jacques was not a sleek, sexy man like the members of Village People. According to some sources, while he was as proud of the group he had created, he was simultaneously frustrated by it. Speaking of Morali, Randy Jones explains, "There had to be an element of frustration for Jacques ... here you are a gay man who has lots of money, surrounded by attractive men, yet you are not one of them. I think that really deep in his heart he wanted to be what we were. That must have been a peculiar form of agony for him." (19)

Village People continued to record and tour into the 1990s, when Randy Jones decided to leave the group for good. By the late 1990s the group's original Leatherman, Glenn, became ill, and he passed away in 2001. He was buried in his leather Village People outfit, as per his final wishes.

Today, over thirty years since the formation of Village People, the music that made the group famous continues to touch audiences around the world. According to Randy Jones, "Even nowadays, whenever people hear about me, they think of me wearing boots, tight jeans, and a cowboy hat, while wiggling my ass and singing 'Y.M.C.A.' And, you know what? I still do that pretty well! Having created such an iconic image that's permeated the public consciousness and achieved such a place in pop culture is what I'll be remembered for even if I run for president some day. It's something I acknowledge, embrace, respect, and then I move on." (19)

The interesting thing about Village People was that no one in the group ever publicly defined themselves as being "gay" or "straight." As Randy Jones explains, "We had people guessing, but we did not want to alienate any portion of our audience, and we attempted to keep our personal lives personal." (19)

Since that time, both the members of Village People and Randy have moved on. A variation of Village People continues to tour with two and sometimes three of the original members in the group: Alex Briley, David Hodo, and Felipe Rose. Randy has graduated from the school of Village People and has gone on to a successful multimedia career. But that is a whole different chapter.

The always-insightful Angela Bowie claims, "As a fully crystallized 1970s idea, Village People was a unit that was a brilliant concept which came with political and social ramifications attached. Perhaps they were meant to suggest gay images to the masses, and they brilliantly succeeded. As individuals, the six Village People were the glittering centerpieces of an excitingly effective marketing campaign of cross promotion: the image sold the group, the legend of the group begat the movie, the movie promoted the music, and round and round it went. And, it was done with what I call: 'stealth precision.' In my mind a 'stealth' promotional campaign keeps the subject constantly in the public's eye, so that your targeted demographic market is constantly anticipating the next media blitz, like a [bell] signaling Pavlov's dogs. Furthermore, the popularization of disco and the sounds that came from the popular dance clubs around the world, signaled a call to invigorate the rally for civil liberties for gays and lesbians. Everyone was dancing to the music of Village People, and while they were dancing, the world was changing." (10)

The members of Village People gave a dynamic voice and a high-profile media presence to a growing gay civil rights movement that was earlier closeted or ignored, but certainly not front and center in American popular culture. They became the welcomed faces of the gay liberation movement, and they proudly took their place in society as media icons. The spotlight on them in the late 1970s burned so brightly that they projected indelible positive images.

Although the disco movement faded as the decade of the 1980s began, the music and the impact of Village People has never gone away. Whenever there is a soundtrack album for a movie that defines the late 1970s, the early 1980s, or just needs to signal a happy upbeat feeling, it almost certainly has to contain at least one Village People song. Films like *Wayne's World II*, *In and Out*, *The Last Days of Disco*, and *Priscilla Queen of the Desert* are amongst the dozens of films where "Y.M.C.A.," "Macho Man," "Go West," or some other classic Village People track is heard somewhere in the film. There has never been a group before or since like Village People. They will be forever remembered for having paved the way for positive gay images to be embraced by the masses and having made a statement through their music, their presence, and their artistry.

Now, more than thirty years after the group's multi-million selling gold and platinum albums appeared, Village People still have a diverse and loyal audience. There are few adults around the world who cannot at least hum the tune to at least one of their popular songs—each of them laden with double-entendre references, especially "Y.M.C.A." and "Macho Man." Village People became the ultimate symbol of the disco era and a positive symbol of gay social progress, not only in America, but also on a global scale.

Chapter 6

Post Disco: After the Ball

As the disco era ended in the 1980s, it seemed the world was now a much better, and a much more liberal, place. Then came HIV/AIDS. It appeared that all of the progress that gay people had made in terms of social acceptance was all going to be lost. When the causes of HIV/AIDS were discovered, and the medical community rallied to isolate the virus, things again evolved. Then HIV/AIDS was found to not be a uniquely gay epidemic, but a new disease that can infect anyone indiscriminately, and society has been able to put it in perspective and to begin to move forward again.

Today there are whole television networks, like LOGO and here!, which are devoted to all-gay programming. And in the twenty-first century, the challenge to legalize and recognize same-sex marriage continues. Even on the 2008 season of the cooking competition show *Top Chef*, there was a lot of gay subtext. There was a lesbian couple who competed against each other. On the season wrap-up, several of the guys seemed to find some gay male bonding, which was termed a case of "BRO-mance!" How progressive is that?

Not long ago things looked quite bleak. Along with all of the positive advancement in human politics and gay liberalization in the early 1980s, the greatest tragedy struck the gay community—on a global basis. When the first HIV/AIDS deaths were reported, it was originally termed "Gay Cancer" by the media, because it was members of the gay male community who first showed the symptoms of the illness. It was clear that something was going terribly wrong, and medical science was facing a virally-caused disease that was relentless.

This caused a social backlash against gay men. Many were treated as though they were responsible for this new epidemic. Time of course has shown that the disease is neither "gay" or "straight" or "bisexual" in nature. It is simply a new mutant strain of disease that affects humans. However, in the early 1980s it was almost exclusively the gay community that was struck with HIV/AIDS first.

HIV/AIDS seemed to be highly isolated and unable to touch the general public. When Rock Hudson was diagnosed with AIDS in 1985 and succumbed from it, a sudden wave of panic swept across Hollywood. The gay backlash was devastating to all of the inroads that in the 1970s gay rights movement. Again, prejudices covered gay life like a dark cloud. In the gay world, the heady sense of freedom which was prevalent in the disco era was replaced by distrust, funerals, and fear.

In the 1970s there was no fear of disease associated with the wave of sexual promiscuity that was underway. Yes, syphilis and gonorrhea existed, but they were treatable with penicillin and other antibiotics. HIV/AIDS changed all of that. Suddenly the topics of condoms and "safe sex" became commonplace in mainstream society.

It was unthinkable at the time, but eventually such topics would be commonly and openly discussed on broadcast television, like they are today.

In the 1990s, Jacques Morali was diagnosed with HIV/AIDS and died. Then came the tragic of death of Glenn Hughes, the Leatherman in Village People, in 2002. Glenn's cause of death was officially listed as "lung cancer." Village People fans mourned their passing.

In the twenty-first century, it is now the heterosexual community where HIV/AIDS represents the greatest danger, especially in Africa. The HIV/AIDS pandemic is in no way over, but in many countries—including the United States and Europe—HIV/AIDS is more often viewed as a chronic, maintainable condition, not unlike diabetes. It is not the guaranteed death sentence it once was.

This being said, the HIV/AIDS epidemic claimed many beloved and talented gay people in its wake. Two whom we would like to discuss are Michael Bennett (the director of *A Chorus Line*) and Freddie Mercury (the brilliant lead singer of the rock group Queen).

RANDY: "In the 1980s we lost a lot of great people due to the HIV/AIDS epidemic."
MARK: "It was horrifying."
RANDY: "And many of them, you and I personally knew."
MARK: "I was really saddened when Michael Bennett died."
RANDY: "He was such a creative talent."
MARK: "When I came to New York City in the early 1970s, Michael Bennett was responsible for one of the greatest Broadway sensations of that era: *A Chorus Line*."

RANDY: "I remember when it started down in the Village at the Public Theater."
MARK: "And, I know that you—being a dancer—really identified with the theme of it depicting a dancer's life."
RANDY: "It was an important theater piece, and Michael was so talented. I'm sorry to have missed the opportunity to work with him."
MARK: "And, we can't forget about his other masterpiece: *Dreamgirls*."
RANDY: "And, I'm telling you: I'm not going!"
MARK: "You tell 'em, Mr. Jones!"

Michael Bennett was the Tony Award-winning musical theater director, writer, choreographer, and dancer behind several of the most important Broadway shows of the later half of the twentieth century, most famously *Chorus Line* and *Dreamgirls*. He was an absolute dynamo of creativity.

Born on April 8, 1943, in Buffalo, New York, Michael Bennett DiFiglia showed dance talent at an early age. He dropped out of high school to go on the road as part of the touring company of *West Side Story*, which took him across the United States and to Europe, portraying the role of Baby John.

His first role in a Broadway show came in 1961 in *Subways Are For Sleeping*, and he was also in Meredith Willson's *Here's Love*. He then landed a job as one of the featured dancers on the classic a-go-go style rock & roll show *Hullabaloo* (ABC-TV; September 16, 1964 to August 29, 1966). For anyone who missed seeing *Hullabaloo*, it was an hour-long show on which the top pop and rock performers would either perform or lip sync their latest Top Ten hits, while go-go-dancers would dance the latest steps in the background.

It was there that he first met fellow *Hullabaloo* dancer Donna McKechnie. In other words, you might have Martha Reeves & The Vandellas singing "Nowhere to Run" in the foreground, and future Tony Award winners Michael Bennett and Donna McKechnie would be doing the Frug, the Pony, or the Shing-A-Ling in the shadows behind them. It was the swinging '60s at their best.

Michael went on to choreograph such high-profile Broadway hits as *Promises, Promises* in 1968, *Twigs* with Sada Thompson, and *Coco* with Katharine Hepburn. When he worked on two of the most highly acclaimed Stephen Sondheim musicals—*Company* and *Follies*—he was truly in the Broadway big league. He codirected *Follies* with Harold Prince and served as the librettist and director of *Seesaw*.

In 1974, he came up with a revolutionary idea for a Broadway show. His concept was to do a Broadway show about the dancers who are the lifeblood of musical productions. He called the show *A Chorus Line*, and it was a breathtaking, Tony Award-winning, box office record-breaking hit. The show won nine Tony Awards, the New York Drama Critics' Circle Award, and the Pulitzer Prize for Drama. Furthermore, Michael made his longtime friend and fellow dancer, Donna McKechnie, the star of the show.

Although she knew that he was bisexual, Donna married Michael in 1976. The marriage only lasted three months. Bennett was brilliantly creative, but he was also semi-self-destructive and reportedly addicted to alcohol and drugs—including cocaine and Quaaludes.

In 1981, he produced another Broadway masterpiece. Directing and choreographing the stunning *Dreamgirls*, he used as its inspiration the story of The Supremes and Motown Records. Again, it was a Tony Award-winning smash.

It was in 1985, while working on the London West End production of *Chess*, that his health failed. He dropped out of sight and moved to Tucson, Arizona. He died on July 2, 1987 of AIDS-related lymphoma. Michael Bennett bequeathed a large portion of his estate to HIV/AIDS research.

RANDY: "Another talented friend we lost was Freddie Mercury."
MARK: "He was unbelievably talented. What a voice, and what an incredible persona."
RANDY: "He was such a lot of fun to be with."
MARK: "I remember you introducing him to me at one of your birthday parties."
RANDY: "My thirtieth. The one at The Underground. One of the milestones!"
MARK: "Exactly! That was a great party."
RANDY: "That party went on until the sun came up."
MARK: "Trust me, I remember it well."

He was born Farrokh Bulsara, on September 5, 1946, of East Indian descent. But as the unmistakably talented Freddie Mercury, he went on to international fame as the lead singer of acclaimed rock group Queen. He was outrageous, outlandish, fun loving, and bigger than life. The songs that he recorded in his years with Queen won them status as one of the top-grossing rock groups in rock & roll history. Their unforgettable hits included "We Will Rock You," "Bohemian Rhapsody," "I Want to Break Free," "Killer Queen," "Somebody to Love," "We Are the Champions," "Crazy Little Thing Called Love," and "Under Pressure"—which they recorded with David Bowie. Throughout the height of their recording career, the group Queen logged more collective weeks on the British Album Charts than any other musical act in rock history, including The Beatles.

Freddie was born on the island of Zanzibar, off of the coast of Africa. As a boy, Freddie spent much of his childhood in India. He was sent there at the age of seven, where he attended a boy's boarding school in Panchgani near Bombay. After attending high school in India, he returned to his native Zanzibar. However, Freddie and his family had to flee for England during the 1964 Zanzibar Revolution.

Having shown musical talent at an early age, he played with a couple of bands in England. In the early 1970s he teamed up with guitarist Brian May, drummer Roger Taylor, and base player John Deacon, to form Queen.

Their appealing hits combined many different styles of music with their own distinctive version of rock & roll—particularly on "Bohemian Rhapsody," which had broad strokes of opera woven into the pounding drums and wailing rock guitars. Not only did all four of the musicians get along incredibly well, but they were all involved in the writing of their music.

In the 1970s and 1980s, they produced a string of gold and platinum Top Ten albums including *A Night at the Opera*, *A Day at the Races*, *News of the World*, *Jazz*, and *The Game*. In 1981, they scored the soundtrack to the adventure film *Flash Gordon*. They were one of the most beloved rock bands in the business.

Freddie also recorded two successful solo albums, *Mr. Bad Guy* in 1985 and *Barcelona* in 1988. Although he had a longtime girlfriend by the name of Mary Austin, he was said to frequent the gay bathhouses in New York City. In 1985, he began a long-term relationship with Jim Hutton, a hairdresser. Freddie was quite a character. He loved to give parties and had a devoted circle of friends and lovers.

Freddie Mercury was diagnosed as having the HIV virus in the spring of 1987, and his visible presence in the public was slowly becoming rare. In November 1990, news reports claimed that Freddie was seriously ill. He fiercely guarded his privacy that last year of his life. Freddie never publicly admitted that he was gay. But, finally he knew that the end was drawing near, and he had to say something to his public. He felt that he owed them that much.

On November 23, 1991, Freddie issued the following public statement to the press: "Following the enormous conjecture in the press over the last two weeks, I wish to confirm that I have been tested HIV positive and have AIDS. I felt it correct to keep this information private to date to protect the privacy of those around me. However, the time has come now for my friends and fans around the world to know the truth and I hope that everyone will join with my doctors and all those worldwide in the fight against this terrible disease. My privacy has always been very special to me and I am famous for my lack of interviews. Please understand this policy will continue."

Freddie Mercury died on the following day, November 24, 1991, at the age of forty-five. The whole rock & roll world was in shock. Many fans had no idea that he was ill, and then suddenly he was gone.

On April 20, 1992, several of Freddie's friends and admirers performed a tribute concert for him at Wembley Stadium, including Annie Lennox, Elton John, David Bowie, George Michael, and Queen. It concluded with Liza Minnelli singing "We Are the Champions." Freddie would have loved it!

MARK:	"You do realize, that as 'Baby Boomers,' we were the first generation who literally grew up in front of a television screen."
RANDY:	"Is that why we turned out the way we did?"
MARK:	"I think it's all Rocky and Bullwinkle's fault."
RANDY:	"*Have Gun Will Travel.*"
MARK:	"*The Monkees.*"
RANDY:	"*The Rifleman.*"
MARK:	"*The Partridge Family.*"
RANDY:	"*Rawhide!*"
MARK:	"And all of the Mouseketeers!"
RANDY:	"Okay, okay.... You know how much I loved the Westerns. This could go on all day, but we have a book to write!"

For members of the so-called baby boomer generation, there is no mass communication or mass culturalization device quite like the television. Who among us—who lived through *The Donna Reed Show* and *Leave it to Beaver*—would have guessed that we would live to see the day when gay people on *Sex and the City*, *Ellen*, *Friends*, and *Will and Grace* would be all the rage. Yet, in the 1990s the mass liberalization of American broadcast television began. Now, in the 2000s, there are television networks like LOGO and here! broadcasting daily programming of primarily gay interest.

When the NBC-TV show *Friends* grew to become one of the most popular global television hits in broadcasting history, and featured prominent gay characters, all bets were off. When the reality show

Queer Eye for the Straight Guy became a huge hit in 2003, television audiences enthusiastically embraced it. America was finally ready to allow gay characters to take their place next to their straight counterparts, in countless millions of living rooms around the planet.

RANDY: "One of my favorite recent television shows is *Friends.*"
MARK: "Well, it ought to be, it takes place in Greenwich Village."
RANDY: "But there is something that I don't understand."
MARK: "What's that?"
RANDY: "How can they have jobs like working in a coffee shop, and yet they have a great apartment . . ."
MARK: "You mean because it looks like the remodeling crew from *While You Were Out* just came in and re-did it?"
RANDY: "Exactly!"
MARK: "That's why it's television!"
RANDY: "Or have you ever heard of rent stabilization!"

Although television situation comedies are not reality, they are often a direct reflection of society's view of reality. Everyone in the 1950s did not live and act like they did on *I Love Lucy*, no more than every twenty-something in America lived and acted like the six stars of *Friends*. However, each of those characters somehow resonated within all of us. Whether it was doofy Ross (David Schwimmer), ditzy Phoebe (Lisa Kudrow), perky Rachel (Jennifer Aniston), sensible Monica (Courtney Cox), bumblingly attractive Chandler (Matthew Perry), or cute but dumb-as-a-rock Joey (Matt LeBlanc), there was something in each of them that all of us somehow found appealing.

In ten solid years of broadcasting (1994–2004), there was not one season on the American TV ratings that *Friends* was not in the Top Ten. The thread of plot was that each of the six lead characters was busy finding him or herself, with ongoing emotional attachments, rivalries, and ultimate friendships.

Although none of the six lead characters was actively gay, a lot of their fictional friends and family members were. It is not that the characters were gay that made them so dramatic; it was that these gay men and women were mixed into the plot without awkwardness or apology. It was truly a first for American primetime network television.

One of the plot threads involved Chandler, whose father was a transsexual, played by actress Kathleen Turner. Then there was Ross, whose first wife left him for another woman. While there were hopes amongst the gay community that eventually Joey would have a fling with another man, it never happened. However, the show's producers handled gay issues without batting an eyelash. It prepared American television viewers for shows that were to follow.

MARK: "Another popular sitcom from that same era that I really enjoyed was the *Ellen* show."

RANDY: "She was great in that sitcom."

MARK: "And she totally made history by starring as the first prime-time television star to 'come out' on her own show."

RANDY: "And, on the cover of *Time* magazine!"

MARK: "I wonder who her publicist was?"

RANDY: "We need that phone number!"

Debuting the same season as NBC-TV's *Friends*, the show that started out being called *These Friends of Mine* (for season one) morphed into the ABC-TV sitcom starring Ellen DeGeneres, which is more commonly known as *Ellen*. It began as just another network situation comedy, but there was an edge to it. Since the star of the series was publicly suspected of being a lesbian herself, there were clear tensions bubbling under the surface of the television show.

Like *Friends*, there was a host of quirky supporting characters who were fictional Ellen's friends. In the first season of the show, Ellen Morgan (DeGeneres) is an employee at the Buy the Book store. In the second season she purchases the store and runs Buy the Book. Her overlapping circle of buddies includes neurotic Paige Clark (Joely Fisher), male roommate Adam Green (Arye Gross), annoyingly cloying friend and coworker Audrey Penney (Clea Lewis), her male cousin Spence Kovak (Jeremy Piven), red-headed gay male friend Peter Barnes (Patrick Bristow), and cuddly and bumbling Joe Farrell (David Anthony Higgins) who runs the coffee counter at the store. Ellen's hapless parents were Harold Morgan (Steven Gilborn) and Lois Morgan (Alice Hirson), and neither of them had a clue of daughter's budding sexual identity crisis.

In 1997, the actress Ellen DeGeneres publicly came out as gay in a most high profile way: on *The Oprah Winfrey Show* and on the cover of *Time* magazine. The question then became: how will her fictional character make the announcement on television? In the famous "Puppy Episode," the fictional character of Ellen announced that she too was a lesbian.

On the episode, she announces to guest star Laura Dern, at an airport: "I'm gay!" What she didn't realize at the time was that she had accidentally leaned into a microphone, and had made her sexual pronouncement over the terminal loudspeaker. In doing so, she made American broadcast television history.

Unfortunately, in the weeks after the disclosure, the once bubbly sitcom became bogged down in the plot. She took on a new girl-friend, Laurie Manning (Lisa Darr), but the comic camaraderie in the old cast was somehow sacrificed in the transition. Once fictional "Ellen" finally "came out," the big mystery was gone as well. How-ever, during its very popular run from 1994 to 1998, it was both entertaining and groundbreaking.

Ellen DeGeneres was seen in another attempt at a sitcom, called *The Ellen Show*, in the 2001–2002 season. However, it was not a suc-cess. But, what was—and is—a huge success, is DeGeneres' appeal-ing new talk show series, *Ellen: The Ellen DeGeneres Show*. She is now heralded as one of the most charming and popular talk show hosts on television, winning multiple Emmys for Outstanding Talk Show Host. She was also a huge hit in the movies, providing the voice to the fish Dory in the cartoon *Finding Nemo* (2003). On August 16, 2008, Ellen married her longtime partner, Portia de Rossi.

RANDY: "Without *Ellen* and *Friends*, we might never have seen the bril-liance of *Will & Grace*."

MARK: "So true. *Will & Grace* was truly a groundbreaking show, and it continues to be seen several times a day in reruns."

RANDY: "Not to mention the fact that several of the subjects of your books made guest appearances on *Will & Grace*."

MARK: "No wonder I have always liked that show."

RANDY: "Let's see, Cher went on *Will & Grace*, not once, but three times. Then there was Madonna who appeared as a girlfriend of Karen's. Then there was Matt Damon. You did a book on him, too. And then there's Barry Manilow and Elton John."

MARK: "I just knew that show was brilliant, the moment I saw it!"

In 1996, when the original *Ellen* show went off the air, NBC-TV debuted their first all-gay sitcom, *Will & Grace*. It was the story of Will Truman (Eric McCormick), a gay lawyer with a history of bad luck with men, and his neurotic Jewish heterosexual best friend Grace Adler (Debra Messing). They share a unique friendship that is rounded out with their friends: gay and goofy-acting Jack (Sean Hayes), and affluent lush of a socialite Karen Walker (Megan Mullally).

Taking over where *Friends* and *Ellen* left off, *Will & Grace* took the gay card and played it winningly over and over again. No longer was the gay character just the best friend—now they were the stars.

In addition, the Karen character did not shy away from taking her character into "lipstick lesbian" arenas.

During *Will & Grace*'s award-winning run, it was a popular program that attracted a sea of guest stars, including the following: Cher, Minnie Driver, Dave Foley, John Cleese, Beau Bridges, Matt Damon, Lily Tomlin, Michael Douglas, Elton John, Barry Manilow, Deborah Harry, Candice Bergen, George Takei, Patti LuPone, Janet Jackson, Hall & Oates, Jennifer Lopez, and Alec Baldwin. Grace's longest suitors were played by Gregory Hines, and then by Harry Connick, Jr. Furthermore, Will and Grace's mothers were played by Blythe Danner and Debbie Reynolds, respectively. Even Madonna made a guest appearance, as Karen's brief lesbian lover.

In the plot of the show, Grace owned her own design firm, which was based in the famed Puck Building in Manhattan. Her one employee was lazy and boozy Karen, who only took the job because she was rich and bored. Karen's prime talent seems to be drinking cocktails at any hour of the day or night. Jack is a would-be actor who changes careers like most people change their socks. Furthermore, Hayes portrays Jack as the silliest "queen" in the history of network prime time. When he mounts his own cabaret act, he entitles it *Just Jack!* And Will is a lawyer who can never seem to find or hold on to a boyfriend. There is also a strange semi-lesbian dynamic between Karen and her devoted El Salvadorian maid Rosario (Shelley Morrison).

The show went on to be nominated for eighty-three Emmy awards, winning sixteen of them. The final episode, which was an hour long, aired May 18, 2006, and was precluded by an hour-long retrospective special. The final broadcast itself drew in an estimated audience of 18.1 million viewers.

RANDY: "I swear, you can't pick up *The National Enquirer* without some new gay rumors."

MARK: "Hey, I read *The National Enquirer*, too. It's usually you who is starting the rumors."

RANDY: "Who, me?"

MARK: "Yes, you!"

Whether buoyed up by the fact that media had not drummed other gay celebrities out of the business, or just ready as a point of personal development, since 1990 several mainstream celebrities have admitted that they are gay or lesbian. Leading the pack are rock star Elton John, fellow rocker Melissa Etheridge, the Pet Shop

Boys, k. d. lang, television personality Rosie O'Donnell, author Clive Barker, Chastity Bono, Tracy Chapman, Alan Cummings, Leslie Gore, Nathan Lane, actor Rupert Everett, and even *Star Trek* star George Takai.

The two stars that we have chosen to profile in this chapter are Elton John and Rosie O'Donnell. Each of these high-profile stars have begun to attempt to live more honest lives after achieving certain success in their careers. They are also deeply involved in various charitable causes.

MARK: "And now we come to one of my all-time favorite performers, Elton John."

RANDY: "Sir Elton!"

MARK: "He is a royal trip all right. I remember going backstage to meet Elton with my publicist, David Salidor, at Madison Square Garden."

RANDY: "Wasn't that the night that Andy Warhol was there?"

MARK: "That was it! That was also the night that Elton came out on stage for his encore dressed in drag as Tina Turner."

RANDY: "I'm speechless! Elton was always capable of giving his turns at 'drag' a good shake!"

The body of music that Elton John has produced includes an incredible list of million-selling songs and hit albums, spanning five decades. He has a long list of hits including "Crocodile Rock," "Your Song," "Daniel," "Island Girl," "Bennie and The Jets," "Goodbye Yellow Brick Road," "Don't Let the Sun Go Down on Me," "The Bitch is Back," and "I Guess That's Why They Call It the Blues." Elton is known as one of the most prolific musicians in the rock world.

On March 25, 1947, Elton John was born Reginald Dwight in Pinner, Middlesex, England, in a council house of his maternal grandparents. At the time, his newlywed parents, Stanley and Sheila Dwight, were living there. Elton became interested in music at an early age. In 1956, when his mother brought home some recordings by Elvis Presley and Bill Haley and His Comets, Reginald heard where his future career would lie.

In 1964, Dwight and a group of his musician friends formed a band that they called Bluesology. In the mid-1960s, Bluesology became the local British band backing touring American soul and R&B musicians including The Isley Brothers, Major Lance, Doris Troy, and Patti LaBelle & The Bluebelles.

After answering an ad in the *New Musical Express* placed by Ray Williams, who at the time was the A&R manager for Liberty Records,

Williams handed him a stack of lyrics written by Bernie Taupin and asked him what he thought of them. This led to the first Elton John/ Bernie Taupin musical collaboration, on a song called "Scarecrow."

Originally, John and Taupin tried out their career as songwriters for other singers. Their first American release was a cover of their song "Lady Samantha," which the group Three Dog Night recorded on their *Suitable for Framing* album in 1969.

The 1970s found popular music segmented into disco, traditional soul, hard rock, pop, and folk music. Elton John proved that he could do it all, and do it with equal success and creative panache. His first album was called *Empty Sky*, and his first big song was the hit "Your Song" which was released in 1970. By the mid-1970s, he was widely acknowledged as the most successful pop and rock star of the decade. His unique writing style, and his ability to jump from sensitive ballads to bawdy rock anthems to campy pop, has made him the most consistently popular across-the-board superstar of the past forty years.

Elton's stylistic versatility, combined with his flamboyant stage shows and outlandish costumes, make him into a flashy combination of John Lennon, Noel Coward, Barry Manilow, and Liberace. In a marketplace that regularly creates "disposable" pop icons, Elton has been able to not only maintain his popularity, but to grow and develop it into brilliant new areas—including Broadway, films, and the new generation of gleaming and bawdy Las Vegas arenas.

Elton John's personal life has been as colorful as his string of million-selling hits. Take, as one example, his close relationship with his heterosexual long-time buddy Rod Stewart—which, back in their native England, has long been the subject of ribald speculation. It is known in music circles that the two men have "drag" names for each other. Elton is known to Rod as "Sharon," and John refers to Stewart as "Phyllis."

In 1976, on the pages of *Rolling Stone* magazine, Elton admitted to being "bisexual." The disclosure ended up hurting his career, losing him both popularity and radio airplay in America. Uncomfortable with the public perception of his own sexuality in the early 1980s, however, Elton entered into a masquerade marriage to a female sound engineer friend of his named Renate Blauel. It was widely known that they never lived together for more than a week or so at a time. After their divorce, Elton returned to sex with men.

In the 1990s, however, when a *Rolling Stone* reporter squeezed out of him the confession that he was indeed gay, Elton found himself speaking publicly about it for the first time. It became a watershed moment for Elton, the occasion for him to deal with long-time substance abuse problems and speak passionately about issues that had long seemed problematic for him to be associated with. Since then Elton has lived very publicly with his longtime boyfriend, designer David Furnish. In 2004, during the global controversy surrounding the legalization of gay marriage, Elton—now Sir Elton, having been knighted by the Queen of England—announced his plans to wed David as soon as England passed provisions to recognize gay unions. He made good his promise on December 21, 2005.

Equally mesmerizing to the public has been Elton's involvement in the lives of fashion designer Gianni Versace and the troubled but glamorous Princess Diana. The year 1997 was a traumatic one for Elton. Early that summer, Versace's murder in Miami Beach developed into a high profile media feeding frenzy for all the dead man's friends and family. No sooner did Elton help bury Versace then Princess Diana was killed in a horrific car crash. Eulogizing Diana in a revamped version of one of his hit songs ("Candle in the Wind"), his recording "Goodbye England's Rose" became the biggest-selling single in the history of recorded music.

Of course, big sellers were nothing new to Elton. He had managed to chart a Top 40 single in England and/or America every single year from 1970 to 2005. During this period, he indeed suffered temporary slumps in creativity and sags in album sales. And, from time to time he has fallen out of favor with music critics. He has also had infamous battles with his long-time lyricist Bernie Taupin, and battled various drug addictions and public scandals. There were even a few suicide attempts. But through it all, Elton John remains one of the most remarkably beloved rock and pop artist of rock history.

Elton has used his time and his money to raise funds to fight AIDS since the late 1980s. In his native England he was knighted for his long and illustrious career in 1998, and in the U.S. he got the Kennedy Center Award. In 1994, he was inducted into the Rock and Roll Hall of Fame.

In the late 1990s, looking for new challenges and opportunities, Elton John began an enormously successful side career as a Broadway and film composer. He wrote the music to two long-running Broadway hits: *The Lion King* and *Aida*. In 2006 he presented the short-lived *Lestat* and in 2008 his new musical *Billy Elliot* debuted on Broadway.

In 2004, in the new, glitzier, and bigger Las Vegas, Elton John made his Red Piano casino debut on the most elaborate stage ever built there. Elton's live concerts—always the occasion for commentary about his flamboyant style and music—are suddenly headline news again. And this move to Vegas closely mimics the career of the only piano playing superstar whose costumes were as gaudy, and whose reputation was as flamboyant: Liberace.

Elton's scandal-filled life of rock & roll excesses has been both colorful and fascinating. Sir Elton's life most closely parallels that of a modern-day Oscar Wilde. He is wild, glitzy, moody, bawdy, and unconventional. From the addictions, the self-doubts, the bad toupees, the affairs, and the scandals, there is no one quite like Elton John. He is the first male rock star to have married both a woman, and then a man!

In his incredible career, Elton John has sold more than 250 million record albums and CDs, and in excess of one hundred million singles. He logged seven consecutive Number One albums on the United States charts, has had forty-nine Top 40 singles, sixteen Top Tens, and nine Number One hits. Elton is acknowledged as being one of the most successful recording artists in the music world, and he is the biggest selling openly gay rock star ever.

MARK: "Without a doubt, one of the most outspoken personalities in modern television is Rosie O'Donnell."
RANDY: "Whether or not you agree with her viewpoint, you are going to listen to her viewpoint."
MARK: "And, she too was a guest star on *Will & Grace*."
RANDY: "I think I sense another Bego book deal coming on!"

Whether you like her or not, you cannot ignore Rosie O'Donnell. In her two decades in the spotlight, she has made herself one of the most outspoken women in show business. She started out as a stand-up comedian, made a highly successful transition into becoming a film star, shifted to television talk show hostess, and then morphed into a radically gay human rights proponent.

Born on March 21, 1962 in Commack, Long Island, New York, Roseann Theresa O'Donnell came from a middle-class background. On March 17, 1973, four days before her eleventh birthday, her mother died of breast cancer, which left a lasting emotional wound. She attended Dickinson College, later transferring to Boston University. However, she dropped out and launched a career as a stand-up comedienne. She toured in small clubs from 1979 to 1984, and received her first big break on the talent contest, *Star Search*.

From the exposure that she received from her stand-up act, she made a successful transition into television sitcoms with her series debut as Nell Carter's neighbor on the show *Gimme a Break!* in 1986.

Rosie made her movie debut in the women's baseball film *A League of Their Own* (1992), which starred Geena Davis, Tom Hanks, and Madonna. Her acting in that film led to a string of highly appealing movie roles. She played Meg Ryan's best friend in the box-office hit *Sleepless in Seattle* (1993). Then she took on the role of Betty Rubble in the live-action adaptation of the cartoon world's *The Flintstones* (1994). She played a nun who loved baseball in M. Night Shyamalan's *Wide Awake* (1998). And Rosie provided the voice of a female gorilla in the Disney cartoon version of Edgar Rice Borough's *Tarzan* (1999).

In 1996, she shifted gears and debuted her own daytime television talk program, the highly successful *The Rosie O'Donnell Show*. She was a breath of fresh air when she started the show, and was dubbed "The Queen of Nice" because of her ability to handle herself so adeptly amidst a sea of different guests.

Slowly, she started to vehemently and passionately speak her own mind about social issues, on the air and off. On April 19, 1999, after the Columbine, Colorado, shootings O'Donnell said to her television audience, "You are not allowed to own a gun, and if you do own a gun, I think you should go to prison." She finally had to tone down her stance on gun ownership, later stating, "I don't personally own a gun, but if you are qualified, licensed and registered, I have no problem." (26)

A month later, when actor Tom Selleck was on her show, she got into an argument with him on the air for his recent television commercials advertising membership to the NRA (National Rifle Association).

Following the September 11, 2001, attacks on the World Trade Center in New York City, Rosie used her program as a platform to lure tourists back to Manhattan. She also donated $1 million of her own money to 9/11 rescue efforts. In 2002, she left her television program to concentrate on other projects. That same year she published her memoir, *Find Me*, which made it to Number Two on *The New York Times'* Best Sellers List.

On February 26, 2004, O'Donnell married her girlfriend Kelli Carpenter. Rosie's decision to go to San Francisco and marry Carpenter was her way of actively protesting against President George W. Bush and his announced support for the Federal Marriage Amendment.

The marriage license was later voided by the California Supreme Court, which was tied up in red tape as part of the same-sex marriage issues in that state.

Together Rosie and Kelli have several adopted children: Parker Jaren (born May 25, 1995), Chelsea Belle (born September 20, 1997), and Blake Christopher (born December 5, 1999). The couple's fourth child, Vivienne Rose, was conceived via artificial insemination, and born on November 29, 2002, to Carpenter.

In 2004, O'Donnell and Carpenter partnered with travel entrepreneur Gregg Kaminsky to launch R Family Vacations. It is the first organization started to provide family-oriented vacation cruises especially catering to gays and lesbians with families. July 11, 2004, was the maiden voyage of the first cruise held aboard Norwegian Cruise Lines' *Norwegian Dawn*, which has a 2,200-passenger capacity. The ship was reportedly 70 percent filled with 1,600 passengers. A documentary was filmed by HBO, called *All Aboard: Rosie's Family Cruise*. It was used to defray the costs of the cruise and to advertise it.

In September of 2006, Rosie joined the cast of the daytime television talk show, *The View*. From the moment she joined the program, she instigated controversy, but she was also great for the show's ratings. She had no problem making her views known about the war in Iraq, gay rights, President Bush, or anything else that was on her mind. In early 2007, she launched into a huge argument in the press with Donald Trump. She left the show in May 2007 and was replaced by Whoopi Goldberg.

In the summer of 2007, Rosie joined *The True Colors Tour*, which traveled to fifteen cities in the United States and Canada, sponsored by television's gay network, LOGO. Also on the tour were Margaret Cho, Cyndi Lauper, Debbie Harry, Erasure, The Gossip, Rufus Wainwright, The Dresden Dolls, The MisShapes, Indigo Girls, The Cliks, and other special guests. Monetary profits from the tour helped to benefit the Human Rights Campaign, the parents-of-gay-children organization: P-FLAG, as well as the Matthew Shepard Foundation.

When it comes to having an opinion about social ills or human rights issues, Rosie O'Donnell has no problem speaking her mind. And she is one "out" lesbian who literally puts her money where her mouth is! Her charity work is unprecedented, and she continues to work actively for gay and lesbian rights.

Of all of the male macho figures that American pop culture has created, the cowboy has symbolized a romantic figure with decidedly sexual overtones. As the Cowboy in the musical group Village People, Randy Jones has become an indelible icon. (Randy Jones Collection)

Since the early part of the twentieth century, Greenwich Village in New York City has been the epicenter of the Bohemian lifestyle and gay culture. (Mark Bego)

In 1969 a riot broke out at The Stonewall Inn on Christopher Street between the police and gay patrons. It symbolized the beginning of the Gay Rights Movement. (Mark Bego)

The singing group Village People became such a huge success in the late 1970s "disco era" that their music made them international stars. Here they are seen receiving a proclamation from the U.S. Navy. (left to right): David Hodo, Alex Briley, Felipe Rose, a Navy official, VP managers Jacques Morali and Henri Belolo, Glenn Hughes, Victor Willis, and Randy Jones. (MJB Photo Archives)

Randy Jones came to New York City in the early 1970s to pursue a career in dance and in acting. He found sudden stardom as the original Cowboy in Village People, through their hit recordings like "Y.M.C.A.," "In the Navy," and "Macho Man." (Sunny Bak/Randy Jones Collection)

In the early 1970s, Angela Bowie became one of the most glamorous figures on the London music scene. Her controversial marriage to glam rocker David Bowie was filled with highly publicized bisexual escapades. (Terry O'Neill/MJB Photo Archives)

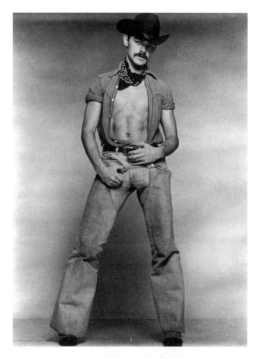

Randy Jones at the height of Village People's fame. Not only did the group sell over 100 million records worldwide, they also starred in the 1980 cult classic film *Can't Stop the Music*. (Randy Jones Collection)

Village People in the 1980s: David Hodo (Construction Worker), Ray Simpson (Cop), Felipe Rose (Indian), Alex Briley (G.I.), Randy Jones (Cowboy), and Glenn Hughes (Leatherman). (MJB Photo Archives)

Mark Bego and artist Andy Warhol at Tavern on the Green in New York City, 1984. Andy revolutionized the public's concept about the meaning of true art. His prints of Campbell's Soup cans, and his colorful portraits of pop culture stars, made him a legend. (Roger Glazer/MJB Photo Archives)

Many of the songs recorded on Village People albums contain gay images and sexual references, including "Ups and Downs," "Hot Cop," "I'm a Cruiser," "Fire Island," and "Liberation." (MJB Photo Archives)

Randy Jones and Mark Bego have been friends since 1978 when Bego became the first journalist to ever interview Village People. Together they have produced shows, stage events, and hosted parties. (Randy Jones)

Randy Jones (left) left Village People in 1980 and went on to record his first solo album. After three European albums the group disbanded. Randy reunited the band in 1987 and remained with the group until the early 1990s. (MJB Photo Archives)

Village People "Leatherman" Glenn Hughes and Mark Bego at a CD release party in New York City, 1988. Glenn remained with the group until the 1990s, and he passed away in 2001. (Lara Donen/MJB Photo Archives)

Still causing a commotion after all these years: Mark Bego and Randy Jones in New York City, 2006. A *New York Times* best-selling author, Mark has written and published over 50 books on rock music and pop culture. Randy continues to record and perform internationally, and he released the CD *Ticket to the World* in 2007. (Photo: Derek Storm)

Chapter 7

Important Gay Movies

Unlike any era that came before it, the twentieth century is completely unique in its ability to chronicle and archive itself. Since the advent of moving pictures in the late 1800s, every aspect of the shifts and changes in human culture has been captured on film. And, what better way to trace the evolution of society's view of gays and lesbians than in movies!

Censorship and the gradual liberalization of society and culture can be directly traced in the motion pictures that have been made throughout the decades. While gay and lesbian images, as we have already traced, span the arc of time, their inclusion and acceptance in mainstream films has been most gradual. It wasn't until the end of World War II that modern society loosened up to the point where homosexuals could be depicted to the general public as anything more than tragic victims.

Today, in the twenty-first century, it would be hard to believe how much things have changed since talking films debuted in the late 1920s. Popular films have traced the changes in the types of stories that the censors have allowed to be released to the general public.

In this chapter, we have selected twenty-five films that have undeniably reflected the times in which they were made, and vividly depicted the evolution of gay history in the past seven decades. Originally, film directors were forced to make certain that any gay characters in their films were portrayed as strange misfits in society who were destined to be arrested, murdered, or shunned by the end of the film.

However, now, in the twenty-first century, the gay or lesbian character might just as likely be the hero, or the protagonist, or the star. This chapter represents our list of "must see" movies that celebrate the gay experience and depict its evolution.

Rope (1948)

Director: Alfred Hitchcock

Writers: Patrick Hamilton (play *Rope's End*), Hume Cronyn (adaptation), Arthur Laurents (screenplay), Ben Hecht (uncredited)

On the surface this little known curiosity of an Alfred Hitchcock film seems like an odd choice for our first entry in gay films. However, it was about as homosexual as it could be as a mainstream film, working around the moral codes of the time. If you delve beyond the one-set play that is unfolding, and look closely at the motivation and the subtleties of the dialogue and the interrelationships, you will find that two of the main characters are indeed jealous, murderous homosexuals. Furthermore, the crime—which occurs in the first five minutes of the film—is the plotted demise of an obvious gay love object/rival of the assailants.

According to screenplay writer Arthur Laurents, Hitchcock, and everyone on the set of this film knew that the two pivotal cast members, Brandon (John Dall) and Phillip (stunningly handsome Farley Granger), were obvious gay lovers. But to get the screenplay past the censors, the actors played their characters as close to homosexual as they could, without ever making mention of it. Furthermore, part of the dynamic was the fact that their teacher, Rupert (James Stewart), was gay as well and had an affair with one of the young men. While watching this slightly stiff drawing room murder, knowing this "conceit" truly adds an interesting viewing dimension.

The other completely unique and historic fact about this 1948 murder mystery classic is the fact that there was absolutely zero editing within the scenes once the film begins. This made for one of the rarest and most uncommonly distinctive looks of all of Hitchcock's amazing body of works. With the knowledge that the maximum time duration of a roll of motion picture film is approximately ten minutes, a clever single interior set was constructed so that a lone camera follows all of the action completely, either "panning," "dollying," or "zooming" to the next speaker or bit of staged action without a single "jump cut." When the ten minutes of film was allotted, the camera shot cleverly reaches a doorway, or an object, the film roll is changed, and the action begins exactly on that same static shot. It is so cleverly and seamlessly done that one has to have the knowledge that this is going on to spot the changes in the roll of the film. Perhaps this technical trick—which was publicized at the time of release—was merely a ruse to mask the gayness of the four main male characters.

Here is the action: Brandon and Phillip are roommates, and—presumably—lovers. In the opening sequence of the film, the two of them murder a third friend of theirs, David Kentley (Dick Hogan). They strangle him with a piece of rope and stuff his body into a trunk in the living room of their Manhattan apartment. We have not given the plot away by telling you this. The mystery is not in identifying the murderer, but discovering which other member of the cast will find that there was a crime to begin with.

In the form of a sick, tongue-in-cheek black comedy, Brandon and Phillip proceed to host a cocktail party in their apartment. The murderous lovers apparently like living life on the edge, because they go so far as to serve their guests drinks and dinner off of the chest where dead David now dwells. To make matters worse, they don't bother to dispose of the rope either, which—naturally— makes a most inconvenient reappearance in the middle of the party.

Just to spice up the proceedings, the deadly duo's guests include David's father (Sir Cedric Hardwicke), his aunt (Constance Collier), his fiancée Jane (Joan Chandler), and their former schoolteacher Rupert (Stewart). Much of the dialogue has to do with "Where is David?" "What can be keeping him from arriving?" Hints, clues, and dangerous puns fly through the air of the party like daggers, making this for a fascinating gay mystery as only Hitchcock could devise.

Naturally, because of the film censors of the day, the concepts of gay and homosexual are never brought up. However, once you start questioning the relationships that exist between David, Brandon, Phillip, and Rupert, it makes for riveting viewing. Furthermore, are the boys really fighting over the attention of clueless Janet? Or, is she merely a pawn in this cat-and-mouse game about jealous homosexual lovers? This film is about as gay as you could get, circa 1948, and a curious Hitchcock classic. And, yes, Alfred makes one of his unbilled cameo appearances in the beginning of the film.

Cast:

James Stewart	Rupert Cadell
John Dall	Brandon Shaw
Farley Granger	Phillip Morgan
Sir Cedric Hardwicke	Mr. Kentley
Constance Collier	Mrs. Atwater
Douglas Dick	Kenneth Lawrence
Edith Evanson	Mrs. Wilson
Dick Hogan	David Kentley
Joan Chandler	Janet Walker

Some Like It Hot (1959)

Director: Billy Wilder

Writers: Robert Thoeren and Michael Logan (story), Billy Wilder and I.A.L. Diamond (screenplay)

Although this is not a gay film, per se, the fact that its two male stars spend the majority of their screen time dressed as women makes this the best-known and most famous transvestite film ever made. And in the middle of all of the action is the seductive singer Sugar Cane (Marilyn Monroe), at her absolutely most gorgeous. What ensues is one of Hollywood's most successful and most sparkling comedies.

Some Like It Hot is the story of two musicians, Jerry (Jack Lemmon) and Joe (Tony Curtis), who accidentally witness the infamous St. Valentine's Day Massacre. Their only foolproof plan involves them masquerading as female musicians on a bawdy train ride to Florida. Now that Jerry is pretending to be "Daphne," and Joe is dressed as "Josephine," both men take to their new personas differently.

Joe takes to this new circumstance like a rooster in a hen house, and he begins courting ditzy Sugar. On the other hand, Jerry finds himself fighting off the advances of wealthy Osgood Fielding (Joe E. Brown). When the group of gangsters they are fleeing from suddenly arrive at the seaside resort their "all-girl" band is booked at, the comic fireworks and the lethal machine guns start to flare.

In the film's final frames, Joe ends up with Sugar, and Osgood proposes marriage to Daphne. When Daphne tries to protest on the grounds that "she" isn't really a woman, Osgood deadpans the classic line, "Nobody's perfect." *Some Like It Hot* is a totally mainstream comedy that ends with a surprisingly gay twist.

Marilyn Monroe	Sugar Kane Kowalczyk
Tony Curtis	Joe/"Josephine"/"Junior"
Jack Lemmon	Jerry/"Daphne"
George Raft	Spats Colombo
Pat O'Brien	Det. Mulligan
Joe E. Brown	Osgood Fielding III
Nehemiah Persoff	Little Bonaparte
Joan Shawlee	Sweet Sue
Billy Gray	Sig Poliakoff
George E. Stone	Toothpick Charlie
Dave Barry	Beinstock

Mike Mazurki	Spats' henchman
Harry Wilson	Spats' henchman
Beverly Wills	Dolores
Barbara Drew	Nellie

The Children's Hour (1961)

Director: William Wyler

Screenplay Writer: Lillian Hellman (adaptation)

Original Play: Lillian Hellman

Awards: Nominated for five Oscars, winning four of them, including Faith Bainter as Best Supporting Actress. Both Shirley MacLaine and Bainter won Golden Globe Awards in the categories of Best Actress and Best Supporting Actress, respectively

The Children's Hour was originally a stage play by the brilliant Lillian Hellman. Although you do pick up on the fact that the two main characters are suspected of being lesbians, this is another case of reading between the lines. Although it is a frank and incredibly plotted drama, this second filmed version of the play is made up of innuendo's and veiled accusations.

The plot has to do with best friends Karen Wright (Audrey Hepburn) and Martha Dobie (Shirley MacLaine), who are a pair of diligent headmistresses at a private school for girls, located in New England. It is a successful venture, and they also employ Martha's slightly dotty Aunt Lily (Miriam Hopkins) as one of their instructors.

While Karen has a beau, Dr. Joe Cardin (James Garner), Martha is single. One of their pupils is the spoiled and willful little Mary Tilford (Karen Balkin), who is used to getting her way. When she is cornered in one of her deceitful lies, she makes up a story that turns the whole school upside down and ultimately ruins lives.

When Mary is caught lying, the evil child goes to her powerful grandmother Amelia (Faye Bainter), and she weaves her biggest fib. According to Mary, she suspects that Karen and Martha are lesbian lovers. Actually these accusations are handled in inaudible whispers, but the viewer clearly gets the picture of what is supposedly going on.

The acting in this film is brilliant. In fact, Balkin plays the role of Mary Tilford with such evil brattiness that you will find yourself thinking out loud, "Would someone please slap that lying little bitch!"

When Grandma Amelia Tilford gets on the phone to all of the other girls' mothers, suddenly the school is emptied of its students, and Karen and Martha find themselves at the eye of a tornado of scandal. Furthermore, the lies ruin the profession of innocent Dr. Cardin as well. The lone character witness who could help Karen and Martha, Aunt Lily, flees the scene as the scandal hits the fan.

This thoughtful and incredibly written play was originally made into a 1936 film called *These Three*. In the original version, the censorship laws were so strict that the whole plot of the film had to be redirected. Instead of accusing that cast's Martha (Miriam Hopkins) and Karen (Merle Oberon) of being lesbians, the plot was rewritten to be about heterosexual jealousy over the love of Dr. Cardin (Joel McCrea). The director of both films was William Wyler.

In a bit of genius casting, he gave Miriam Hopkins the role of Aunt Lily in this 1961 version of the film. He also offered Merle Oberon the chance to play Grandma Tilford, but she declined. It is also worth noting that in the roles of Martha and Karen, he originally approached Doris Day and Katharine Hepburn.

Reportedly, there were several scenes where the lesbian accusations were more specifically filmed, but the censorship of the times caused Wyler to leave them on the cutting room floor. Still, this slightly edited version makes the action and the lesbian subtext apparent to the viewer.

Please note that we are not giving away the "No! She didn't just do that!" kind of ending that this classic film has. It's a real lesbian dilly of a dramatic conclusion. Go buy the DVD and find out what one of the characters admits to, and how they ultimately handle this disclosure. This film is a brilliantly acted "must see" gay classic.

Cast:

Audrey Hepburn	Karen Wright
Shirley MacLaine	Martha Dobie
James Garner	Dr. Joe Cardin
Miriam Hopkins	Mrs. Lily Mortar
Fay Bainter	Mrs. Amelia Tilford
Karen Balkin	Mary Tilford
Veronica Cartwright	Rosalie Wells
Mimi Gibson	Evelyn

Reflections in a Golden Eye (1967)

Director: John Huston

Writers: Carson McCullers and Gladys Hill

Original novel: Carson McCullers

Few actors play more convincingly close-to-the-edge crazy better than Marlon Brando. Likewise, no actress does a better job at portraying a frustrated Southern woman in heat better than Elizabeth Taylor. She had a lot of practice in her Tennessee Williams-based films like *Suddenly, Last Summer* and *Cat on a Hot Tin Roof*. That being said, few actresses excel at "I'm terrified" and "coming unglued" quite like Julie Harris. Here all three of these seasoned pros take a turn at letting their libidos run wild in the same film.

In *Reflections in a Golden Eye*, director John Huston sets this trio of Oscar winners loose in a film about homophobia, sexual repression, frustration, and just a dash of lunacy. Set on a U.S. Army post, in a Southern town in the late 1940s, you are not quite sure which member of this trio has been smoking more "loco weed," and the craziness of it all keeps the viewer riveted to the screen.

Major Weldon Penderton (Brando) is a career soldier on the verge of finally coming out of the closet. And, what better place to do it than at a military base populated by hunky young men. While watching all of the enlisted young "eye candy" on the base during the day, he has plenty of beefcake to ogle. His best friend is Lt. Col. Morris Langdon (Brian Keith), who lives next door to the Pendertons. When they come home each night to their wives it is strictly "drama central."

Penderton's wife, Leona (Taylor), is a frustrated woman who has no trouble letting anyone who will listen know that her husband has zero interest in sleeping with her. How convenient that she is living at a military base full of studs for her to bed. In addition, she is having a sexual affair with Lt. Langdon.

Things are even less well in the Langdon household. Alison Langdon (Harris) has already been to the "funny farm" once and is strangely attracted and attached to her mincing queen of a houseboy, Anacleto (Zorro David). In fact, Alison once became so unglued that she cut off her own nipples with a pair of gardening shears. Once the film sets up its characters, you just know that someone, if not everyone, is headed for a giant mental meltdown.

Leonora does her best to drive her husband to the brink at a cocktail party, whipping him with a riding crop in front of all of her guests, announcing to everyone who will listen what an impotent weasel she has as a husband. Meanwhile, there is a hot enlisted man by the name of Private L.G. Williams (Robert Forster), who has taken to riding through the local woods on horseback, stark naked and in full view of Major Penderton. To further push the envelope, Williams has taken to walking into the Langdon house at night, where he sneaks into Leonora's bedroom to watch her sleep. Or, is he really trying to entice the man of the house?

Major Penderton can't stop thinking about the naked Private Williams. You know that he wants him, but is he finally dealing with his gay desires? A fascinating train wreck of a film, everyone seems like they are destined to let their personal demons get the best of them. And, they do just that.

Cast:

Elizabeth Taylor	Leonora Penderton
Marlon Brando	Major Weldon Penderton
Brian Keith	Lt. Col. Morris Langdon
Julie Harris	Alison Langdon
Zorro David	Anacleto
Gordon Mitchell	Stables Sergeant
Irvin Dugan	Capt. Murray Weincheck
Fay Sparks	Susie
Robert Forster	Pvt. L.G. Williams

Valley of the Dolls (1967)

Director: Mark Robson

Writers: Jacqueline Susann, Helen Deutsch, and Dorothy Kingsley

Original novel: Jacqueline Susann

Awards: Nominated for Oscar for Best Music, Scoring of Music, Adaptation or Treatment, John Williams

Although this is not a gay film, per se, it could be on our list of favorite films merely because it is camp classic. What brings it merit on this particular list is the fact that its dealings with its homosexual characters start to mirror the growing tolerance of the times. The primary gay/bisexual character, film costume designer Ted Casablanca (Alex Davion), doesn't end up killed, committed, or blamed for some heinous crime in the end of the film. His sex life is dealt with in a matter-of-fact fashion, unless you are his pill-popping wife Neely O'Hara (Patty Duke).

The original novel, *Valley of the Dolls*, when it was first published in the late 1960s, became one of the biggest selling book of all time, excluding the Bible. To devoted fans of Jacqueline's delightfully decadent book, *Valley of the Dolls* IS the Bible of trashy novels.

This is the story of three young girls who are drawn to New York City, seeking fame and fortune. They are career girl Anne Welles (Barbara Parkins), talented goldmine of a singer Neely O'Hara, and gorgeous sex bomb Jennifer North (Sharon Tate). Neely is so talented that she is instantly perceived as a threat to the mature warhorse of a Broadway star Helen Lawson (Susan Hayward).

Like the novel, this film is just filled with interesting characters like handsome crooner Tony Polar (Tony Scotti) and his latent lesbian sister Miriam (Lee Grant). Along the way, it's the "dolls," the lovely prescription pills in dreamy M&M's style colors, which ultimately hook Neely, Anne, and Jennifer. That is a common thread linking the characters. The "uppers" and "downers" aren't the only "ups" and "downs" in these girls' lives, as they ascend and descend their career ladders.

When Neely complains to Jennifer about her bisexual husband, Casablanca, Jennifer offers the poolside advice, "You know how bitchy fags can be."

The real classic is the ladies room showdown between Helen and Neely. It includes the following classic dialogue:

Helen Lawson: Look. They drummed you right outta Hollywood! So ya come crawlin' back to Broadway. Well, Broadway doesn't go for booze and dope. Now you get outta my way, I got a guy waitin' for me.
Neely O'Hara: That's a switch from the fags you're usually stuck with!
Helen Lawson: At least I never had to MARRY one!

This is a must-see romp that visibly shows the changing mores toward sex and sexuality, and it's thoroughly modern views toward homosexuality. This is a glitzy show business extravaganza, which also features a Hitchcock-like cameo role for Jacqueline Susann, who plays a small part as a television reporter.

Cast:

Barbara Parkins	Anne Welles
Patty Duke	Neely O'Hara
Sharon Tate	Jennifer North Polar
Susan Hayward	Helen Lawson

Paul Burke	Lyon Burke
Tony Scotti	Tony Polar
Martin Milner	Mel Anderson
Charles Drake	Kevin Gillmore
Alex Davion	Ted Casablanca
Lee Grant	Miriam Polar
Noami Stevens	Miss Steinberg
Robert H. Harris	Henry Bellamy
Jacqueline Susann	First Reporter
Robert Viharo	Film director
Joey Bishop	MC at Cystic Fibrosis telethon
George Jessel	MC at Grammy Awards, aka Toastmaster General

The Damned (1969)

Director: Luchino Visconti

Writers: Luchino Visconti, Nicola Badalucco, and Enrico Medioli

The decadence of the Nazi regime was one of power and anarchy. In this film, the action traces the effects of the war through the eyes and lives of one particular family. *The Damned* takes matters way beyond the things you see on the History Channel; in fact, by the last hour of this delightfully twisted film, one can see plot elements of a bisexual *Hamlet*, a dramatic touch of *Oedipus*, plus just a little dash of Lady Macbeth thrown in.

It opens during the birthday celebration of the patriarch of the Von Essenbeck family, grandfather Joachim (Albrecht Schoenhals). Just as his grandson Martin (Helmut Berger) scandalizes the family by performing a Marlene Dietrich song in drag, news of the burning of the Reichstag is announced, and the party erupts into pandemonium.

After a night of dramatic power shifts, the family heir apparent is suddenly Martin, who is the child of Joachim's deceased son, a World War I war victim. Martin's mother is the conniving Black Widow of a woman, Sophie Von Essenbeck (Ingrid Thulin). While she promotes her son's ascent to power, Sophie is in love with Friedrich Bruckmann (Dirk Bogarde) and plans to use Martin as a pawn to promote Bruckmann's elevation to power as the head of the lucrative family steel business.

As the war commences and escalates, the family behaves like the Germanic precursors to the Carringtons of television's *Dynasty*, and the Ewings of *Dallas*, all rolled together. There is a big Nazi homosexual orgy involving Martin's Uncle Konstantin (René Koldehoff). It is a wild sequence of man-on-man sexual excesses, which leads directly into the slaughter of a gay faction of the Nazi "brown shirts," on a murderous occasion known as the infamous Night of Long Knives.

Sophie has done her best to nurture her son Martin's many vices. It is her way of controlling him. She takes delight in his many kinks, and even derives amusement from his forays as a transsexual. She also turns her head to his dark streaks, including his bent as a child molester. Although he dresses in drag, he also has a thing for little girls. He even has a strangely incestuous obsession for his mother. By the end of the movie, Martin's debauchery runs the gamut from Adultry-to-Z.

Amidst *The Damned's* many family power struggles, there are several depictions of homosexual sex and lust. The lengthy sequence depicting the gay sex orgy takes part of this film down a fascinatingly perverse *Boys of the Third Reich* path. As the members of the Von Essenbeck family vie for power and survival, all of their sexual passions are brought to the forefront. This is not director Visconti's only film to deal with homosexual lust and desires. However, here he crystallizes it into some sort of *Nazis Gone Wild*, with everyone in the cast wearing their sexual lusts and their passions for power on their sleeves.

Cast:

Dirk Bogarde	Frederick Bruckmann
Ingrid Thulin	Sophie Von Essenbeck
Helmut Griem	Aschenbach
Helmut Berger	Martin Von Essenbeck
Renaud Verley	Gunther Von Essenbeck
Umberto Orsini	Herbert Thallman
René Koldehoff	Konstantin Von Essenbeck
Albrecht Schönhals	Joachim Von Essenbeck
Florinda Bolkan	Olga
Nora Ricci	Governess
Charlotte Rampling	Elisabeth Thallman

The Boys in the Band (1970)

Director: William Friedkin

Writer: Mart Crowley

Original Play: Matt Crowley

Released a year after the Stonewall Riots in New York City, this controversial movie is an unabashed all gay mainstream film, and as such was the first of its kind. It doesn't apologize for any of the cast members' lifestyles, as they all convene at the apartment of Michael (Kenneth Nelson) to throw a party for birthday boy Harold (Leonard Frey). Just like the Sharon Tate line in *Valley of the Dolls* ("You know how bitchy fags can be"), this film is just that. As the party guests get drunker and drunker, the sniping just gets sharper and more cutting.

This film shows the subculture of professional gay men in Manhattan circa 1970, operating in a two-edged society of their own. Just about every male gay type is personified here, including the not-quite-out-of-the-closet straight man, Hank (Laurence Luckinbill); and Cowboy (Robert LaTourneaux), a hapless hustler with an I.Q. that is barely above the number consigned to "room temperature."

Everyone lets their hair down and reveals their true inner-workings as they play a cruel and biting party game. According to the rules of the party game, each man present must pick up the telephone and tell someone they have never told before that they love him. Although the film shows its theatrical roots via its one-set staginess, the dialogue and revealing monologues brilliantly show the psyche of each of the characters.

Cast:

Kenneth Nelson	Michael
Peter White	Alan
Leonard Frey	Harold
Cliff Gorman	Emory
Frederick Combs	Donald
Laurence Luckinbill	Hank
Keith Prentice	Larry
Robert La Tourneaux	Cowboy
Reuben Greene	Bernard

Something for Everyone (1970)

Director: Harold Prince

Writers: Harry Kressing and Hugh Wheeler

Original Novel: Harry Kressing

This sinister black comedy of a film opens with a picturesque sequence of handsome Conrad (Michael York) bicycling through the lovely scenery of postwar Austria. As he glides to a stop for a rest, he gazes up at a stunning storybook castle on a majestic mountain.

It is the lovely *schloss* of a widowed Countess (Angela Lansbury) and her just-waiting-to-be-seduced two teenagers. Former wealthy aristocrats, the war has left them cash-poor. In fact, the Countess is so broke that she must now worry about the price of strawberries.

Conniving Conrad develops a plan to place himself in the Castle Ornstein household, so that he can live the life of luxury that he has always wanted. To make certain that there is a spot for him at the castle, he murders the family's butler.

To further ingratiate himself into the family, he systematically seduces everyone in it, including the Countess' son (Anthony Corlan) and daughter (Jane Carr). Along the way he makes his presence invaluable to all of them. A hysterically funny bisexual romp through the Austrian hills, this is clearly no G-rated *Sound of Music*.

Seducing the family is not the only cat-and-mouse game that clever Conrad performs. He also figures out a way to channel some more wealth into the household through another gay affair. A little-known classic, *Something for Everyone* is truly a fun and funny bisexual romp of a film ripe for revival.

Cast:

Angela Lansbury	Countess Herthe von Ornstein
Michael York	Konrad Ludwig
Anthony Corlan	Helmuth Von Ornstein
Heidelinde Weis	Anneliese Pleschke
Jane Carr	Lotte Von Ornstein
Eva Maria Meineke	Mrs. Pleschke
John Gill	Mr. Pleschke
Wolfried Lier	Klaus
Klaus Havenstein	Rudolph
Walter Janssen	Father Georg
Erik Jelde	Bit Part

Sunday Bloody Sunday (1971)

Director: John Schlesinger

Writers: Penelope Gilliatt and David Sherwin

Awards: Nominated for four Oscars including Best Actor and Actress

A divorced woman by the name of Alex (Glenda Jackson) has the same telephone answering service as a prominent Jewish doctor by the name of Daniel Hirsh (Peter Finch). The woman who answers their phones for them (Bessie Love) seems like their only common thread. However, unbeknownst to them both is the fact that they also share the same male lover, artist Bob Elkin (Murray Head).

Neither party is willing to make their own relationships with Bob permanent. That would be too much of a commitment for either of them, so they just let it go on as it is, unaware that Bob is "playing for both teams." A proper British film of manners, its content was very telling about the changing moral structure of society. Why should any member of this modern day triangle give up his or her independence, when in reality, they all have the best of all worlds?

It was the dawning of the "Me" decade of the 1970s, and in a way everyone got what they wanted, and Bob adeptly lived his life on both sides of the fence. It is interesting to note that the telephone operator is the same Bessie Love of silent film fame. And, Murray Head was also enjoying a lot of popularity during this era as the star of the first Andrew Lloyd Webber/Andrew Rice rock opera, *Jesus Christ Superstar*.

Although the subject matter seems a bit tame nowadays, at the time of its release, *Sunday Bloody Sunday* caused quite a stir. It brilliantly showed how society's attitudes toward gay male sexuality, and bisexuality, were indeed changing drastically.

Cast:

Peter Finch	Dr. Daniel Hirsh
Glenda Jackson	Alex Greville
Murray Head	Bob Elkin
Peggy Ashcroft	Mrs. Greville
Tony Britton	George Harding
Maurice Denham	Mr. Greville
Bessie Love	Telephone Operator
Vivian Pickles	Alva Hodson
Frank Windsor	Bill Hodson

Cabaret (1972)

Director: Bob Fosse

Writer: Christopher Isherwood

Original Novel: Christopher Isherwood

Awards: Winner of eight Oscars including Best Film and Best Actress

This sharp and witty adaptation of the hit Broadway show of the same name, *Cabaret* was made revolutionary and vastly popular in the hands of the great director Bob Fosse. The casting of talented and highly appealing Liza Minnelli was right on target. *Cabaret* made her a superstar and a film commodity. She was literally catapulted into the spotlight in this tailor-made role.

The story takes place in late-1930s Berlin, a city that was a hotbed of "anything goes" morality. However, Adolf Hitler was positioning himself to take over the world and was exercising his ability to send to the concentration camp anyone he didn't like: not only Jews, but people with mental problems, and homosexuals as well.

Right before it is all about to change for the worse, we are introduced to an American expatriate by the name of Sally Bowles (Minnelli), who is a singer in a divinely decadent cabaret called the Kit Kat Club. At the nightclub is an M.C. (Joel Grey) whose sharp edged observations in song perfectly mirror what is going on throughout Germany at the time.

In the Kit Kat Club there are drag queens and scantly clad dancers. It is there that Sally hopes to find the kind of fame she longs for. The majority of the very evocative songs are set in the cabaret, so that they blend seamlessly into the action. When a dashing young British citizen, Brian Roberts (Michael York), comes to town, intending to teach English to interested citizens, Sally falls in love with him. However, he is reluctant to "complicate" the relationship with sex. That is before handsome Maximilian von Heune (Helmut Griem) comes to town to complicate matters further. Both Sally and Brian have sex with Max, and then a divinely decadent bisexual love triangle is set into action.

Meanwhile, one of Brian's prime students, Fritz Wendel (Fritz Wepper), wants to learn English to impress beautiful Natalia Landauer (Marisa Berenson), who turns out to be Jewish, at a time and place where that is not a good thing at all. As the Nazis take power in Berlin, everyone's tune changes from happy-go-lucky, to brutality and terror.

With the teaming of Kanter and Ebb's succinct and appealing songs and Bob Fosse's unique and beautiful choreography, *Cabaret* is a film that holds up well to this day. And, its depiction of the changing social mores of the day make this a must-see movie.

Cast:

Liza Minnelli	Sally Bowles
Michael York	Brian Roberts
Helmut Griem	Maximilian von Heune

Joel Grey	Master of Ceremonies
Fritz Wepper	Fritz Wendel
Marisa Berenson	Natalia Landauer
Elisabeth Neumann-Viertel	Fraulein Schneider
Helen Vita	Fraulein Kost
Sigrid Von Richthofen	Fraulein Mayr
Gerd Vespermann	Bobby
Ralf Wolter	Herr Ludwig

La Cage Aux Folles (French 1978)

Director: Edouard Molinaro

Writer: Jean Poiret (play "La Cage Aux Folles")

Based on earlier screenplay by Francis Veber, Edouard Molinaro, Marcello Danon, and Jean Poiret

This hysterically funny French film was a big hit in art houses in America in 1979, following a successful run in Europe the previous year. It was such a hit that it was made into a hit sequel (*La Cage Aux Folles II*), a long-running Broadway musical, an American film starring Robin Williams and Nathan Lane (*The Birdcage*), and a 2004 hit Broadway revival starring Robert Goulet and Gary Beach.

It was truly one of the first purely gay films to deal with the subject matter of drag queens in an unapologetic fashion, in the context of ludicrous comedy. It centers on the mad household of a gay male couple: Renato Baldi (Ugo Tognazzi) and Albin Mougeotte (Michel Serrault) who live in St. Tropez in the south of France. They are also the owners of a notorious and very popular transvestite nightclub called La Cage Aux Folles.

Renato is a stylish gay gentleman who runs the club, and Albin spends half of his time in his drag queen persona: "Zaza Napoli." Renato is a sane businessman, and Albin is flighty, flaming, temperamental, and a true diva. Their household is peopled with a colorful coterie of gays: from butch boys to hysterical queens. However, all of the sexuality here is played for laughs.

It seems that in his youth Renato had a heterosexual fling, which produced his only offspring, a son named Laurent Baldi (Rémi Laurent). When Laurent shows up to announce his engagement to a young woman, he also announces that his future in-laws are coming to dinner to meet his parents, whom he has fabricated new facts about. Suddenly, his father has to "play it straight" for the evening, and Alban has to convincingly portray a matriarch instead of a diva.

Whereas American films often have to go out of their way to make their gay characters fit into careful molds, European films just let their characters be who they are. This is very true when comparing *La Cage Aux Folles* with the later American film *The Birdcage*. While this French original film shows its characters off with more grittiness, and the American film has more of the homogenized feel of a television sitcom at times, both succeed in garnering the laughs. Both are also successful at instilling the final message for everyone to just "live and let live." And, each film has its cinematic merits as being an important gay film.

Cast:

Ugo Tognazzi	Renato Baldi
Michel Serrault	Albin Mougeotte/"Zaza Napoli"
Claire Maurier	Simone Deblon
Rémi Laurent	Laurent Baldi
Carmen Scarpitta	Louise Charrier
Benny Luke	Jacob
Luisa Maneri	Andrea Charrier
Michel Galabru	Simon Charrier
Venantino Venantini	Le chauffeur de Charrier
Carlo Reali	The bouncer
Guido Cerniglia	The doctor
Liana Del Balzo	Mme. Charrier

Can't Stop the Music (1980)

Director: Nancy Walker

Writers: Allan Carr and Bronte Woodard

This is the story of Village People reinterpreted into a big glitzy musical extravaganza. Partially due to the massive success of *Saturday Night Fever* and *Thank God It's Friday*, it seemed that traditional movie musicals could be synthesized into disco epics. On one hand, this pastiche perfectly took its plot from the formation of Village People and succeeded in bringing it to the general public. Yet, on the other hand, its 1980 release also coincided with the demise of the disco craze, and didn't become the huge box-office hit that the producers had hoped it would become.

The story had enough gay tongue-in-cheek elements to make it a fun romp about six macho men living in Greenwich Village in the late 1970s. It centers on a fictional music producer, Jack Morell (Steve Guttenberg), putting together the ultimate all-male disco group. Along the way, just like the legend of the group, he encounters six preconceived characters: a cowboy (Randy Jones), a G.I. (Alex Briley), a construction worker (David Hodo), a leather-clad biker (Glenn Hughes), an Indian brave (Felipe Rose), and a singing cop (Raymond Simpson).

The costars include June Havoc (the sister of Gypsy Rose Lee), Altovese Davis (Mrs. Sammy Davis, Jr.), and Broadway singing sensation Tammy Grimes (the original star of *The Unsinkable Molly Brown*). Village People's "sister group," singing trio The Ritchie Family, are also on hand to perform their own number.

Another thing that this film had going for it was that it presented a bona fide musical comedy star—Nancy Walker—as its director. To add the right amount of female sex appeal, there is Jack's brainy roommate Samantha (Valerie Perrine), and a hunky lawyer named Ron (Bruce Jenner). The musical numbers did their best to channel Busby Berkeley, and it all ends with a concert climax in the gayest big city in 1970s America: San Francisco.

Although the words "gay" and "homosexual" are never mentioned in the script, there is little question that this is the biggest, gayest big-budget Hollywood musical ever filmed. *Can't Stop the Music* is to this day considered a sheer camp classic.

Cast:

Randy Jones	Randy the Cowboy
Alex Briley	Alex the G.I.
David Hodo	David the Construction Worker
Glenn Hughes	Glenn the Leatherman
Felipe Rose	Felipe the Indian
Ray Simpson	Ray the Police Officer
Valerie Perrine	Samantha Simpson
Bruce Jenner	Ron White
Steve Guttenberg	Jack Morell
Paul Sand	Steve Waits
Tammy Grimes	Sydney Channing
June Havoc	Helen Morell
Barbara Rush	Norma White
Altovise Davis	Alicia Edwards
Marilyn Sokol	Lulu Brecht

Russell Nype	Richard Montgomery
Jack Weston	Benny Murray
Leigh Taylor-Young	Claudia Walters
Dick Patterson	Mr. Schultz, Record Store Manager
Bobo Lewis	Bread Woman
Paula Trueman	Stick-up Lady
Portia Nelson	Law Office Receptionist
Selma Archard	Mrs. Williams
Murial Slatkin	Mrs. Slatkin
Aaron Gold	TV Reporter
Vera Brown	Ritchie Family member
Jacqui Smith Lee	Ritchie Family member
Dodie Draher	Ritchie Family member
Greg Zadikov	Singing Vendor
Danone Camden	Stewardess in Record Store
Rasa Alileen	Mime
Gabriel Barre	Mime
Donald Blanton	Relief DJ
Roger LeClaire	Disco Photographer
Cindy Roberts	Jean Harlow mannequin
Maggie Brendler	Marilyn Monroe mannequin
Bradley Bliss	Betty Grable mannequin
Bill Bartman	Wino
Victor Davis	Buster Sirwinski, Auditioning Bodybuilder
William L. Arndt	Construction Commercial Director
Jerry Layne	Ventriloquist
Terry Dunn	James the Flame
Maria Rodsakos	Steve Waits' secretary
Mike Kulik	Milk Commercial Director
Richard Bruce Friedman	Recording Technician
Bill Anagnos	Moped Rider

Taxi Zum Klo (1981)

Director: Frank Ripploh

Writer: Frank Ripploh

A completely off-the-wall German gay comedy, *Taxi Zum Klo* literally interprets into English as "Taxi to the toilet." The main character in this amusing movie is Frank (Frank Ripploh). He is a bearded schoolteacher with shaggy hair and an interest in filmmaking. Living in Berlin, he has an active sex life, which he somehow manages to keep separate from his teaching career. However, he has taken to correcting his student's work papers in public toilets, so that he can "cruise" while getting his work done. One night he meets Bernd (Bernd Broaderup) and there is an instant attraction. They become lovers, and in the relationship that develops it is Bernd who is the attentive and caring one.

Not content to have the satisfaction of a loving partner, Frank soon gets bored, and he is up to his old habits of cruising public men's rooms. How long can Frank keep his relationship with Bernd going? How long can he keep his secret sex life apart from his career? The morning after the annual Berlin Queen's Ball, every aspect of Frank's life collides. An amusing and voyeuristic film, *Taxi Zum Klo* was a critical hit when it was originally released, and still holds up as an entertaining cinematic experience.

Cast:

Frank Ripploh	Frank Ripploh
Bernd Broaderup	Bernd
Orpha Termin	Female neighbor
Peter Fahrni	Gas station attendant
Dieter Godde	Masseur
Klaus Schnee	Teacher
Bernd Kroger	Teacher
Markus Voigtlander	Teacher
Irmgard Lademacher	Teacher
Gregor Becker	Teacher

Making Love (1982)

Director: Arthur Hiller

Writers: A. Scott Berg and Barry Sandler

When *Making Love* was originally released, it was heralded as the first major Hollywood gay love story. And, with an appealing cast, a mainstream director (Arthur Hiller), and an appealing soundtrack (complete with a hit Roberta Flack theme song), it accomplished its goals on many levels. The plot centers on the life of a successful young Los Angeles dweller named Zach Elliot (Michael Ontkean) and his high-powered television producer wife Claire (Kate Jackson) who have the ideal marriage, at least on the surface. That is until he finally comes out of the closet with regard his attraction to the same sex.

The man who awakens Zach's need to cross the fence is a highly attractive novelist, Bart McGuire (Harry Hamlin). For Zach, it's "love at first sight." For Bart, it's just another hot night in West Hollywood. As Zach keeps blowing off plans with Claire, she begins to suspect that there is another woman. Imagine her surprise when she finds that she is being jilted for another man.

Claire isn't sure what she is going to do when Zach finally confesses to her that he is gay. She seeks the opinion of her elderly confidante, Winnie Bates (Wendy Hiller), who offers her some sage advice. Although this film is a bit of a soap opera, its appealing cast and a strong script keep it from becoming a maudlin cliché of a film. It is an important film in that *Making Love* was one of the first gay themed films by a major studio. Furthermore, it dealt with gayness as a matter of love, and not just a matter of sex.

Cast:

Michael Ontkean	Zach Elliot
Kate Jackson	Claire Elliott
Harry Hamlin	Bart McGuire
Wendy Hiller	Winnie Bates
Arthur Hill	Henry
Nancy Olson	Christine
John Dukakis	Tim
Terry Kiser	Harrington
Dennis Howard	Larry
Asher Brauner	Ted
John Calvin	David
Gwen Arner	Alrene
Gary Swanson	Ken

Personal Best (1982)
Director: Robert Towne
Writer: Robert Towne

The idea of some female athletes being lesbians in their personal lives was hardly a stretch of the imagination. However, this premise was never explored in a mainstream motion picture. In this case, *Personal Best* both confronts and humanizes the subject matter both tastefully and provocatively.

Telling the story of a classic relationship triangle—in this case a bisexual one—and setting it in the competitive world of women's sports sets up the premise for a highly entertaining mainstream film.

The plot involves a trio of athletes, one of whom switches sexual teams in the middle of the movie.

Chris Cahill (Mariel Hemingway) has a highly dysfunctional relationship with her father, who happens to be a sports coach. While that dynamic is not working for her in a supportive way, she finds an extended family in her new coach Terry Tingloff (Scott Glenn), and her friend and competitor Tory Skinner (Patrice Donnelly). There is an undeniable female bonding between Chris and Tory, and it isn't long before their strong friendship becomes sexual. This sets off a new competition: that between Chris and her coach, Chris and her female lover, as Tory and Terry vie for Chris' love and attention.

A sensitive and thoughtful film, set against the backdrop of women's sports, *Personal Best*, like *Making Love*, was Hollywood's attempt at making films about homosexual protagonists both mainstream and entertaining. Ultimately, it is a human drama more than a gay film, yet its undeniable lesbian content makes *Personal Best* both unique and compelling.

Cast:

Mariel Hemingway	Chris Cahill
Scott Glenn	Terry Tingloff
Patrice Donnelly	Tory Skinner
Kenny Moore	Denny Stites
Jim Moody	Roscoe Travis
Kari Gosswiller	Penny Brill
Jodi Anderson	Nadia "Pooch" Anderson
Maren Seidler	Tanya
Martha Watson	Sheila
Emily Dole	Maureen
Pam Spencer	Jan
Deby Laplante	Trish
Mitzi McMillin	Laura

Victor Victoria (1982)

Director: Blake Edwards

Writers: Blake Edwards, Hans Hoemburg (concept), Reinhold Schünzel (1933 script)

Awards: Oscar Nomination for Best Supporting Actress, Lesley Ann Warren

Director Blake Edwards is no stranger to comedies with twisted plots. His famed *Pink Panther* series of films alone have made him one of the most famous directors of movies where silliness, mistaken identity, and bumbling characters are behind the steering wheel of the action. He has made of some of Hollywood's zaniest classics.

Here, Edwards takes his masterful comedy dynamics and goes gay with them. Starring his delightful wife, Julie Andrews, he layers plot twist upon plot twist to come up with a delightfully gay farce of sexual manners.

It is Paris in the 1930s, and our heroine, Victoria (Andrews) is a struggling opera singer in search of a career and an income. She is aided by a charming gay cabaret performer named Toddy (Robert Preston). Since he is the host of a transvestite club in the City of Lights, he strikes upon a comedy supposition to turn Victoria into the toast of the town. If gay men are amused by men pretending to be women in elaborate "drag," why not pass off a woman masquerading as a man, pretending to be a woman? What ensues is one of Blake Edwards' goofiest plot-twisting, gender-tweaking cinematic laugh riots.

Just like Toddy predicted, Victoria becomes the delight of the Paris underground as she cuts her hair short and passes herself to French society as an effete young man named "Victor." It all goes without a hitch until a Chicago mobster named King Marchand (James Garner) breezes into the plot, and the mistaken identities start to have Marx Brothers-styled plot turns.

When King finds himself falling in love with Victor and "Victoria," he begins to doubt his own sexuality. Seeing this, his bodyguard, "Squash" Bernstein (Alex Karras), is inspired to admit that he is a closet homosexual who admires his macho boss' ability to "come out." However, none of this is taken lightly by his ditzy blonde gun moll of a girlfriend, Norma Cassady (Leslie Ann Warren). If ever there was a perfect role for Warren, this is it. She is an absolute scream from start to finish, and she was nominated for an Academy Award for her performance.

Naturally, since Julie Andrews is the grand diva of some of the most famous movie musicals of all times, here she is awarded several of the best singing and dancing numbers of her career. Her snappy singing of "Le Jazz Hot" is worth backing up the DVD for time and time again. *Victor/Victoria* is a sheer cavalcade of goofiness, and its gay theme is treated as just another twist in the vast canvas of human comedy.

Cast:

Julie Andrews	Victoria Grant, aka Count Victor Grezhinski
James Garner	King Marchand
Robert Preston	Carroll "Toddy" Todd
Lesley Ann Warren	Norma Cassady
Alex Karras	"Squash" Bernstein
John Rhys-Davies	Andre Cassell
Graham Stark	Waiter
Peter Arne	Labisse, Che Lui Nightclub Owner
Sherloque Tanney	Charles Bovin, Private Investigator
Michael Robbins	Manager of Victoria's hotel
Norman Chancer	Sal Andratti
David Gant	Restaurant Manager
Maria Charles	Madame President

The Adventures of Priscilla, Queen of the Desert (1994)

Director: Stephan Elliott

Writer: Stephan Elliott

Awards: Won Oscar for Best Costume Design—Lizzy Gardiner and Tim Chappel

Take one transsexual, two drag queens, put them in a tour bus in the Australian outback with some of the most outrageously over-the-top costumes ever to grace the cinematic screen, mix it with several songs by ABBA, and yes even a Village People number ("Go West"), and you have the unlikely-but-winning formula for the delightful *The Adventures of Priscilla, Queen of the Desert*. It was so successful that it even inspired a hit soundtrack album, an American take-off (*To Wong Fu, Thanks for Everything! Julie Newmar*), and a sparkling twenty-first century stage adaptation in Australia.

As the three stars of a crazy touring company of lip-synching performers, this trio of queens play out their very human drama in the blazing sun of the scenic and remotest areas of "the land down-under," lots of zaniness and glitz abounds. They are Ralph/Bernadette Bassenger (Terence Stamp), the mother of all transsexuals, and her cohorts in drag: Anthony "Tick" Belrose/Mitzi Del Bra (Hugo Weaving) and Adam Whitely/Felicia Jollygoodfellow (Guy Pearce).

Things are all fun and games until the pink bus, christened "Priscilla," pulls into the resort town of Alice Springs, and Anthony runs smack-dab into his estranged wife and young son. Not wanting to make a fool of himself in front of his little boy, he does a bit of gender-questioning himself, with comic results. It is the young son who is more adjusted with Dad's homosexuality than Dad is.

Never before has a film so expertly mixed drag, bitchy funny dialogue, musical numbers, homophobia, and ABBA so adeptly. There are some completely crazy bits in this bizarre hit of a film, including one of the characters guarding his prize possession/good luck charm, an actual "ABBA turd" rescued from a toilet stall.

Cast:

Terence Stamp	Ralph/Bernadette Bassenger
Hugo Weaving	Anthony "Tick" Belrose/Mitzi Del Bra
Guy Pearce	Adam Whitely/Felicia Jollygoodfellow
Bill Hunter	Bob
Rebel Russell	Logowoman
John Casey	Bartender
June Marie Bennett	Shirley
Murray Davies	Miner
Frank Cornelius	Piano Player
Bob Boyce	Petrol Station Attendant
Leighton Picken	Young Adam
Maria Kmet	Ma
Joseph Kmet	Pa
Alan Dargin	Aboriginal Man
Julia Cortez	Cynthia

To Wong Fu, Thanks for Everything! Julie Newmar (1995)

Director: Beeban Kidron

Writer: Douglas Carter Beane

With an eclectic and talented cast, and several casting surprises, *To Wong Fu, Thanks for Everything! Julie Newmar*, is on one hand a garish train wreck of a film, yet on the other hand it ultimately succeeds with its quirky casting, garish drag costumes, snappy dialogue, and excitingly lively musical soundtrack. When Vida Boheme (Patrick Swayze) and Noxeema Jackson (Wesley Snipes) share the top prize in a Manhattan drag competition, they each win an expense paid trip to Hollywood. When they take pity on a Hispanic drag novice who calls herself Chi-Chi Rodriguez (John Leguizamo), they decide to hock their plane tickets, purchase an enormous Cadillac convertible, and sweep Chi-Chi up for their high-heeled cross-country adventure.

When the drag queen mobile breaks down in redneck Middle America, Vida, Noxeema, and Chi-Chi find that their greatest challenge isn't finding the right mascara at Walmart, it's standing up for who they are, and inspiring others to stand up for themselves as well. A crazy film with several holes in the plot, it remains a comically explosive cavalcade of colorful costumes and sage advice, dished out in a goofy sense of drag fury. In addition to the over-the-top performances Snipes, Swayze, and Leguizamo, there is a brilliant supporting cast—including Stockard Channing and Blythe Danner—and surprise appearances by RuPaul, Lady Bunny, and an all-too-brief glimpse at the real Julie Newmar.

Wesley Snipes	Noxeema Jackson
Patrick Swayze	Vida Boheme
John Leguizamo	Chi-Chi Rodriguez
Stockard Channing	Carol Ann
Blythe Danner	Beatrice
Arliss Howard	Virgil
Jason London	Bobby Ray
Chris Penn	Sheriff Dollard
Melinda Dillon	Merna
Beth Grant	Loretta
Alice Drummond	Clara
Marceline Hugot	Katina
Jennifer Milmore	Bobby Lee
Jamie Harrold	Billy Budd
Mike Hodge	Jimmy Joe
RuPaul	himself
Lady Bunny	himself
Julie Newmar	herself

Birdcage (1996)

Director: Mike Nichols

Writer: Jean Poiret (play "La Cage Aux Folles")

> Based on earlier screenplay by Francis Veber, Edouard Molinaro, Marcello Danon, and Jean Poiret

Award Nominations: Nominated for an Oscar: Best Art Direction/Set Decoration

It took nearly two decades from the release of the original *La Cage Aux Folles* for a major studio to produce an American version. Here, with the resulting *Birdcage*, director Mike Nichols hit a homerun with both a winning cast and over-the-top art direction. In many ways, this is one of the all-time most appealing and hysterical gay films ever made in Hollywood.

Cinematic chameleon Robin Williams is perfect at breathing realism and appeal to his portrayal of Armand Goldman, the owner of a successful drag nightclub. Here the setting has been transposed from St. Tropez to South Miami Beach, with its pastel deco hotels and its permissively gay locale.

The star of Armand's nightclub, The Birdcage, is his long-time lover Albert (Nathan Lane) who transforms himself nightly into Starina, his drag alterego. Although Armand dresses like something of a gay dandy, he is the most sane and centered half of the duo. On the other hand Albert is a true diva, both on stage and off.

Together, Armand and Albert have raised the son that Armand had after a one-night heterosexual fling twenty-some years before. When the son, Val (Dan Futterman), shows up to announce his engagement to the daughter of a U.S. senator, this madly gay household is turned upside down.

When Val explains to Armand that he has invited his fiancée Barbara (Calista Flockhart) and her parents to meet his mom and dad, all hell breaks loose. Val's future in-laws aren't just conservative, they are from the high-profile political elite. Her father, Senator Kevin Keeley (Gene Hackman), is not only the vice president of "The Coalition for Moral Order," he is concurrently embroiled in his own brewing Washington, DC, scandal. To escape the heat that the press is putting on him, he feels that a trip to Miami is just what he needs to get out of the tabloid crossfire. Big mistake.

Robin Williams has his best scene demonstrating choreography to an air-headed hunk. Prancing around on stage he instructs the dense hunk to do, "Fosse, Fosse, Fosse; Martha Graham, Martha Graham, Martha Graham; Twyla Tharp, Twyla Tharp, Twyla Tharp; Michael Kidd, Michael Kidd, Michael Kidd; Madonna, Madonna, Madonna!" As he dances away his demonstration he perfectly nails each dance legend in a five second imitation, concluding with some Madonna "vogueing."

The supporting cast is absolutely perfect here, including Mrs. Keeley (Diane Weist), Val's birth mother Katherine (Christine Baranski), and fruity Cuban houseboy Agador (Hank Azaria). Ridiculously goofy

Agador is a wannabe drag queen who considers himself to be "a little bit Ricky and a little bit Lucy."

Cast:

Robin Williams	Armand Goldman
Gene Hackman	Sen. Kevin Keeley
Nathan Lane	Albert Goldman
Dianne Wiest	Louise Keeley
Dan Futterman	Val Goldman
Calista Flockhart	Barbara Keeley
Hank Azaria	Agador
Christine Baranski	Katherine Archer
Tom McGowan	Harry Radman
Grant Heslov	*National Enquirer* Photographer
Kirby Mitchell	Keeley's Chauffeur
James Lally	Cyril
Luca Tommassini	Celsius

In & Out (1997)

Director: Frank Oz

Writer: Paul Rudnick

Awards: Oscar Nomination for Best Supporting Actress, Joan
Cusack

One of the best mainstream American comedies to deal with homosexuality, *In & Out* is a very funny film on every level. The premise of
the film is based on the Oscar acceptance speech that Tom Hanks gave
when the won the Best Actor award for playing a dying gay man in the
film *Philadelphia*. On television Hanks took his trophy and thanked one
of his gay drama teachers for inspiration in his portrayal.

In this film Kevin Kline plays a midwestern teacher, Howard
Brackett, whose star pupil, Cameron Drake (Matt Dillon), wins
a nationally televised award and thanks his "gay" teacher,
Mr. Brackett. Suddenly Brackett's entire life is thrown into small-
town chaos. It seems that everyone in town seems to know that
Brackett is gay, everyone but Brackett that is.

Although Howard is fastidious, fussy, and a die-hard Barbara
Streisand fanatic, he has yet to explore his own sexuality. Now that
he is thrust into the national spotlight, his past, present, and future
all collide with comic results. As he publicly denies his gayness, he
also begins to doubt his straightness. One of the funniest scenes

involves Howard listening to a "butch it up" style self-help tape. It is a routine right out of a Goofy cartoon.

When Howard instantly becomes a nationally known character, an openly gay television reporter named Peter Malloy (Tom Selleck) shows up to get the story, and he does all he can to convince Brackett to come out of the closet. When Selleck plants a big kiss on Klein's mouth, poor Howard Brackett doesn't know what to think.

Speaking of not knowing what to think, his "fiancée," Emily (Joan Cusack) is truly left in the dark. Gee, and she thought that Howard not wanting to have sex with her until they were married was so charming and respectful.

The supporting cast in this charming and very funny film are especially key to its success. Debbie Reynolds, as Bernice, Howard's surprised mother, is perfect. And, as the hapless principal at Howard's school, Tom Halliwell, Bob Newhart is comically nonplussed.

Included on the musical soundtrack for *In & Out* are a fun mixture of hit makers and gay icons including Ethel Merman ("Everything's Coming up Roses"), Diana Ross ("I Will Survive"), Patsy Cline ("Crazy"), and Village People ("Macho Man").

Cast:

Kevin Kline	Howard Brackett
Joan Cusack	Emily Montgomery
Tom Selleck	Peter Malloy
Matt Dillon	Cameron Drake
Debbie Reynolds	Berniece Brackett
Wilford Brimley	Frank Brackett
Bob Newhart	Tom Halliwell
Gregory Jbara	Walter Brackett
Shalom Harlow	Sonya
Shawn Hatosy	Jack
Zak Orth	Mike
Lauren Ambrose	Vicky
Alexandra Holden	Meredith

The Talented Mr. Ripley (1999)

Director: Anthony Minghella

Writer: Anthony Minghella

Original novel: Patricia Highsmith

Awards: Nominated for five Oscars

A deliciously twisted murder mystery, with a homoerotic walk on the wild side, *The Talented Mr. Ripley* is riveting from start to finish. This story is so ripe with murderous delight that Alfred Hitchcock himself would find it irresistible. In fact, novelist Patricia Highsmith is also the authoress who created the book that Hitchcock's classic *Strangers on a Train* was based. It too had gay twists to it. However, in this case, in the late 1990s the gay angle could be confronted face-on, whereas in the 1950s when *Strangers on a Train* was made, its sexual identity twists had to be handled as a subtle undercurrent.

Here we have the story of Tom Ripley (Matt Damon) as a New York City lavatory attendant who spots his golden opportunity to spin a web of lies and deception from which he can benefit. When he borrows a Princeton jacket and plays piano at a posh garden party he chats up a wealthy man, whose son is a recent Princeton grad, and he fabricates a friendship with the man's son, Dickie Greenleaf (Jude Law).

The wealthy father has a business proposition for Tom. What if Tom receives an expense-paid trip to Italy and $1,000 to convince Dickie to return to the States? Tom leaps at the opportunity, and soon he is Europe-bound. Basking in the sumptuous Italian setting, he ingratiates himself to Dickie, and Dickie's highly cultured fiancée Marge Sherwood (Gwyneth Paltrow). There is undeniable homosexual chemistry between Tom and Dickie. However, when Dickie's interest in Tom wanes, scorned potential lover Tom murders Dickie; that's when the plot intrigue really begins to spin.

Hooked on this new European lush life that he is now leading, Dickie finds himself caught in a dense labyrinth of lies. As one lie leads to the next, Tom finds himself having to fabricate more lies to substantiate the first one and to hide the fact that he is now a murderer. This is a delightfully brilliant maze of murder, gay attraction, and lush scenery, layered one upon another. *The Talented Mr. Ripley* is a dazzling film from start to finish. Not only does Tom Ripley get away with seducing male lovers, he also gets away with murder.

Cast:

Matt Damon	Tom Ripley
Gwyneth Paltrow	Marge Sherwood
Jude Law	Dickie Greenleaf
Cate Blanchett	Meredith Logue
Philip Seymour Hoffman	Freddie Miles
Jack Davenport	Peter Smith-Kingsley
James Rebhorn	Herbert Greenleaf

The Closet [English Title]
Le Placard (French 2001)
Director: Francis Veber
Writer: Francis Veber

Written by Francis Veber, one of the men responsible for *La Cage Aux Folles*, *The Closet* is a very funny twenty-first century gay comedy. Set in a French condom factory, *The Closet* reflects the new millennium stance on homosexuality. The laughs here center around the fact that gays and "metrosexuals" are suddenly considered so "in," that some straight men are willing to pretend to be gay to be "hip."

The central character of *The Closet*, François Pignon (Daniel Auteuil), is such a boring milquetoast man that no one wants to hang out with him. A boring accountant at the condom factory, Pignon has his coworkers laughing behind his back. Furthermore, he overhears coworkers talking about how he is moments away from losing his job. His snotty ex-wife left him and now doesn't even want to talk to him on the telephone. And his teenage son wants absolutely nothing to do with him.

When Pignon's new next-door neighbor, Belone (Michel Aumont), finds him on the terrace of his apartment contemplating suicide, he comes up with a plan. Belone does a little "cut and paste" on a couple of photos, and voila: pix of Pignon in bare-assed chaps being caressed by a male buddy in a gay bar. When the incriminating photos are sent to the president of Pignon's company, his whole power base shifts. Suddenly the company is afraid to fire him for fear that he will sue on the grounds of sexual discrimination.

Instead of firing him, Pignon is now a revered minority at the company. Even his bigoted coworker, Félix Santini (Gérard Depardieu) suddenly courts his favor. When an overzealous public relations officer at the condom factory hatches a scheme for Pignon to ride atop the company's float in the Gay Pride parade—with a giant condom on his head no less, suddenly everyone in his life wants to know what is going on. Even his ex-wife is calling him on the phone, and his son wants to drop by to smoke a joint with him. Pignon has gone from "nerd" to "hip" in everyone's eyes.

A silly and fun comedy of errors, *The Closet* shows that people's sexual perceptions can be changed, bigotry can be dissolved, and what is considered to be scandalous one day, can suddenly be viewed as "hip" and "cool" the next day.

Cast:

Daniel Auteuil	François Pignon
Gérard Depardieu	Félix Santini
Thierry Lhermitte	Guillaume
Michèle Laroque	Mlle. Bertrand
Jean Rochefort	Kopel, the director
Alexandra Vandernoot	Christine
Stanislas Crevillén	Franck
Michel Aumont	Belone, the neighbor
Edgar Givry	Mathieu
Thierry Ashanti	Victor
Armelle Deutsch	Ariane
Michèle Garcia	Madame Santini
Laurent Gamelon	Alba
Vincent Moscato	Ponce
Irina Ninova	Martine

Adam and Steve (2005)

Director: Craig Chester

Writer: Craig Chester

If *National Lampoon* were to do a gay love story, *Adam and Steve* would most likely be it. The biggest milestone in this goofy New York City romantic comedy is the fact that it is able to deal with the homosexual theme in a frank and funny way, which results in a frothy comedy of circumstance and very human silliness. In this clever film, two romantic couples are paralleled with amusing results: one gay couple and one straight couple.

The plot concerns gay men Adam (Craig Chester) and Steve (Malcolm Gets), who have an embarrassing one-night-only sexual encounter in the 1980s. Two decades later they meet up, fall in love, and fail to recognize the fact that they had been disastrous sexual partners years before. Amusingly, their comical straight best friends, Rhonda (Parker Posey) and Michael (Chris Kattan), fall in love as well, giving the title characters riotous heterosexual counterpoints to play against. It is the nature of modern human relationships that becomes the zaniest part of the plot.

Much of the strength in *Adam and Steve* lies in the many plot twists the film has, and in many of the loony supporting characters who people this film. This includes the always-delightful 1986 Academy Award-nominated Sally Kirkland as eccentric spiritual leader, Mary. An ordained minister, Mary performs a commitment ceremony at the end of the film, but we are not going to reveal which couple gets joined.

One of the most groundbreaking aspects of this quirky little film is that the gay characters in it don't have to be the victims, the murderous outlaws, the AIDS patients, or the tragically doomed heroes. They are depicted here as being just as silly and hapless as their heterosexual counterparts. In the seven decades since *These Three* had to be rewritten to become a straight love triangle before it could be shown to the general public, *Adam and Steve* shows that homosexuality is nothing more than a viable lifestyle choice.

Cast:

Malcolm Gets	Steve Hicks
Cary Curran	Cary/Cherry Dazzle
Craig Chester	Adam Bernstein
Parker Posey	Rhonda
Chris Kattan	Michael
Noah Segan	Twink
Sally Kirkland	Mary
Jackie Beat	Herself
Mario Diaz	Orlando
Lisa Frederickson	Fiona
Sandy Martin	Biker Chick

Brokeback Mountain (2005)

Director: Ang Lee

Writers: Larry McMurtry and Diana Ossana

Short Story Writer: Annie Proulx

Awards: Won Oscar for Best Achievement in Directing, Ang Lee

Won Oscar for Best Achievement in Music Written for Motion Pictures, Original Score, Gustavo Santaolalla

Won Best Writing, Adapted Screenplay, Larry McMurtry and Diana Ossana

Award nominations: Nominated Oscar, Best Achievement in Cinematography Rodrigo Prieto

Nominated Oscar, Best Motion Picture of the Year, Diana
Ossana And James Schamus

Nominated Oscar, Best Performance by an Actor in a
Leading Role, Heath Ledger

Nominated Oscar, Best Performance by an Actor in a
Supporting Role, Jake Gyllenhaal

Nominated, Best Performance by an Actress in a Supporting Role, Michelle Williams

In terms of box-office appeal and mainstream theatrical release,
this unabashed gay romantic drama went from being a potentially
small film with only a limited impact, to becoming a major motion
picture winning three Academy Awards, with three of its lead
characters vying for the top acting trophies. It certainly didn't
hurt the film's success that it starred a pair of the sexiest male
actors in the twenty-first century Hollywood roster: Jake Gyllenhaal
and the late Heath Ledger.

A surprisingly frank, touching, and compelling film, *Brokeback
Mountain* is winning on several levels. It is at once a highly sexual
love story, an edgy social commentary, a thoughtful and beautifully
filmed visual epic, and ultimately: a heart-tugging drama.

It is the summer of 1963, and the film's lead characters, Ennis Del
Mar (Ledger) and Jack Twist (Gyllenhaal), are a pair of work-for-hire
sheepherders in a fictional setting in rural Wyoming. Nineteen-year-
old Ennis is engaged to be married the following autumn. He is on
the path to becoming a rancher just like his parents had been.
Unfortunately, he and his sister were orphaned when their mom
and dad perished in a tragic car crash.

Jack Twist is approximately the same age, and his aspirations are
aimed toward becoming the most successful rodeo cowboy alive.
Both young men harbor feelings of being essentially alone in the
world. When they are hired to tend to a herd of sheep for the
summer, they are virtually isolated from the outside world, with
the exception of a weekly shipment of food and provisions. Being
alone for the summer without outside guidance, their loneliness and
sexual desires soon come to the surface, as they become each other's
sole source of emotional—and physical—attention.

The man who originally hired them for their jobs is the typical
macho rancher by the name of Joe Aguirre (Randy Quaid). It is his
instruction that one man was supposed to sleep where the sheep

are, to protect them from wolves and coyotes, and the other man was supposed to position himself at a nearby solitary campsite. However, unexpected cold weather one night facilitates them both remaining in camp around the campfire. For the sake of survival against the freezing elements, and following an ample amount of liquor, Jack entreats his friend Ennis to share the tent with him.

What might have started out as a ploy to stay warm in the tent quickly progresses from "spooning" for body heat, to full-fledged man-on-man sex. Clearly it is Jack who, of the two, is more mentally adjusted to his "gay side." However, what blossoms between the pair is a lifelong emotional bond that time and distance does not diminish.

The summer ends, and the pair remains in contact. Although Ennis carries out his plans to marry his fiancée Alma (Michelle Williams), and the couple has two daughters, part of his heart and his lust still belongs to Jack. It is Jack who remains unmarried the longest, but finally he meets an independent rodeo cowgirl, Lureen (Anne Hathaway), marries her, and accepts a job from his new father-in-law.

It has been four years since their summer of gay sexual awakening, but when Jack gets in touch with Ennis and proposes a Brokeback Mountain fishing trip together, again their affair blossoms. After Alma spies her husband passionately kissing Jack in a lip-locking embrace, she realizes that more than fishing is going on during their recurring "fishing" trips. Eventually Alma divorces Ennis, but the two men don't exactly go off into the sunset together. It is rural America, and there is fear that if they come completely out of the closet, trouble will ensue.

Unfortunately, as secretly as they intend on living their lives, the outside world and the prevailing prejudices of rural America lead to a sudden tragedy. Without giving the plot of the film away, in the final reel, Ennis has an emotionally touching scene that reveals the fact that there has been only one true love in his life, and it is Jack. Homosexual themes aside, *Brokeback Mountain* became one of the most successful and groundbreaking films of 2005, or for that matter, any film of the new century.

Cast:

Heath Ledger	Ennis Del Mar
Jake Gyllenhaal	Jack Twist
Randy Quaid	Joe Aguirre
Valerie Planche	Waitress
David Trimble	Basque

Victor Reyes	Chilean Sheepherder #1
Lachlan Mackintosh	Chilean Sheepherder #2
Michelle Williams	Alma
Larry Reese	Jolly Minister
Marty Antonini	Timmy
Tom Carey	Rodeo Clown
Dan McDougall	Bartender #1
Don Bland	Biker #1
Steven Cree Molison	Biker #2
Anne Hathaway	Lureen Newsome
Michael Panes	Lou
Jennifer Echols	Triage Nurse
Jack Guzman	Security Guard
Chris Kattan	Michael
Sergio Rubini	Inspector Roverini
Philip Baker Hall	Alvin MacCarron
Celia Weston	Aunt Joan
Rosario Fiorello	Fausto
Stefania Rocca	Silvana
Ivano Marescotti	Colonnello Verrecchia
Anna Longhi	Signora Buffi
Alessandro Fabrizi	Sergeant Baggio

The Bubble (2006)

Director: Eytan Fox

Writers: Eytan Fox and Gal Uchovsky

An ambitious, engrossing, and thoroughly fascinating Israeli film, *The Bubble* follows the lives of a group of young people in modern-day Tel Aviv. It starts when a handsome Israeli soldier by the name of Noam (Ohad Knoller) is doing a stint of duty at a checkpoint on the Palestine border. It is there that he first lays eyes upon a handsome Palestinian man by the name of Ashraf (Yousef "Joe" Sweid). Little does he know at the time, but it becomes a life-changing occurrence.

When a pregnant Palestinian woman goes into labor at the border, Noam comes to her aid. However, in doing so, he loses his ID card. When Ashraf finds it, he reads the address on the card, and he comes to return the card to where Noam lives. He meets Noam's roommates, a gay man named Yelli (Alon Friedman) and a straight woman named Lulu (Daniela Virtzer). It isn't long before Asraf and Noam begin a gay love affair, and their lives intertwine.

The film's title, *The Bubble*, refers to the bubble of safety that Noam and Ashraf exist in, within the protective walls of Noam's apartment. When they are there together they can openly share their love. For Palestinian Ashraf, gay sex is strictly forbidden. For Israeli citizen Noam, sleeping with a member of his political and religious foe is radically taboo. Yet, when they are alone together in bed, they find that love can bridge the abyss of the world.

Meanwhile, Lulu is something of a political activist, who is involved in a rave party for the cause of peace. All three of her gay male friends—Ashraf, Yelli, and Noam—help her to organize it. However, as the story unfolds, the viewer is left questioning whether the love that Noam and Ashraf share forms an alliance of peace, or will the political conflicts between their countries prove an insurmountable obstacle?

A highly modern and thought-provoking film, *The Bubble* is entertaining, controversial, and surprisingly enjoyable to watch. It also has a surprising twist at the end.

Ohad Knoller	Noam
Yousef "Joe" Sweid	Ashraf
Daniela Virtzer	Lulu
Alon Friedman	Yelli
Zohar Liba	Golan
Tzion Baruch	Shaul
Oded Leopold	Sharon
Roba Blal	Rana, Ashraf's Sister
Shredi Jabarin	Jihad
Yael Zafrir	Orna
Noa Barkai	Ella
Yotam Ishay	Chiki
Eliana Bakier	Dalfi
Avital Barak	Dana

Chapter 8

Take a Walk on the Wild Side: Important Gay Rock Songs

Rock songs have tackled edgy themes since the birth of rock & roll in the 1950s. Rock was always supposed to be a bit controversial, and ever since Elvis Presley crooned to a fellow cellmate/"jailbird" on his 1956 song "Jailhouse Rock," there has been a bit of double-entendre contained in several of rock's greatest hits.

Naturally, the gender-bending early 1970s brought in a new wave of bisexual and homosexual awareness to the rock & roll arena. Song's like Bowie's "Boys Keep on Swinging," Mott the Hoople's "All the Young Dudes," Alice Cooper's "Muscle of Love," and Tim Curry's "Sweet Transvestite" from *The Rocky Horror Picture Show*, threw the spotlight onto gay life in a whole new way.

In this chapter, we explore some obvious songs about sex, like Frankie Goes to Hollywood's "Relax," and LaBelle's "Going Down Makes Me Shiver," and we unearth some little-known gay facts about some of the most seemingly mainstream songs.

PETER ALLEN: "Bi-Coastal"
> Written by: Peter Allen, David Foster, and Tom Keane
> 1980 A&M Records
> From the album: *Bi-Coastal*

Peter Allen was a wildly energetic, magnetically compelling, clever singer/songwriter who dazzled audiences whenever he performed. He was the first husband of Liza Minnelli, which no one seems to be able to explain, and he was also gay.

In the early 1960s, Peter and his friend, Chris Bell, had a duet act, singing as the Allen Brothers. They appeared on the television show

American Bandstand in 1960, and had a hit single in their native Australia. By 1964, their big musical career fizzled, and they found themselves as a lounge act in Hong Kong. According to legend, that is where Judy Garland caught their act and brought them back to London to be her opening act.

Marrying Judy's daughter, Liza Minnelli in 1967 immediately thrust Peter into the spotlight. However, their marriage lasted just two years. In 1969, he left both Liza and Chris to launch his solo act. From that time forward, Peter remained in New York City where he became a songwriter. His first big hit came when Olivia Newton-John recorded his composition "I Honestly Love You."

While other people turned his songs into hits, Peter became a flamboyant stage performer, and his shows were excitingly extravagant events. Some of the crowning achievements of his career were his shows at Radio City Music Hall, in which he even put the renowned chorus girls, the Rockettes, in his act. His tongue-in-cheek song "Bi-Coastal" could have been entitled "Bi-Sexual," because that is what the content of the song is about. In it Allen sings that he cannot decide who he loves more, the California "girls" on television, or the East Coast "boys" on Broadway.

His AIDS-related death in 1992 robbed the entertainment world of a talented songwriter who left behind a wealth of songs including "I Go to Rio," "Don't Cry Outloud," "I'd Rather Leave While I'm In Love," and his Academy Award-winning "Arthur's Theme," in which he sings of getting caught between the moon and New York City. In 2003 Hugh Jackman portrayed Peter Allen on Broadway in the award-winning tribute to the singer/songwriter, *The Boy From Oz*.

THE BEATLES: "You've Got to Hide Your Love Away"
Written by: John Lennon and Paul McCartney
1965 Capitol Records
From the album: *Help!*

In 1965 one would never suspect that this song from The Beatles' million-selling Number One album, the soundtrack for *Help!*, was actually about the quartet's gay manager, Brian Epstein. Several sources claim this was John Lennon's way of tweaking Epstein's dilemma of having to proceed secretly with his sex life.

Epstein had a crush on Lennon, and often longed for Beatle John to respond to his obvious attraction. John never did reciprocate the

affection that Epstein lavished on him. Even though Lennon unmer-
cifully teased Epstein about being gay, they were also good friends.

In 1963, following the birth of John and Cynthia Lennon's son,
Julian, John had gone with Brian on a twelve-day holiday to Spain.
However, when he returned to London, he found that there were all
sorts of rumors at The Beatle's management office that he had gone
off to have an affair with Brian in Spain. Lennon was livid to hear
that these rumors were circulating.

Apparently, writing "You've Got to Hide Your Love Away" about
Brian wasn't the only time Lennon and he clashed on the point of
Epstein's secret sexuality. According to Ray Coleman's 1984 biogra-
phy, *Lennon*, when Epstein penned his own autobiography under the
title *A Cellarful of Noise*, Lennon began snidely referring to it publicly as "*A Cellarful of Boys*." (27)

DAVID BOWIE: "Rebel Rebel"
> Written by: David Bowie
>
> 1974 RCA Records
>
> From the album: *Diamond Dogs*

A full overview of David Bowie's notorious pansexuality is discussed earlier in this book. However, we need to point out that the
whole 1974 *Diamond Dogs* album was recorded from the stance of
"gender bending."

When David sings of this rebel of a boy, he also sings that the lad
has torn his dress, and that his face is a mess. Clearly it's time for a
new shot of make-up and glitter. Furthermore, the young man's poor
mother has a hard time figuring out whether he's a boy or a girl.
Why not just let him be a little bit of both?

DAVID BOWIE: "Boys Keep on Swinging"
> Written by: David Bowie and Brian Eno
>
> 1979 RCA Records
>
> From the album: *Lodger*

On this song from Bowie's final album of the 1970s, he goes out
on a bisexual highpoint. The song "Boys Keep on Swinging" finds
David extolling the merits of being a boy. Most notably: other boys
check you out when they see you on the street.

To further drive his point home, in the video that accompanies this song, Bowie dresses up as not one, but three separate drag queens, all three of whom appear on the split screen ending the song. One of the "drag Davids" wears a flared 1950s style patterned skirt, the second one is a vamp, and the third one is a matronly blonde. Nobody does bad drag better than Bowie, and at the end of the video all three of them pull off their wigs and smear their lipstick with the back of their hands. Such a pretty dress. Such a pretty mess!

GARTH BROOKS: **"We Shall Be Free"**
                          Written by: Stephanie Brooks and Garth Brooks
                          1992 Capitol Records
                          From the album: *The Chase*

Although this seems like an odd song to be included on this list, especially since the country music world has been traditionally homophobic, it deserves very honorable mention here. First of all, Garth Brooks has always marched to his own drummer. He is actually more of a rocker with country and cowboy leanings than he is a product of Nashville. Furthermore, his own sister, Betsy, is an "out" lesbian whose voice is often heard on his records.

So, it comes as no surprise that when he released this cheery anthem-like song of self-expression, it seemed innocuous and harmless on the outside. However, when Garth produced a video for the song, and it depicted black people, white people, Asian people, gay men, and lesbians, in a "could-we-all-just-love-each-other-without-prejudice?" sort of way, country radio freaked out and refused to play the song. Furthermore, when Garth was scheduled to play at the *Superbowl* halftime show on January 31, 1993, NBC-TV refused to play the video either, although Brooks insisted that they do so. Ultimately, he won his case, and gay and lesbian groups saluted him for standing up and holding his ground, regardless of what the controversy caused him in the country community.

The controversy seemed to help the single, which made it up to Number 12 on the Country Chart, and the album it came from, *The Chase*, hit Number One on the *Billboard* Hot 200 Albums chart. Brooks reveled in the fact that the video caused such a stir that it went on to win Video of the Year at the 1993 Academy of Country Music Awards.

BRONSKI BEAT: **"Smalltown Boy"**

Written by: Jimmy Somerville, Larry Steinbachek, and Steve Bronski

1984 MCA Records

From the album: *Age of Consent*

When the group Bronski Beat first released their *Age of Consent* album, and their hit single, "Smalltown Boy" in 1984, they became the first mainstream rockers to admit that they were all openly gay. Their danceable song about a gay boy running away from a small town and into the big city was instantly compelling. The song ultimately made it up to Number 48 on the U.S. charts. The accompanying video starred the lead singer, Jimmy Somerville, who was depicted as being persecuted for being gay in the small town, and then finds himself amidst the urban sprawl of very permissive London.

ALICE COOPER: **"Muscle of Love"**

Written by: Michael Bruce and Alice Cooper

1973 Warner Brothers Records

From the album: *Muscle of Love*

Alice Cooper [aka Vince Furnier] may be a heterosexual male, but when a man wearing full make-up records an album entitled for his penis, you gotta suspect that something is going on. This title track is aimed right at the "I'm Eighteen" kind of audience whom Alice Cooper had in the palm of his hand. Cooper was at the height of his gender-bendingest phase of his career when this Top-Ten certified gold album, *Muscle of Love*, became the follow-up to his Number One *Billion Dollar Babies* album, which was released that same year. The first line of the title song asks who the "queen" of the locker room is; the one who is currently the "cream of the crop?"

On this particular sex organ anthem, in the lyrics "teenage" Alice ponders his age, hitting puberty, and the fact that he suddenly finds "everything" incredibly "hot." It's pretty obvious that this "queen" of the locker room is up to some homosexual or bisexual adventures.

Alice was on an unbeatable hot streak at the time that *Muscle of Love* was on the charts, and although this album failed to produce a huge hit single, it got a lot of media attention. Originally the album was packaged in a brown corrugated cardboard box, as though it contained illicit material.

Of additional trivial note: this is the one Alice Cooper album that features the campy likes of Liza Minnelli, who provides background vocals on two of the album's tracks.

TIM CURRY: **"Sweet Transvestite"**
Written by: Robert O'Brien
1975 Rhino Records
From the album: *Rocky Horror Picture Show*

At the height of the whole glam rock movement, a London stage show was mounted to capitalize on it. It was called *Rocky Horror Show*. It was such a big hit in England that the show, with its lead star, Tim Curry, was also brought to New York and Los Angeles. Not long afterward, the film version, called *Rocky Horror PICTURE Show* was made, and it has been running in midnight movie theaters ever since.

Actors assuredly choose the roles that they play in front of the cameras, but they have absolutely no control over which roles they are most remembered for by the public. When Curry reprised his stage persona as drag queen mad professor, Frank-N-Furter, he had no idea that it would eclipse every other role he ever played in life. Dressed in a Merry Widow corset, fishnet stockings, and enough make-up to stock a drug store counter, Tim Curry brought this campy, queeny, totally gay take-off on Dr. Frankenstein vividly to life.

Audiences still delight in doing "The Time Warp" to this outlandish film and soundtrack album. The 1970s were literal "drag queen heaven" for cross-dressers, and the song "Sweet Transvestite" is truly their campiest anthem ever.

ROBERTA FLACK: **"Ballad of the Sad Young Men"**
Written by: Frances Landesman
and Thomas J. Wolf, Jr.
1969 Atlantic Records
From the album: *First Take*

When Roberta Flack became the toast of the music world in 1972, the masses had not heard of her, although she had already recorded and released three excellent albums. However, when Clint Eastwood put her 1969 song "The First Time Ever I Saw Your Face" in his hit 1972 film *Play Misty For Me*, she became an "overnight success."

The song "Ballad of the Sad Young Men" is actually from a nearly forgotten musical play from 1959 called *The Nervous Set*. It was all about the beatnik scene in Greenwich Village, and clearly this very touching and hauntingly somber song captures the mood of "the desperate hour" at a gay bar. A song of loneliness, it is about the end of a night for many gay men, who face going home alone.

Flack's success with "The First Time Ever I Saw Your Face" catapulted the *First Take* album to Number One in the United States. While it was on top of the chart for five consecutive weeks, countless record buyers became familiar with this somber gay classic.

FRANKIE GOES TO HOLLYWOOD: **"Relax"**
Written by: Frankie Goes to Hollywood
1984 ZTT Records
From the album: *Welcome to the Pleasure Dome*

When this electrifying song about relaxing and having an orgasm was banned by the BBC in 1984, the song "Relax" instantly hit Number One on the British charts, where it sat for five solid weeks. It sold over a million copies in England alone, and in the United States it made it to Number Ten, and became a pansexual anthem. The album it came from, *Welcome to the Pleasure Dome*, hit Number One in England when it was released later that year, peaking at Number 33 in the United States.

Suddenly, Frankie Goes to Hollywood was a huge mid-1980s hit. And, the quintet's two lead members, Holly Johnson and Paul Rutherford, instantly came out in the press as proudly being gay. There was even a popular t-shirt on the marketplace that year which read in big black letters: "Frankie Say Relax."

BOY GEORGE: **"The Crying Game"**
Written by: Geoff Stephens
1992 SBK/Virgin Records
From the album: *At Worst ... The Best of Boy George and Culture Club*

Although this song was not originally recorded in any sort of a gay context, by the time Boy George got hold of it, the Pet Shop Boys produced it, and it was used as the theme song to the surprise hit 1992 transvestite espionage film *The Crying Game*, it was heard in a whole new context. The first version of the song, in 1964, became a Number Five British hit for Dave Berry. However, this rendition, which made it to Number 22 in Britain, was even more effective.

Boy George first came to fame as the distinctive transvestite lead singer of the 1980s British band who called themselves Culture Club. Defying all odds, America took George and his band to their hearts, and soon both boys and girls were dressing like him. George's most famous quote was heard at the Grammy Awards in 1984, when he announced, "America, you know a good drag queen when you see one."

Boy George recorded this track a decade after his groundbreaking group, Culture Club, swept the globe in 1982 and then broke up in 1987. This song became the peak of Boy George's post-Culture Club solo recording career. In the context of the film, the song perfectly personifies the anguish that was felt by the mysterious transvestite character played by Jaye Davidson.

Having fallen into phases of drug use, and bad times, Boy George [aka, George O'Dowd] enjoyed a career upswing because of this universally touching ballad of love lost. Part of the song's success was that it also resonated true, as heartbreak was something he was obviously familiar with. George's career continues in peaks and valleys, but he will always be remembered as the transvestite singer who would be welcomed into just about everyone's living room as the leader of Culture Club.

ELTON JOHN: "Daniel"
Written by: Elton John and Bernie Taupin
1972 MCA Records
From the album: *Don't Shoot Me, I'm Only the Piano Player*

Daniel is apparently flying tonight on a plane, and Elton is clearly going to miss him—a lot. Although this "Honky Cat" views Daniel as his "brother," it has always sounded very suspiciously like he is in reality a lover who is leaving a heartbroken Elton for Spain. Since this came from a time when Elton was not making any pronouncements about his sex life, it's pretty obvious that he is in fact in love with Daniel. Regardless, the song became a huge Number Two hit for Elton in the United States, and Number Four in the United Kingdom.

Although Taupin later claimed that the inspiration for this song was a blind stranger he once saw at an airport, we think otherwise. The song resonates too deeply as one man's love for another man, as Elton emphatically and convincingly laments that he is going to miss Daniel "soooooo much!"

ELTON JOHN: **"All the Girls Love Alice"**
Written by: Elton John and Bernie Taupin
1973 MCA Records
From the album: *Goodbye Yellow Brick Road*

Elton John and Bernie Taupin were never afraid to court controversy, even as early as 1973. Here Elton sings about all of the young girls being in love with Alice. The album that "All The Girls Love Alice" comes from, *Goodbye Yellow Brick Road*, spent eight weeks at Number One in America. This elaborately packaged two-disc set was released at the absolute height of Elton's international stardom, so the package was his lushest release to date. It came with a fully illustrated booklet by artist Ian Beck. Next to the lyrics for "All the Girls Love Alice" is a drawing of pretty blonde "Alice," flanked by two very tailored looking lesbian school matrons, looking at Alice with an obvious glance of desire. This was Elton's first public acknowledgement of any of the characters in his songs being gay and expressing such blatant homosexual love.

ELTON JOHN: **"Big Dipper"**
Written by: Elton John and Gary Osborne
1978 MCA Records
From the album: *A Single Man*

Like Rainer Werner Fassbinder's outlandish and totally gay "sailors-in-love" film *Querelle* (1982), here we find Elton singing about a friend of his cruising a cute sailor boy who has a "Big Dipper"—which is presumably in his pants. He then proclaims that the sailor has his own eye on his friend's "Big Dipper." The next thing you know, he's "squeezin'" his friend's "Big Dipper." This is a very thinly disguised song about homosexuals cruising the streets with nautically gay abandonment and then having sex at the top of the local amusement park's ferris wheel. "Big Dipper" was included on *A Single Man*, a million-selling platinum album that reached Number 15 in *Billboard* in the United States, and Number Eight in England. This was the first album Elton had done without his longtime lyricist, Bernie Taupin. The album was released after Elton publicly admitted to being "bisexual," so he must have figured "What the hell?" and recorded this blatantly gay song. Hey, sailor!

CHAKA KHAN: **"Free Yourself"**
> Written by: Sami McKinney, Denise Rich, and Warren McRae
>
> 1974 MCA Records
>
> From the album: *To Wong Fu, Thanks for Everything! Julie Newmar* (Movie Soundtrack)

This is another song of liberation and self-actualization, sung in the typically soulful and scorching style of Chaka Khan. Recorded for the transvestite film *To Wong Fu, Thanks for Everything! Julie Newmar*, on "Free Yourself" Chaka let's loose as she dishes out sage advice to "be yourself" and "find yourself" in a whole different pose. Without any heavy messages attached to the lyrics, the song is a marvelous track about gay boys expressing themselves without shame. This is a little-known Chaka classic, and we heartily recommend giving it a listen. Khan sings her heart out on this bouncy and liberating song.

LaBELLE: **"You Turn Me On"**
> Written by: Nona Hendryx
>
> 1974 Columbia Records
>
> From the album: *Nightbirds*

As a trio, by 1974 Patti LaBelle, Nona Hendryx, and Sarah Dash had been singing since they were young girls in the Philadelphia area in the early 1960s as "Patti LaBelle & The Bluebelles." Their two really big hits were "I Sold My Heart to The Junkman" in 1962, and "Down the Aisle" the following year. Originally Cindy Birdsong was in the group as well. However, when Florence Ballard dropped out of The Supremes, Cindy joined Mary Wilson and Diana Ross in that group.

Left as a trio, and managed by music industry maverick Vicki Wickham, Patti LaBelle & The Bluebelles were in a position where it was time to reinvent themselves as a trendsetting triad. As the 1970s began, Wickham orchestrated a new image for the group. Instead of singing classic R&B girl group songs, she pushed them into doing straight rock & roll. They also shortened their name to "LaBelle." They recorded three albums in the early 1970s which featured their expressive versions of rockers like "Wild Horses," "Won't Get Fooled Again," and a searing version of Cat Steven's "Moon Shadow."

In 1974 the trio took things one step beyond, and while wearing glittering and futuristic outfits, they launched their *Nightbirds* album and the mega-hit of their career—"Lady Marmalade," which soared to Number One in America, and Number 17 in the United Kingdom. That landmark album was produced by New Orleans music legend Allen Toussaint. Group member Nona wrote half of the album's tracks. One of the most talented women in rock & roll, Hendryx has been an especially outspoken supporter of gay rights.

One of the songs on this album was the envelope-pushing last track, "You Turn Me On," which has definite gay undertones. On this song, Patti, Nona, and Sarah sing of a lover turning them "on" so much that they "come" just like the "pouring rain." They certainly didn't ever sing anything as frank and liberated as that back in 1962 Philadelphia as The Bluebelles.

This was just the beginning of the group's material having strong homoerotic images. [See the next entry for further developments.]

LaBELLE: "Going Down Makes Me Shiver"
Written by: Nona Hendryx
1976 Columbia Records
From the album: *Chameleon*

Two albums later [see above entry for preclusion to this story], LaBelle was amidst their final full album as a '70s trio. Patti LaBelle, Nona Hendryx, and Sarah Dash were each about to launch solo recording careers following 1976's highly exciting *Chameleon* LP.

On this particular disc, Hendryx composed six of the eight released songs, including the very frank "Going Down Makes Me Shiver." While the above "You Turn Me On" could be construed as a heterosexual love affair, here the girls are singing about "going down" to another person's "river." Do we have to spell this one out? The girls are actively "going down" to this river on this seductive song, we somehow think you can fill in the details from there. Here's a clue: they were not singing of going down on the East River here!

LaBELLE: **"Turn It Out"**
Written by: Shep Pettibone and Steve Feldman
1995 MCA Records
From the album: *To Wong Fu, Thanks for Everything! Julie Newmar* (Movie Soundtrack)

On a rare reunion, Patti LaBelle, Nona Hendryx, and Sarah Dash came together for this tasty dance track for the soundtrack album for *To Wong Fu, Thanks for Everything! Julie Newmar*. A rare reteaming, here the trio finds their voices stronger than ever. This film was America's answer to Australia's Academy Award-winning *The Adventures of Priscilla: Queen of the Desert*, and its three main characters were outrageous drag queens stuck in Midwest farm country. This up-tempo song about dressing up in drag features Patti, Nona, and Sarah in rare form, with Ms. LaBelle adlibbing her make-up tips at the end of song, advising the listener on how to look "fierce."

Sarah Dash laughingly recalls, "We had a ball doing that song for the soundtrack. Shep Pettibone talked us into doing it. From listening to it, you could never tell that we recorded that whole track in Shep's tiny apartment in Queens!" (29) Patti's comments here about lipstick and "pumps" are priceless. What else could LaBelle's campy ode to transvestite drag emerges as?—but nothing-less-than totally "fierce!"

CYNDI LAUPER: **"True Colors"**
Written by: Tom Kelly and Billy Steinberg
1986 Columbia Records
From the album: *True Colors*

Cyndi Lauper is one of the most talented women in rock & roll. Although her "Girl's Just Wanna Have Fun" made her an instant cult figure, with her ever-changing hair—supposedly fashioned from a box of Crayola crayons, and her eccentric thrift store outfits, time-after-time Ms. Cyndi has proven than she is a singer/songwriter, and innovator to be reckoned with.

When the "rainbow" flag became the symbol of gay liberation and acceptance, Cyndi's touching "True Colors" seemed to go brilliantly along with it. In 2007 and 2008, when a gay pride concert series was launched by LOGO television and toured North America, Lauper was aboard for it. It was appropriately dubbed the "True Colors" tour.

The lyrics of the song "True Colors" proclaim of the merit of one being one's own self and letting go of convention. What an appropriate song it still is, especially when sung by the sexually liberated Cyndi Lauper.

CYNDI LAUPER: **"Brimstone and Fire"**
Written by: Cyndi Lauper and Jan Pulsford
1996 Columbia Records
From the album: *Sisters of Avalon*

While her entire career has been one of liberation and self-actualization, Cyndi Lauper has also written and performed songs about gay love, and specifically about lesbian affairs. Although she is well known for whimsical songs, her little-known *Sisters of Avalon* album from 1996 took matters much further.

The title song, "Sisters of Avalon" opens the album with a very sisterly anthem. However, it is the final track on the album, "Brimstone and Fire," that finds Cyndi singing about falling in love with a woman she met at a Laundromat, and playing house with her. The next thing you know, they're making spaghetti and making love. Girls just wanna have fun—indeed!

MADONNA: **"Vogue"**
Written by: Madonna and Shep Pettibone
1990 Sire Records
From the album: *I'm Breathless*

Perpetual "Karma Chameleon" Madonna has reinvented herself so many times at this point that you would think she was one of those shape shifter characters from a rock & roll science fiction movie. The summer she was about to explode on the silver screen in the big budgeted Warren Beatty film, *Dick Tracy*, she needed a sure-fire hit to launch her latest album, which featured her Stephen Sondheim composed songs from the soundtrack album.

She reached into concurrent gay culture to ape the latest transsexual dance craze: "Vogueing." Madonna brilliantly took the craze to new "strike a pose" heights with the video and red hot track to this irresistible song: "Vogue."

Using the dancers from her 1990 *Blonde Ambition* tour on the video, "Lady" Madonna had a huge Number One hit with this song,

and the album it came from, *I'm Breathless* logged in at Number Two
in the United States. Suddenly, every gay boy from West Hollywood
to Greenwich Village was "Vogueing" on the dance floor along with
Madonna.

Furthermore, this was the era in which Madonna was really playing up the implied lesbianism in her act and her music. She and actress Sandra Bernhard were seen on television together flirting
outrageously with each other, and she was just prepping to launch
her outlandish *Sex* picture book (1992), where she was seen in com-
promising poses with men, women, and even a dog or two.

MADONNA: "Justify My Love"
                      Written by: Lenny Kravitz, additional
                      lyrics by Madonna
                      1990 Sire Records
                      From the album: *The Immaculate Collection*

The year 1990 had already been a headline grabbing one for
Madonna, and she finished it off by being banned on MTV for the
video that accompanied this bisexually charged song. Filmed in a
Paris hotel room, Madonna is seen in the video disrobing with
actor Tony Ward, and as he prepares to mount her, she pushes
him away. In the next scene we see a woman in short hair and
heavy eye makeup on top of Madonna, passionately kissing her.
While this is happening, Tony kneels on the side of the bed, obviously getting into watching the lesbian action. As the song progresses, the viewer is also treated to scenes of a female couple
drawing moustaches on each other, male couples in drag fondling
each other, and Madonna watching as Tony—who is tied up in a
chair—gets worked over by a dominatrix who is wearing only sus-
penders as her top. It's a five-minute cavalcade of sex, sex, sex, as
only Madonna could serve it up.

As proven throughout her career, trying to ban Madonna was like
trying to put out a fire with gasoline. The single version of "Justify
My Love" instantly shot up the U.S. song charts to Number One, and
in the United Kingdom it was Number Two.

As soon as the video was banned, clever Madonna stuck a deal to
have the offensive music video marketed commercially to her fans.
Furthermore, the "greatest hits" album that "Justify My Love" was
taken from—*The Immaculate Collection*—hit Number One in England, and stayed on the top of the charts for an astonishing nine

weeks. In the United States it peaked at Number Two and was certified sextuple platinum for six million copies sold.

Gay sex, lesbian sex, any kind of sex: nobody markets it better than Madonna. The money she made from "Justify My Love" justified every move she made, and every breath she took.

MELANIE: "Wear It Like a Flag"
Written by Melanie Safka

1993 Lonestar Records

From the album: *Freedom Knows My Name*

Classic folk singer Melanie, who is most remembered by radio for her 1972 roller skating ode, "Brand New Key," in 1993 penned what is undoubtedly the best gay anthem ever recorded. According to her, she originally intended it to be a simple song of self-realization and free love. However, when she played the song to some of her gay friends, they went crazy for the message behind the song.

On "Wear It Like a Flag," Melanie sings of being proud of loving whomever she wants to love and openly wearing her expression of love like she is dressed in a flag for all to see. Suddenly she realized that it was a colorful gay rainbow flag that she had just draped upon herself.

This absolutely delightful song is performed like a joyous celebration that is embraceable by anyone who hears it, whether gay or straight. On the track, Melanie sounds as joyfully excited as she did when she recorded her huge hit, "Candles in the Rain" in 1970 about being one of the stars of the famed Woodstock Music Festival.

The great thing about this song is that it carries the same "can't-we-all-just-love-each-other?" message that her early 1970s recordings—like "Beautiful People"—carried. However, this time around Melanie has gaily ventured into territory where no other Woodstock alumnus has ever gone, and the "Beautiful People" she is singing about are gay and lesbian. If ever there was a perfect gay anthem, this is it!

BETTE MIDLER: "Friends"
Written by: Mark Klingman and Buzzy Linhart

Released: 1972 Atlantic Records

From the Album: *The Divine Miss M*

When Bette Midler first came to national prominence in 1973, she arrived on the scene with a well-developed stage act, and several personas who would be recurring characters in her shows. When one writer asked her how she saw herself, she replied, "I am all my fantasies." She became exactly that, a product of all of her wildest fantasies.

The legend of her road to stardom was highly publicized, as were stories of her days at the infamous gay bathhouse, the Continental Baths on the Upper West Side of Manhattan. It was there, with Barry Manilow as her piano player, that she first became the bawdy den mother to all of those gay boys in towels who came to catch her act.

She explained of her days at the Continental playing to an all-gay audience, "The Baths is a male health club in New York. It's kind of kitschy, decorated to death. And on Friday and Saturday nights, they have the distinction of being one of the only health clubs in the world that has entertainment. It's like a lounge. They pack these guys in, on the floor, in chairs, in their bathrobes or towels or whatever, and they just watch the show and enjoy themselves. Working at the Baths allowed me a chance to really stretch out and grow in a way I had not been able to before. I was able to work with a piano player and a drummer every week and I didn't have to pay for it. And I had a big built-in captive audience. I mean, where were they going to go? They were practically naked." (30) In 1972, the newly liberated gay New York audience needed a diva/goddess to call their own, and it was Bette Midler.

She would sing old Andrews Sisters songs, and rock & roll camp classics like "Da Doo Ron Ron." Bette also had her own anthems. The song "Friends" was her theme song. The song itself was written for her by Mark "Moogy" Klingman and Buzzy Linhart. The lyrics of the song proclaim that one has to have "friends" to get through life. It was the perfect song of gay life, an existence where one's friends become one's family.

As her fame took her from the Continental Baths to Radio City Music Hall and the Palace Theater on Broadway, she took the song "Friends" with her, and her gay audience came to expect it to be in her act. She never disappointed her fans, and to this day the song "Friends" is as much a part of her history and legend, as Bette's devoted gay following.

BETTE MIDLER: **"My Knight in Black Leather"**
                  Written by: Jerry Ragovy and Estelle Levitt
                  Released: 1979 Atlantic Records
                  From the Album: *Thighs and Whispers*

After her first burst of stardom, as her alter ego "The Divine Miss M," Bette Midler continued to delve into cutting-edge songs that would tickle and delight the same gay audience that had made her a star to begin with. She had, and has a brilliant formula by which all of her albums are plotted. She can sing bawdy, sex-charged songs as one track, and then the next song on the album might be an emotional ballad that deeply touches your heart. Her 1979 LP, *Thighs and Whispers*, too followed this delightfully schizophrenic formula.

As her bawdiest song offering on *Thighs and Whispers*, came the very gay, and very campy cut, "My Knight in Black Leather." Other than another biker chick, who else but a gay man who was "into leather," could this song be about?

The lyrics to the song are an absolute riot, especially when Bette sings about her new leather-clad lover, proclaiming that he "smells" just like "a new car." Dressed in leather chaps, leather boots, and a leather vest, this is the ultimate "Leatherman" song, and so totally gay.

JONI MITCHELL: "Two Grey Rooms"
                            Written by: Joni Mitchell
                            Released: 1991 Geffen Records
                            From the Album: *Night Ride Home*

Joni Mitchell has never been afraid to speak her mind when it comes to life, love, or her politics. She is also a damn good storyteller. Her reputation was built on her ability to take pieces of her own life and turn them into some of the most personal lyrics ever recorded. In her landmark *Blue* album she not only wrote about her love affairs with Graham Nash and with James Taylor, she also wrote about the baby she had to give up for adoption in the 1960s: "Little Green."

On her 1991 album, *Night Ride Home*, Joni was telling other people's stories as well. Speaking of the gay-themed song "Two Grey Rooms," she explained that she had written the music seven years before she recorded it. She wasn't sure what the lyrics were going to be about, but suddenly she heard a bittersweet tale of gay love that touched her, and it became "Two Grey Rooms." According to her, "I finally found a story in some magazine about a German aristocrat, a homosexual and a friend of [film director Rainer Warner] Fassbinder who had a lover in his youth that he never got over. He lost track of him for many years. One day he discovered that his old flame was working on the docks. He moved out of his fancy digs and into a couple of dingy rooms that overlooked the route where, with his hard hat and his lunch pail, his ex-lover walked to work. He lived to glimpse him twice a day, coming and going. He never approached him." (28)

"Two Grey Rooms" is a touching masterpiece of a song, which deserves and receives an effective and absolutely poignant treatment by this "Lady of the Canyon." The whole album *Night Ride Home* is one of Joni's best ever, and this particular song about a gay love lost, is sensitive and haunting.

JONI MITCHELL: "Tax Free"
> Written by: Joni Mitchell and Larry Klein
>
> Released: 1985 Geffen Records
>
> From the Album: *Dog Eat Dog*

In a glittering recording career that has spanned five decades, *Dog Eat Dog* was the one album where Joni divided her crowd in half. Fans of her more folky stylings had a problem with the fact that this was her "new wave"/electronica album, with Thomas Dolby ["You Blinded Me With Science"] as a creative consultant/coproducer. Others loved this album as a bit of stylish stretching out for her.

On the song "Tax Free," which criticized the hypocrisy of televangelists like Jimmy Swaggart and James Baker, Joni thumbs her nose at them, claiming that she is going to go out dancing with "the drag queens" and the "punks." To drive her anti-"Religious Right" point even further in this song, she has actor Rod Steiger doing an over-the-top mock televangelist monologue. Joni has always appreciated her devoted gay fans, and this song and 'Two Grey Rooms" are her salute to them.

MOTT THE HOOPLE: "All the Young Dudes"
> Written by: David Bowie
>
> Released: 1972 Columbia Records
>
> From the Album: *All the Young Dudes*

Released at the height of the glam rock phase, the song "All the Young Dudes" went on to become the anthem of the movement, and placed Mott the Hoople at its apex. The band, with its lead singer Ian Hunter, was on the verge of disbanding when David Bowie came into the picture, with a deal to revitalize their career: he wanted to produce their next album. When they agreed, Bowie made good on his promise and in doing so, he gave them the biggest LP of their entire career.

Originally, Bowie had come to the band and offered them a song he had just composed called "Suffragette City," but they turned it down, choosing instead "All the Young Dudes." The minute it came out, it was a radio smash, peaking at Number 37 in the United States. At one point Hunter sings that he wants to race a "cat" to bed, and in the "fade" of the song he claims he wants to kiss him. He also sings about his friend, "Billy," who dresses like "a queen." The album the hit came from, also entitled *All the Young Dudes*, contained several songs of an equally gender-bending sexual nature. On the song "Jerkin Crocus," Hunter sings of enticing someone to "lick" his "ice cream cone."

WILLIE NELSON: "Cowboys Are Secretly, Frequently
(Fond of Each Other)"
Written by: Ned Sublette
2006 iTunes Originals/Lost Highways Records
Download Only

There are few people in country music, let alone the entire music business, who couldn't care less what Nashville, let alone the rest of the music industry thinks of him. Willie Nelson has been the subject of controversy several times in his career, and he regularly thumbs his nose at convention. Although he is not gay himself, Willie has always stood up for righteousness and nonconformity. That is why, on Valentine's Day 2006, he debuted his unquestionably gay song, "Cowboys Are Secretly, Frequently (Fond of Each Other)," on the most controversial radio show he could choose, *The Howard Stern Show* on the Sirius Radio Network.

While in America, the public debate about the rights for homosexual marriage was blazing at its brightest, the film *Brokeback Mountain* was released. Willie contributed one of the many songs on the movie soundtrack: his version of The Byrds' "He Was a Friend of Mine." The song "Cowboys Are Secretly, Frequently (Fond of Each Other)," was written by Ned Sublette in 1981 and had been floating around for a while. Meanwhile, twenty-five years later Willie felt that the time was right for him to record and release his own version of the song.

In 2004, Willie Nelson's longtime friend and tour manager for thirty years, David Anderson, announced to Willie that he was gay. Nelson decided that the best way to tell David that this disclosure was fine with him was to record this song.

According to Anderson, "This song obviously has special meaning to me in more ways than one, I want people to know more than anything—gay, straight, whatever—just how cool Willie is and . . . his way of thinking, his tolerance, everything about him." (31)

Willie Nelson continues to be someone who has always stood for human rights, and has always marched to his own drummer. He also filmed an amusing video to support the song, which costarred his friend, film star Burt Reynolds. Kudos to both of them for taking such a "no apologies" stand for gay rights. Country radio may have thought that Willie personified the embodiment of his song "Crazy," but with "Cowboys Are Secretly, Frequently (Fond of Each Other)" he became a hero to gay cowboys everywhere! Randy Jones plans to include his version on an upcoming CD.

LOU REED: "Walk on the Wild Side"
              Written by: Lou Reed
              1972 RCA Records
              From the album: *Transformer*

A full discussion of the lyrics of this song can be found in the Lou Reed section of this book. In 1972, with David Bowie producing the track and the album, at the height of the glam rock phase, this song was irresistible to listen to, and was all about the gay "gender bending" that was going on at Andy Warhol's notorious Factory in New York City.

One of the most delightful aspects of this song about drag queens and hustlers, is Reed's commanding his background girls—the "colored girls"—to sing their hearts out. They beautifully complied. This was the first undeniably gay drag queen song to ever hit the American record charts. It is still a rock & roll radio classic to this very day.

TOM ROBINSON BAND: "Glad to Be Gay"
                      Written by: Tom Robinson
                      1977 Razon & Tie Records
                      From the album: *Power in
                      the Darkness*

An active member of the 1970's Rock Against Racism organization, Tom Robinson prided himself in being outspoken, and in being gay. A firebrand for gay liberation, this song became his career-long anthem. Although the album containing "Glad to be Gay"—*Power in the Darkness*—only made it up to Number 144 on the *Billboard* charts in America, Robinson made a name for himself, and for his cause with this "say it loud and say it proud" song.

DIANA ROSS: "I'm Coming Out"
   Written by: Nile Rodgers and Bernard Edwards
   1980 Motown Records
   From the album: *Diana*

Miss Ross was looking for a new direction in her music in 1980, and by going in the recording studio with the two masterminds of the disco group Chic—Nile Rodgers and Bernard Edwards—she found it. "I'm Coming Out" was an instant smash in the gay dance clubs when it was released that year. It became one of Diana's biggest hits of her post-Supremes days, reaching Number Five in the United States.

RuPAUL: "Supermodel (You Better Work)"
   Written by: RuPaul, Larry Tee, and Jimmy Harry
   1993 Tommy Boy Records
   From the album: *Supermodel of the World*

In the early 1990s, when the outrageously tall drag queen calling himself/herself "RuPaul" first burst onto the scene, he did so with such panache and élan, that some television viewers were shocked to find out that he was actually a man. A real glamour queen, transvestite RuPaul had a brief but notable recording career that decade. His one hit was the Number 24 peaking tongue-in-cheek classic "Supermodel (You Better Work)."

RuPaul's other recorded hit was his campy teaming with Elton John. The pair sang "Don't Go Breaking My Heart" on Elton's winning 1993 *Duets* album.

SISTER SLEDGE: "We Are Family"
   Written by: Nile Rodgers and Bernard Edwards
   1979 Cotillion/Atlantic Records
   From the album: *We Are Family*

The quartet of singing siblings, Sister Sledge, were undeniably talented when they signed with Cotillion Records in the mid-1970s. However, their first recordings lacked snap and panache. When they were wisely teamed up with the boys from the disco group Chic—Nile Rodgers and Bernard Edwards—it instantly hooked them up with just the kind of juicy material the girls had previously lacked. While on one hand, "We Are Family" is an autobiographical song about the four sisters themselves, it also rang true for the gay community. It has been an appealing anthem ever since it hit Number Three on the American music charts in 1979. A disco hit, and a gay classic, "We Are Family" still sounds as fresh and appealing three decades after it was originally recorded.

LUTHER VANDROSS: "If I Didn't Know Better"
Written by: Luther Vandross, Reed
Vertelney, and Ezekiel Lewis
2003 J Records
From the album: *Dance With My Father*

Although Luther Vandross never publicly admitted that he was gay, everyone in the music business knew that he was. He was so brilliant at singing love songs, that in so many instances, it didn't matter what gender he was singing to, he was so talented and so appealing that it was a moot point. His 2003 recording of "If I Didn't Know Better" is all about when the line blurs between two people being friends, and the same two people suddenly becoming lovers. In this song, especially, it seems highly suspicious that the person who seems to be in love with Luther, is another man. While Luther admits that he is a "friend" and "brother" to this other person, clearly, if he "didn't know better," this other person loves him much deeper than they previously admitted.

Well, if we didn't know better, we'd swear that this is a totally gay song!

VILLAGE PEOPLE: "Fire Island"
Written by: Jacques Morali, Henri Belolo,
Phil Hurt, and Peter Whitehead
1977 Casablanca Records
From the album: *Village People*

For many decades, the two beach communities of Cherry Grove and The Pines on Fire Island have been summer enclaves of the gay community. This song was Village People's way of saluting that sandbar of sun and fun. One of the most amusing aspects of this song is the chorus warning about going into "the bushes," a notorious thicket of vegetation known for clandestine sexual trysts.

VILLAGE PEOPLE: "**Hot Cop**"
                     Written by: Jacques Morali, Henri Belolo,
                     and Victor Willis
                     1978 Casablanca Records
                     From the album: *Cruisin'*

Sometimes naughty boys just need to be handcuffed! And sometimes, it's a "hot cop" who is doing it. It is acknowledged that some gay men "get off" on the whole uniform trip. And, what could be more uniform-oriented that a handsome man in full police regalia? In the group Village People, the lead singer played this role. The first one was Victor Willis, who was replaced by Ray Simpson. In 1982, Miles Jaye replaced Ray for the Europe-only album *Sex Over the Phone*. Then Ray rejoined the group in 1988. If you are going to have Village People, you have to have a "Hot Cop."

VILLAGE PEOPLE: "**I Am What I Am**"
                     Written by: Jacques Morali, Henri Belolo,
                     and Peter Whitehead
                     1978 Casablanca Records
                     From the album: *Macho Man*

This was the group's earliest "gay liberation" song. It extols of the merits of being one's self, and this includes, but is not limited to being gay or lesbian or transgender, or wearing peacock feathers on your head, as long as you aren't hurting anyone else. These lyrics are words to live by!

VILLAGE PEOPLE: "**I'm a Cruiser**"
                     Written by: Jacques Morali, Henri Belolo,
                     and Victor Willis
                     1978 Casablanca Records
                     From the album: *Cruisin'*

For anyone who has lived under a rock for the last three decades, "cruising" is driving or walking down the street, and checking out a member of the same sex, with the idea of "picking them up" for some fun. This song has nothing to do with playing shuffleboard on the deck of a cruise ship. That is a totally different kind of cruising!

VILLAGE PEOPLE: **"In the Navy"**
Written by: Jacques Morali, Henri Belolo, and Victor Willis
1979 Casablanca Records
From the album: *Go West*

This song from Village People extols of all the benefits of being in the Navy. "Where can you find pleasure, search the world for treasure, learn science, technology?" The history of the world's navies is one of many men on ships at sea for long periods of time with no women. Not unlike the environments that exist in other all-male populations like prisons, except on ship personal behavior is not quite as closely monitored. We are not saying that all sailors are gay, just maybe some. How does one in ten sound? This is one of Village People's most pointedly tongue-in-cheek songs, indeed. Ahoy matey!

VILLAGE PEOPLE: **"Key West"**
Written by: Jacques Morali, Henri Belolo, and Peter Whitehead
1978 Casablanca Records
From the album: *Macho Man*

Like Fire Island, New York, and Provincetown, Massachusetts; Key West, Florida has long been a well-known gay-friendly resort. Hell, when Florida seceded from the Union in the Civil War, Key West remained in the Union. That's how different-thinking that southern-most island of the Continental United States is, and historically has always been.

VILLAGE PEOPLE: **"Liberation"**
Written by: Jacques Morali, Peter Whitehead, and Phil Hurt
1980 Casablanca Records
From the album: *Can't Stop the Music*

This was Village People's second foray of recording a gay liberation theme song. This song from the soundtrack of *Can't Stop the Music* preached tolerance, not judgment. In a way, that is what Village People have always stood for as well.

VILLAGE PEOPLE: **"Macho Man"**
Written by: Jacques Morali, Henri Belolo,
and Peter Whitehead
1978 Casablanca Records
From the album: *Macho Man*

"Macho Man" was the perfect personification song for the group Village People. It was the trademark, the theme song, and the ideal description of how the six characters in Village People were conceived and executed.

VILLAGE PEOPLE: **"Y.M.C.A"**
Written by: Jacques Morali, Henri Belolo,
and Victor Willis
1978 Casablanca Records
From the album: *Cruisin'*

The single only made it to Number 24 in the United States, but it stayed on the music charts for an incredible sixty-nine weeks.

If we had to pick one single Village People song that has complete universality, it is "Y.M.C.A." No rock & roll wedding band is worth its salt if it can't play "Y.M.C.A.," and it is as irresistibly as much fun to listen to as it was the day it was recorded.

As a hit single, it made it to Number One in the United Kingdom, and to Number Three in the United States.

THE WHO: **"Fiddle About"**
Written by: John Entwistle
1969 MCA Records
From the album: *Tommy*

The plot of The Who's rock opera masterpiece, *Tommy*, is so imaginative and so off-the-wall that one must simply suspend all logic while listening to it, or for-that-matter while watching the all-star film that was made of it. Young Tommy, the deaf, mute, and blind boy who becomes a "Pinball Wizard" has to encounter some bizarre behavior in his world of silence and darkness. One of the most confusing things that he endures is being molested by his crazy and perverted Uncle Ernie. "Fiddle About" is Uncle Ernie's song in *Tommy*, and it was played in the 1975 film of the same name, by The Who's bisexual drummer, the late and loony Keith Moon. Regardless of gender issues, Uncle Ernie is clearly every parent's babysitter nightmare. Fiddle about! Fiddle about!

MARY WILSON: "Red Hot"
> Written by: Frank Busey and John Duarte
> 1979 Motown Records
> From the album: *Mary Wilson*

When Mary Wilson left The Supremes in 1977 to pursue a solo career, after being the centerpiece of the ultimate girl-group, she aimed her first full album right at the boys in the discotheques, who were amongst her staunchest supporters. The song "Red Hot" was the way that every gay boy on the disco dance floors felt about themselves, so that is no wonder that she debuted the song at the Manhattan disco nightclub: New York New York. Both Randy Jones and Mark Bego were in the audience that night.

As far as the gay community is concerned, Mary Wilson was always "red hot" as a Supreme, as a person, and as a supporter of gay causes. This was the prefect single to launch her solo career, and it was a disco hit for her on Motown Records.

According to Mary Wilson, "I was especially happy when the single 'Red Hot' became very popular with the fans from Fire Island to Key West. I heard it in the clubs wherever I went, from Studio 54 to Studio One." (32) Miss Mary: You are "red hot!"

Chapter 9

As the World Turns

In his career spanning four decades, before, with, and since Village People, Randy has become an American Music Award winner, a multi-platinum recording artist (selling in excess of 100 million units), an actor on television, on film, and on stage, as well as the original cowboy and one of the founding members of Village People. He continues in his career as an actor, singer, and dancer begun before Village People.

His latest solo CD, *Ticket to the World*, was released in 2007, to rave reviews.

Syndicated columnist Liz Smith has said: "Who, among all of the Village People, did you think might become a solo star? My choice was always Randy Jones!" The notorious TMZ.com website put it this way: "Randy Jones can turn the world on with his smile." The Insider.com simply stated: "Randy Jones is Amazing!"

Randy continues to perform his own solo concerts worldwide, where he has appeared before such diverse audiences as a Royal Command Performance to Trump's Taj Mahal in Atlantic City to a 2005 inaugural ball performance in Washington, DC. Mark Bego wrote of his 2005 Atlantic City Taj Mahal performance for *People* magazine: "The real treat of the evening was the appearance of Randy Jones, best known as the original Cowboy from the hit-making group Village People. The evening marked the major debut of Jones' new concert performance. Seen on film, television, and stage since his 1991 exit from the group with whom he made 'Y.M.C.A.,' 'Macho Man,' and 'In the Navy' famous, Jones enjoyed a welcome return to prominence. In addition to singing a medley of his Number One hits, Randy also debuted his fresh new single release, 'New York City Boy.' How great it is to see Randy Jones back on stage, looking and sounding better than ever. The full standing ovation he received attested to his popularity among the crowd of more than five thousand disco mavens. Randy's still youthful and handsome looks, his dazzling smile, and his winning personality, made his presence one of the evening's true high points."

In addition, he has appeared onstage in musicals and plays in New York City and elsewhere, including *Joseph and the Amazing Technicolor Dreamcoat, Music Man, Chicago, The Madonna Whore: Confessions of a Dirty Mind, Applause!, Camelot,* and *42nd Street* among many others. Included in the list of motion pictures he has starred in are *Against the Wind* (where he portrays the American president), *The Gentleman, Three Long Years, Beyond the Façade, A Tale About Bootlegging, My Guaranteed Student Loan,* and *Can't Stop the Music.*

He can be seen and heard in various documentaries such as *Roxy: The Last Dance, When Ocean Meets Sky, Disco: Spinning the Story,* VH1's *RockDoc NY77: The Coolest Year in Hell, The Godfather of Disco, Behind the Music,* VH1's *Sex: The Revolution* and others as narrator and interview subject. In 2009, a new video game, *POSTAL 3* will be released in which Jones creates yet another new character, the leader of a gay biker gang, on a Segway!

Meanwhile, a variation of the original group now tours as "Village People" with two and sometimes three original members. After years of ups and downs, original Village People lead singer, Victor Willis, has re-energized his solo performing and recording career, once again appearing as the singing "Cop."

Asked about his unique position as an original Village Person, Jones explains, "I'm the only Village People member to actually live in Greenwich Village. I've had an apartment in the Village since 1975. I couldn't imagine living elsewhere!" (19)

Much has changed in relation to gay issues in the last twenty years. Since 2000, the movement for equal rights in America has seen the scales of justice tilting in both directions. On a tragic note, there was the murder of Matthew Shephard. Says Randy, "There will always be senseless hate crimes in this world. But hopefully public opinions will change if we help to make them change." (19)

Then on the hopeful side of things, as mentioned, several major celebrities have recently "come out" without adverse consequences to their career, including Elton John, Melissa Etheridge, George Michael, Rosie O'Donnell, Lance Bass, Ellen DeGeneres, Rupert Everett, k.d. lang, Clay Aiken, Lindsay Lohan, and even *Star Trek* star George "Sulu" Takei. Randy was invited to appear at Takei's bachelor party on the popular *Howard Stern Show* and to sing for the groom-to-be. He did his personal rendition of a medley of the theme from *The Mary Tyler Moore Show* and "Y.M.C.A." The lighted up switchboards attested to another smash appearance. One of the more fascinating events of the new century came when Randy threw his best ten-gallon cowboy hat into the controversial arena of "same-sex marriage."

On May 7, 2004, Randy married his long-time partner, executive consultant Will Grega, in a high-profile ceremony at the club "Rumor" (the former Gerde's Folk City) in (where else?!) the Village. Mark Bego exuberantly filled the role of "best man" at their wedding. With the issue of "same-sex marriage" used for political expediency by the Republican Party to divide America, Randy took another stand for gay rights. *People* magazine ran an item on his surprise wedding; Jay Leno commented on it for two nights in his monologue on *The Tonight Show*; the couple appeared on the wildly popular "VH-1's Best Week Ever;" and a general media frenzy followed.

The Netherlands legalized same-sex marriage in 2001, with Belgium following in 2003. Spain, Canada, and even Iceland came onboard with similar legalizations in 2005. As of this writing, Massachusetts and California are the only states in the union that have legitimized same-sex marriage in the U.S. On the other hand, Michigan first banned same-sex marriage, then they took a further measure and banned benefits for gay partners or for heterosexual couples who were not married. (10)

As the controversy about "same-sex marriage" rights raged, American President George W. Bush publicly renounced the idea, and threatened to put forth a constitutional amendment banning same-sex unions. In doing so, Bush would have been the first president in American history to propose creating an amendment that would revoke the rights of American citizens, instead of extending or guaranteeing rights. Fortunately, he was unable to create any real traction for the divisive proposal on the federal level.

And then came the phone call . . .

In a moment of unexpected irony, Randy was invited by producer Debra Moreno Lowther to appear at one of the 2005 presidential inaugural balls in Washington, DC, to mark the narrow re-election of George W. Bush. Conflicted, but upon confirming that the inaugural event was one intended to raise money for the support of returning veterans of the Iraq War and not solely to celebrate the victory of a man who is an opponent to the equal marriage rights issue, Jones decided to take the high road and made the appearance anyway, in respect for the office of the president of the United States, and not as an endorsement for Bush's policies. It was an ultimate victory for the Village Cowboy, to sing "Y.M.C.A.," and when the chorus to the well-known song arrived, to see hundreds of the ball gown- and tuxedo-wearing GOP faithful down in front of the stage doing the letters with their hands in the same manner as elementary school children everywhere. What is the state of gay rights in America today? Like the title of one of the earliest Village People songs, says Jones: "I Am What I Am." (19)

Randy Jones will always be associated with the iconic '70s disco music that he recorded and made famous with Village People. It is a legacy of music of which he is perpetually proud. "When someone hears 'Y.M.C.A.' or 'Macho Man,' or any of those great Village People songs, suddenly they smile. Now, that's an incredible legacy to have and to be part of having created. We helped change the world, and to bring our music into homes where gay culture may never have been invited inside otherwise." (19)

Perhaps without the advent of the disco era, and the celebratory music that Village People recorded from 1977 to 1987, the evolution of society would have taken even longer to get to where it is today. And society continues to evolve. According to Randy Jones, "I am proud to have made the contributions to pop culture that I have. I try to live my life in the light, to provide a positive image and to be compassionate to those I meet. While there will always be conflict and friction in society as far as acceptance, tolerance, and sexual issues are concerned, I believe that love and compassion always win out in the end." (19)

Quote Sources

(1) Cowan, Thomas. *Gay Men and Women Who Enriched the World.* Boston: Alyson Publications, 1992.

(2) Evans, Richard J. *Rituals of Retribution: Capitol Punishment in Germany 1600–1987.* Oxford, UK: Oxford University Press, 1996.

(3) Asprey, Robert B. *Frederick the Great: The Magnificent Enigma.* New York: Ficknor and Fields Publishing, 1986.

(4) Statements by Lord Alfred Douglas, cited on http://www.wiki pedia.com.

(5) Court transcript from the Oscar Wilde "gross indecency" trial of 1895.

(6) Tiber, Elliot and Monte, Tom. *Taking Woodstock.* Garden City, NY: Square One Publishers, 2007.

(7) Bankhead, Tallulah. *Tallulah.* Jackson: University Press of Mississippi, 2004.

(8) *Tallulah Bankhead,* http://www.wikipedia.com (accessed 2007).

(9) Israel, Lee. *Miss Tallulah Bankhead.* New York: Dell Publishers, 1972.

(10) Angela Bowie, in discussion and written dialogues with Mark Bego, March and April, 2007, Tucson, AZ.

(11) Connor, William. "Cassandra" column. *The Daily Mirror,* London, 1957.

(12) Bego, Mark. *Rock Hudson: Public and Private.* New York: Signet Books, 1985.

(13) *Time* magazine. "I Am a Homosexual: The Gay Drive for Acceptance." September 8, 1975.

(14) Bowie, Angie. *Free Spirit.* London: Mushroom Books, 1981.

(15) Bowie, Angela with Patrick Carr. *Backstage Passes.* New York: Putnam Publishers, 1993.

(16) Hopkins, Jerry. *Bowie.* New York: MacMillian Publishers, 1985.

(17) *WPA Guide to New York City,* 1939.

(18) Chauncey, George. *Gay New York—Gender, Urban Culture, and the Making of the Gay Male World 1890–1940.* New York: Basic Books/ Harper Collins, 1994. This particular extract is from a 1917 public record transcript detailing an investigation about the sexual habits of sailors near the Brooklyn Navy Yard, Box 25, COF.

(19) Randy Jones and Mark Bego, discussion between authors, January– December 2007.

(20) Village People, interview by Mark Bego, April 13, 1974, the offices of Can't Stop Music, New York City. Excerpt from Bego's memoir *Paperback Writer* © 2008 Mark Bego.

(21) Phillip, Matthew. "FEEL THE LOVE: Village People Cowboy Randy Jones Talks about Hot '70s Sex, His Disco Days, Kylie, Robbie's Butt, Pet Shop Boys and His New Album." *DNA* magazine. Lindcombe, Australia, 2007.

(22) Glenn Hughes, in discussion with Mark Bego, Glenn's apartment in New York City, January 1998.

(23) *E! True Hollywood Story*. Village People, first broadcast 2000 by E!

(24) *Time Out London Movie Guide*, as quoted on http://www.rotten tomatoes.com, 2006.

(25) Reed, Rex. *Rex Reed's Guide to Movies on TV & Video*. New York: Warner Books, 1992.

(26) *The Rosie O'Donnell Show*, television program transcripts.

(27) Coleman, Ray. *Lennon*. New York: McGraw Hill, 1984.

(28) Mitchell, Joni. *Joni Mitchell: The Complete Geffen Recordings*. Liner notes. Geffen Records/Universal, 2003.

(29) Sarah Dash, interview by Mark Bego, November 1998, Tucson, AZ.

(30) Bego, Mark. *Bette Midler: Still Divine*. Lanham, MD: Cooper Square Press; Rowman & Littlefield, 2002.

(31) Tarradell, Mario. "Willie Opens Closet with 'Cowboys.'" *The Dallas Morning News*. February 14, 2006.

(32) Wilson, Mary and Patricia Romanowski [with Mark Bego credited on the book's interior]. *Supreme Faith: Someday We'll Be Together*. New York: HarperCollins Publishers, 2000.

Gayography

RANDY:	"When we came to the end of this book, we realized that there were several terms, people, and references that we couldn't fit in anywhere else."
MARK:	"So, we came up with this running list we call our 'Gayography.'"
RANDY:	"In no particular order, here are some terms that might come in handy, amidst our cavalcade of gay pop culture."
JUDY GARLAND:	For some unknown reason, Judy Garland has become acknowledged as the pop star patron saint of gay boys all over the planet. Was it her musical flamboyance or her traumatic personal life that made her such a fascinating star? From her performance in *The Wizard of Oz*, to the tragic end of her career, she remains the Number One gay icon in pop culture.
LIPSTICK LESBIAN:	While many lesbian women choose to sport very "butch" clothing, others choose to play up their femininity. The lesbian women who favor make-up, nylons, and dresses are known as "lipstick lesbians."
METROSEXUALS:	This term is strictly from the twenty-first century and defines a certain strata of modern man. The word "metrosexual" refers to heterosexual men who have the fashion sense that is often attributed to gay men. It has nothing to do with their expression of sexuality, but a fascination with manicures, expensive hair products, big jewelry, and designer clothes.
DRAG QUEEN:	The idea of men dressing up as women goes back at least as far as Elizabethan England, when Shakespearean actors would dress in female clothing to perform the women's roles

193

in theater. In the twentieth century, the idea of men becoming transsexuals took on all new meaning.

FRIEND OF DOROTHY'S: This term comes right from the 1939 film, *The Wizard of Oz*. For whatever reason, that film has become a touchstone of gay culture. The term "friend of Dorothy's" is a code term for a homosexual man.

DONNA SUMMER: When the disco era was in full swing in the 1970s and early 1980s, Donna Summer became the new Judy Garland. She was a patron saint for discothequeing gay men. Her music seemed to express the era perfectly. She still remains a gay pop icon, even if her "born again" philosophies stalled her career in the AIDS-era 1980s. Since that time she has kissed and made up with gay culture and remains a glittering gay icon.

RENT BOYS: This is a British term for male prostitutes. The term first made headlines in the 1980s when British tabloids proclaimed that Elton John was hiring them for his "entertainment." What can we say? Boys just wanna have fun!

ON THE DOWNLOW: A twenty-first century term for living a "straight" lifestyle publicly, yet secretly being gay in private. In other words the homosexual behavior is kept "on the downlow," and out of the public eye.

Discography

VILLAGE PEOPLE/RANDY JONES DISCOGRAPHY

Village People

(LP/USA/Casablanca/1977)
(CD/USA/Polygram/1996)

- –"San Francisco"
- –"You Got Me"
- –"Fire Island"
- –"Village People"

Macho Man

(LP/USA/Casablanca/1978)
(CD/USA/Polygram/1996)

- –"Macho Man"
- –"I Am What I Am"
- –"Key West"
- –"Just a Gigolo"
- –"I Ain't Got Nobody"
- –"Sodom and Gomorrah"

Cruisin'

(LP/USA/Casablanca/1978)
(CD/USA/Polygram/1996)

- –"Y.M.C.A."
- –Medley: "The Women"/"I'm a Cruiser"

–"Hot Cop"

–"My Roommate"

–"Ups and Downs"

Go West

(LP/USA/Casablanca/1979)
(CD/USA/Polygram/1996)

–"In the Navy"

–"Go West"

–"Citizens of the World"

–"I Wanna Shake Your Hand"

–"Get Away Holiday"

–"Manhattan Woman"

Live and Sleazy

(2LP/USA/Casablanca/1979)
(CD/USA/Polygram/1998)

–"Fire Island"

–"Hot Cop"

–Medley: "San Francisco (You've Got Me)"/"In Hollywood (Everybody Is a Star)"

–"Macho Man"

–"In the Navy"

–"Y.M.C.A."

–"Sleazy"

–"Rock & Roll is Back Again"

–"Ready for the '80s"

–"Save Me" (Ballad)

–"Save Me" (Up tempo)

Can't Stop the Music/ Original Movie Soundtrack Album

(LP/USA/Casablanca/1980)
(CD/USA/Polygram/1986)

-"Can't Stop The Music" by Village People

-"Samantha" by David London

-"Give Me a Break" by The Ritchie Family

-"Liberation" by Village People

-"Magic Night" by Village People

-"The Sound of the City"

-"Milkshake" by Village People

-"Y.M.C.A." by Village People

-"I Love You to Death"

-"Sophistication"

The Very Best of Village People

(CD/USA/Polygram/1998)

-"Y.M.C.A."

-"In The Navy"

-"Macho Man"

-"In Hollywood (Everybody Is a Star)"

-"Village People"

-"San Francisco (You've Got Me)"

-"Key West"

-"Go West"

-"Ready for the '80s"

-"Can't Stop the Music"

20th Century Masters, The Millenium Collection/The Best Of Village People

(CD/USA/Universal 2001)

-"Y.M.C.A."

-"In the Navy"

-"Macho Man"

-"In Hollywood (Everybody Is a Star)"

-"Village People"

-"San Francisco (You've Got Me)"

–"Key West"

–"Go West"

–"Ready for the '80s"

–"Can't Stop the Music"

–"Y.M.C.A." (12" Mix)

RANDY JONES SOLO DISCOGRAPHY

RANDY JONES Albums

Randy Jones

(LP/USA/Zoo York Records 1983)

Terrorist Attack

(LP/USA/Europe/ZYX Records 1986)

Ticket to the World

(CD/USA/Europe/ Pop Front Records 2007)

Bibliography

The following books and Web sites were used in the research and writing of this manuscript. Unless otherwise noted, the author's text was not quoted.

Asprey, Robert B. *Frederick the Great: The Magnificent Enigma.* New York: Ficknor and Fields Publishing, 1986.

Bego, Mark. *Bette Midler: Still Divine.* Lanham, MD: Cooper Square Press; Rowman & Littlefield, 2002.

Bego, Mark. *Joni Mitchell.* Lanham, MD: Taylor Trade Publishing; Rowman & Littlefield Publishers, 2005.

Bego, Mark. *Madonna: Blonde Ambition.* Lanham, MD: Taylor Trade Publishing; Rowman & Littlefield Publishers, 2000.

Bego, Mark. *Rock Hudson: Public & Private.* New York: Signet Books, 1986.

Bego, Mark. *TV Rock—The History of Rock & Roll on Television.* Toronto: PaperJacks Publishing, 1988.

Bowie, Angie. *Free Spirit.* London: Mushroom Books, 1981.

Bowie, Angela, with Patrick Carr. *Backstage Passes.* New York: Putnam Publishers, 1993.

Bray, Alan. *Homosexuality in Renaissance England.* London: Gay Men's Press, 1982.

Brooke, C. F. Tucker. *The Life of Marlowe and "The Tragedy of Dido, Queen of Carthage.* London: Methuen Press, 1930.

Chauncey, George. *Gay New York—Gender, Urban Culture, and the Making of the Gay Male World 1890–1940.* New York: Basic Books/HarperCollins, 1994.

Coleman, Ray. *Lennon.* New York: MacMillian Publishers, 1984.

Cowan, Thomas. *Gay Men and Women Who Enriched the World.* Boston: Alyson Publications, 1992.

Crompton, Louis. *Homosexuality & Civilization.* Cambridge, MA and London: Belknap Harvard Publishers, 2003.

Douglas, David. *Presenting David Bowie!* New York: Pinnacle Books, 1975.

Duberman, Martin. *Stonewall.* New York: Plume/Putnam Group, 1994.

Evans, Richard J. *Rituals of Retribution: Capitol Punishment in Germany 1600–1987.* London: Oxford University Press, 1996.

Hogan, Steve and Lee Hudson. *Completely Queer: The Gay and Lesbian Encyclopedia.* New York: Henry Holt Publishers, 1998.

Hopkins, Jerry. *Bowie.* New York: MacMillian Publishers, 1985.

Marlowe, Christopher. *Complete Works of Christopher Marlowe.* Rowland, Oxford: Clarendon Press, 1994.

Packard, Chris. *Queer Cowboys: And Other Erotic Male Friendships in Nineteenth-Century American Literature.* New York: Palgrave; MacMillian Publishers, 2005.

Reed, Rex. *Rex Reed's Guide to Movies on TV & Video.* New York: Warner Books, 1992.

Rees, Dafydd and Luke Crampton. *VH1 Rock Stars Encyclopedia.* New York: DK Publishing, 1999.

Studer, Wayne. *Rock on the Wild Side: Gay Male Images in Popular Music of the Rock Era.* San Francisco: Leyland Publications, 1994.

Summers, Claude J. *The Queer Encyclopedia of the Visual Arts.* San Francisco: Cleis Press, 2004.

Tiber, Elliot with Tom Monte. *Taking Woodstock.* Garden City, NY: Square One Publishers, 2007.

Whitburn, Joel. *Top 40 Albums.* New York: Billboard Books, 1995.

Whitburn, Joel. *Top Pop Singles 1955–1996.* New York: Billboard Books, 1997.

Wilson, Mary and Patricia Romanowski [with Mark Bego credited on the book's interior]. *Supreme Faith: Someday We'll Be Together.* New York: Harper Collins Publishers, 1990.

Film casts and crews were either taken from the actual film credits, DVD or VHS packaging, or the following Internet Web sites:

www.imdb.com

(Note: This is a comprehensive Web site devoted to everything to do with films and is a wonderful resource for movie trivia.)

www.Amazon.com

(Note: Although this is primarily a commercial sales Web site, it also provides many details about the films and books it sells.)

Index

About the Authors

RANDY JONES, an American Music Award winner and multi-platinum recording artist, is the original Cowboy and a founding member of Village People. In his career spanning four decades before, with, and since Village People, he has sold 100 million units. The group, perhaps best known for hits like "Macho Man," "In the Navy," and "Y.M.C.A.," earned 65 gold and platinum record certificates, toured worldwide, starred in its own camp classic film, made the cover of *Rolling Stone*, and garnered a star on Hollywood's Walk of Fame. Continuing a career as an actor, singers, and dancer, Jones has released solo CDs, performs his own solo concerts worldwide and has appeared in musicals and plays in New York City and elsewhere, including *Joseph and the Amazing Technicolor Dreamcoat, Music Man, Chicago, The Madonna Whore: Confessions of a Dirty Mind, Applause, Camelot*, and *42nd Street*, among many others. Included in the motion pictures he has starred in are *Against the Wind* (in which he portrays the American president), *The Gentleman, Three Long Years, Beyond the Façade, A Tale About Bootlegging, My Guaranteed Student Loan* and *Can't Stop the Music*. He appears in various documentaries such as *Roxy: The Last Dance, When Ocean Meets Sky, Disco: Spinning the Story,* VH-1's *RockDoc NY77: The Coolest Year in Hell, The Godfather of Disco, Behind the Music,* VH1's *Sex: The Revolution*, and others as narrator and interview subject. He has appeared in countless magazines and publications worldwide in every language. With Will Grega, he is the co-author of *Outsounds: The Gay and Lesbian Music Alternative* (1996). His official Web site is: www.RandyJonesWorld.com. You can write to him at: vpcowboy1@yahoo.com.

MARK BEGO is a professional writer who is called "the No. 1 Best-Selling Pop Biographer" in *Publisher's Weekly* and has been referred to in the press as "the Prince of Pop Music Bios." He has authored over fifty published books involving rock & roll and show business. He has penned two *New York Times* bestsellers, a *Los Angeles Times* bestseller, and the *Chicago Tribune* bestseller *Dancing in the Street: Confessions of a Motown Diva* written with its subject, Martha Reeves of the beloved recording group: Martha & the Vandellas. He has also written books with Micky Dolenz of The Monkees (*I'm a Believer*), Debbie Gibson (*Between the Lines*), and Jimmy Greenspoon of Three Dog Night (*One Is the Loneliest Number*). Bego's subjects have ranged from Elvis Presley, Michael Jackson, Madonna, Bonnie Raitt, Julia Roberts, Joni Mitchell, Billy Joel, to Leonardo DiCaprio. In 1994, his more general books published included *Country Gals* (life stories of Reba McEntire, Dolly Parton, Tanya Tucker, and other famed women in country music) and *Country Hunks* (spotlighting Vince Gill, Billy Ray Cyrus, George Strait and others). Bego also authored the reference books *TV Rock* [The History of Rock & Roll on Television] and *The Rock & Roll Almanac*. He has also written books about Hollywood in its heyday: *The Best of "Modern Screen"* and *Rock Hudson: Public and Private*. He penned his own memoir, *Paperback Writer*. His official Web site is: www.MarkBego.com. You can write to him at: MarkBego@aol.com.